EVERYMAN'S LIBRARY
EDITED BY ERNEST RHYS

ESSAYS & BELLES-LETTRES

PAST AND PRESENT
BY THOMAS CARLYLE · APPRE-
CIATION BY RALPH WALDO EMERSON

THOMAS CARLYLE, born in 1795 at
Ecclefechan, the son of a stonemason.
Educated at Edinburgh University. School-
master for a short time, but decided on a
literary career, visiting Paris and London.
Retired in 1828 to Dumfriesshire to write.
In 1834 moved to Cheyne Row, Chelsea,
and died there in 1881.

PAST AND PRESENT

THOMAS CARLYLE

LONDON: J. M. DENT & SONS LTD.
NEW YORK: E. P. DUTTON & CO. INC.

PRINTED AND BOUND IN CANADA
T. H. Best Printing Co., Limited, Toronto

INTRODUCTION

Being an appreciation from " The Dial "[1]

By RALPH WALDO EMERSON

HERE is Carlyle's new poem, his *Iliad* of English woes, to follow his poem on France, entitled the *History of the French Revolution*. In its first aspect it is a political tract, and since Burke, since Milton, we have had nothing to compare with it. It grapples honestly with the facts lying before all men, groups and disposes them with a master's mind, and, with a heart full of manly tenderness, offers his best counsel to his brothers. Obviously it is the book of a powerful and accomplished thinker, who has looked with naked eyes at the dreadful political signs in England for the last few years, has conversed much on these topics with such wisemen of all ranks and parties as are drawn to a scholar's house, until such daily and nightly meditation has grown into a great connection, if not a system of thoughts; and the topic of English politics becomes the best vehicle for the expression of his recent thinking, recommended to him by the desire to give some timely counsels, and to strip the worst mischiefs of their plausibility. It is a brave and just book, and not a semblance. "No new truth," say the critics on all sides. Is it so? Truth is very old, but the merit of seers is not to invent but to dispose objects in their right places, and he is the commander who is always in the mount, whose eye not only sees details, but throws crowds of details into their right arrangement and a larger and juster totality than any other. The book makes great approaches to true contemporary history, a very rare success, and firmly holds up to daylight the absurdities still tolerated in the English and European system. It is such an appeal to the conscience and honour of England as cannot be forgotten, or be feigned to be forgotten. It has the merit which belongs to every honest book, that it was self-examining before it was eloquent, and so hits all other men, and, as the country people say of good preaching, " comes bounce down into every pew." Every reader shall carry away something. The scholar shall read and write, the farmer and mechanic shall toil, with new resolution, nor forget the book when they resume their labour.

Though no theocrat, and more than most philosophers a believer in political systems, Mr. Carlyle very fairly finds the calamity of the times, not in bad bills of Parliament, nor the remedy in good bills, but the vice in false and superficial aims of the people, and the remedy in honesty and insight. Like every work of genius, its great value is in telling such simple truths. As we recall the topics, we are struck with force given to the plain truths; the picture of the English nation all sitting enchanted, the poor, enchanted so that they cannot work, the rich, enchanted so that they cannot enjoy, and are rich in vain; the exposure of the progress of fraud into all arts and social activities; the proposition that the labourer must have a greater share in his earnings; that the principle of permanence shall be admitted into all contracts of mutual service; that the state shall provide at least schoolmaster's education for all the citizens; the exhortation to the workman that he shall respect the work and not the wages; to the scholar that he shall be there for light; to the idle, that no man shall sit idle; the picture of Abbot Samson, the true governor, who " is not there to expect reason and nobleness of others, he is there to give them of his own reason and nobleness; " and the assumption throughout the book, that a new chivalry and nobility, namely the dynasty of labour, is replacing the old nobilities. These things strike us with a force which reminds us of the morals of the Oriental or early Greek masters, and of no modern book. Truly in these things is great reward. It is not by sitting still at a grand distance and calling the human race *larvæ*, that men are to be helped, nor by helping the depraved after their own foolish fashion, but by doing unweariedly the particular work we were born to do. Let no man think himself absolved because he does a generous action and befriends the poor, but let him see whether he so holds his property that a benefit goes from it to all. A man's diet should be what is simplest and readiest to be had, because it is so private a good. His house should be better, because that is for the use of hundreds, perhaps of thousands, and is the property of the traveller. But his speech is a perpetual and public instrument; let that always side with the race and yield neither a lie nor a sneer. His manners,—let them be hospitable and civilising, so that no Phidias or Raphael shall have taught anything better in canvas or stone; and his acts should be representative of the human race, as one who makes them rich in his having, and poor in his want.

It requires great courage in a man of letters to handle the contemporary practical questions; not because he then has all men for his rivals, but because of the infinite entanglements of the problem, and the waste of strength in gathering unripe fruits. The task is superhuman; and the poet knows well that a little time will do more than the most puissant genius. Time stills the loud noise of opinions, sinks the small, raises the great, so that the true emerges without effort and in perfect harmony to all eyes; but the truth of the present hour, except in particulars and single relations, is unattainable. Each man can very well know his own part of duty, if he will; but to bring out the truth for beauty, and as literature, surmounts the powers of art. The most elaborate history of to-day will have the oddest dislocated look in the next generation. The historian of to-day is yet three ages off. The poet cannot descend into the turbid present without injury to his rarest gifts. Hence that necessity of isolation which genius has always felt. He must stand on his glass tripod, if he would keep his electricity.

But when the political aspects are so calamitous that the sympathies of the man overpower the habits of the poet, a higher than literary inspiration may succour him. It is a costly proof of character, that the most renowned scholar of England should take his reputation in his hand and should descend into the ring; and he has added to his love whatever honour his opinions may forfeit. To atone for this departure from the vows of the scholar and his eternal duties to this secular charity, we have at least this gain, that here is a message which those to whom it was addressed cannot choose but hear. Though they die, they must listen. It is plain that whether by hope or by fear, or were it only by delight in this panorama of brilliant images, all the great classes of English society must read, even those whose existence it proscribes. Poor Queen Victoria—poor Sir Robert Peel—poor Primate and Bishops—poor Dukes and Lords! There is no help in place or pride or in looking another way; a grain of wit is more penetrating than the lightning of the night-storm, which no curtains or shutters will keep out. Here is a book which will be read, no thanks to anybody but itself. What pains, what hopes, what vows, shall come of the reading! Here is a book as full of treason as an egg is full of meat, and every lordship and worship and high form and ceremony of English conservatism tossed like a football into the air, and kept in the air, with merciless kicks and rebounds, and yet not a word is punishable by statute. The wit has eluded all official zeal; and yet these dire jokes, these cunning thrusts, this flaming sword of Cherubim waved high in air, illuminates the whole horizon, and shows to the eyes of the universe every wound it inflicts. Worst of all for the party attacked, it bereaves them beforehand of all sympathy, by anticipating the plea of poetic and humane conservatism, and impressing the reader with the conviction that the satirist himself has the truest love for everything old and excellent in English land and institutions, and a genuine respect for the basis of truth in those whom he exposes.

We are at some loss how to state what strikes us as the fault of this remarkable book, for the variety and excellence of the talent displayed in it is pretty sure to leave all special criticism in the wrong. And we may easily fail in expressing the general objection which we feel. It appears to us as a certain disproportion in the picture, caused by the obtrusion of the whims of the painter. In this work, as in his former labours, Mr. Carlyle reminds us of a sick giant. His humours are expressed with so much force of constitution that his fancies are more attractive and more credible than the sanity of duller men. But the habitual exaggeration of the tone wearies whilst it stimulates. It is felt to be so much deduction from the universality of the picture. It is not serene sunshine, but everything is seen in lurid storm-lights. Every object attitudinises, to the very mountains and stars almost, under the refraction of this wonderful humorist; and instead of the common earth and sky, we have a Martin's Creation or Judgment Day. A crisis has always arrived which requires a *deus ex machina*. One can hardly credit, whilst under the spell of this magician, that the world always had the same bankrupt look, to foregoing ages as to us—as of a failed world just re-collecting its old withered forces to begin again and try to do a little business. It was perhaps inseparable from the attempt to write a book of wit and imagination on English politics, that a certain local emphasis and love of effect, such as is the vice of preaching, should appear,—producing on the reader a feeling of forlornness by the excess of value attributed to circumstances. But the splendour of wit cannot out-dazzle the calm daylight, which always shows every individual man in balance with his age, and able to work out his own salvation from all the follies of that, and no such glaring contrasts or severalties in that or this. Each age has its own follies, as its majority is made up of foolish young people; its superstitions appear no superstitions to itself; and if you should ask the contemporary, he would tell you, with pride or with regret (according as he was practical or poetic), that he had none. But after a short time, down go its follies and weakness and the memory of them; its virtues alone remain, and its limitation assumes the poetic form of a beautiful superstition, as the dimness of our sight clothes the objects in the horizon with mist and colour. The revelation of Reason is this of the unchangeableness of the fate of humanity under all its subjective aspects; that to the cowering it always cowers, to the daring it opens great avenues. The ancients are only venerable to us because distance has destroyed what was trivial; as the sun and stars affect us only grandly, because we cannot reach to their smoke and surfaces and say, Is that all?

And yet the gravity of the times, the manifold and increasing dangers of the English State, may easily excuse some over-colouring of the picture; and we at this distance are not so far removed from any of the specific evils, and are deeply participant in too many, not to share the gloom and thank the love and the courage of the counsellor. This book is full of humanity, and nothing is more excellent in this as in all Mr. Carlyle's works than the attitude of the writer. He has the dignity of a man of letters, who knows what belongs to him, and never deviates from his sphere; a continuer of the great line of scholars, and sustains their office in the highest credit and honour. If the good heaven have any good word to impart to this unworthy generation, here is one scribe qualified and clothed for its occasion. One excellence he has in an age of Mammon and of criticism, that he never suffers the eye of his wonder to close. Let who will be the dupe of trifles, he cannot keep his eye off from that gracious Infinite which embosoms us.

As a literary artist he has great merits, beginning with the main one that he never wrote one dull line. How well-read, how adroit, what thousand arts in his one art of writing; with his expedient for expressing those unproven opinions which he entertains but will not endorse.

by summoning one of his men of straw from the cell,—and the respectable Sauerteig, or Teufelsdröckh, or Dryasdust, or Picturesque Traveller, says what is put into his mouth, and disappears. That morbid temperament has given his rhetoric a somewhat bloated character; a luxury to many imaginative and learned persons, like a showery south-wind with its sunbursts and rapid chasing of lights and glooms over the landscape, and yet its offensiveness to multitudes of reluctant lovers makes us often wish some concession were possible on the part of the humorist. Yet it must not be forgotten that in all his fun of castanets, or playing of tunes with a whip-lash like some renowned charioteers,—in all this glad and needful venting of his redundant spirits, he does yet ever and anon, as if catching the glance of one wise man in the crowd, quit his tempestuous key, and lance at him in clear level tone the very word, and then with new glee return to his game. He is like a lover or an outlaw who wraps up his message in a serenade, which is nonsense to the sentinel, but salvation to the ear for which it is meant. He does not dodge the question, but gives sincerity where it is due.

One word more respecting this remarkable style. We have in literature few specimens of magnificence. Plato is the purple ancient, and Bacon and Milton the moderns of the richest strains. Burke sometimes reaches to that exuberant fullness, though deficient in depth. Carlyle, in his strange, half-mad way, has entered the Field of the Cloth of Gold, and shown a vigour and wealth of resource which has no rival in the tourney-play of these times—the indubitable champion of England. Carlyle is the first domestication of the modern system, with its infinity of details, into style. We have been civilising very fast, building London and Paris, and now planting New England and India, New Holland and Oregon—and it has not appeared in literature; there has been no analogous expansion and recomposition in books. Carlyle's style is the first emergence of all this wealth and labour with which the world has gone with child so long. London and Europe, tunnelled, graded, corn-

lawed, with trade-nobility, and East and West Indies
for dependencies, and America, with the Rocky Hills
in the horizon, have never before been conquered in
literature. This is the first invasion and conquest.
How like an air-balloon or bird of Jove does he seem
to float over the continent, and stooping here and there
pounce on a fact as a symbol which was never a symbol
before. This is the first experiment, and something of
rudeness and haste must be pardoned to so great an
achievement. It will be done again and again, sharper,
simpler; but fortunate is he who did it first, though
never so giant-like and fabulous. This grandiose
character pervades his wit and his imagination. We
have never had anything in literature so like earth-
quakes as the laughter of Carlyle. He "shakes with
his mountain mirth." It is like the laughter of the
Genii in the horizon. These jokes shake down Parlia-
ment-house and Windsor Castle, Temple and Tower,
and the future shall echo the dangerous peals. The
other particular of magnificence is in his rhymes.
Carlyle is a poet who is altogether too burly in his
frame and habit to submit to the limits of metre. Yet
he is full of rhythm, not only in the perpetual melody
of his periods, but in the burdens, refrains, and grand
returns of his sense and music. Whatever thought or
motto has once appeared to him fraught with meaning,
becomes an omen to him henceforward, and is sure to
return with deeper tones and weightier import, now as
threat, now as confirmation, in gigantic reverberation,
as if the hills, the horizon, and the next ages returned
the sound.

BIBLIOGRAPHY

Life of Schiller (*Lond. Mag.*, 1823-4), 1825, 1845. (Supplement published in the People's Edition, 1873) Wilhelm Meister's Apprenticeship, 1824. Elements of Geometry and Trigonometry (from the French of Legendre), 1824. German Romance, 1827. Sartor Resartus (*Fraser's Mag.*, 1833-4), 1835 (Boston), 1838. French Revolution, 1837, 1839. Critical and Miscellaneous Essays, 1839, 1840, 1847, 1857. (In these were reprinted Articles from *Edinburgh Review, Foreign Review, Foreign Quarterly Review, Fraser's Magazine, Westminster Review, New Monthly Magazine, London and Westminster Review, Keepsake, Proceedings of the Society of Antiquaries of Scotland, Times.*) Chartism, 1840. Heroes, Hero-worship, and the Heroic in History, 1841. Past and Present, 1843. Oliver Cromwell's Letters and Speeches; with Elucidations, 1845. Thirty-five Unpublished Letters of Oliver Cromwell, 1847 (Fraser). Original Discourses on the Negro Question (Fraser, 1849), 1853. Latter-day Pamphlets, 1850. Life of John Sterling, 1851. History of Friedrich II. of Prussia, 1858-65. Inaugural Address at Edinburgh, 1866. Shooting Niagara; and After? 1867 (from *MacMillan*). The Early Kings of Norway; also an Essay on the Portraits of John Knox, 1875.

There were also contributions to Brewster's *Edinburgh Encyclopædia*, vols. xiv., xv., and xvi.; to *New Edinburgh Review*, 1821, 1822; *Fraser's Magazine*, 1830, 1831; *The Times*, 19 June, 1844 (Mazzini); 28 November, 1876; 5 May, 1877; *Examiner*, 1848; *Spectator*, 1848.

First Collected Edition of Works, 1857-58 (16 vols.).

Reminiscences (ed. J. A. Froude), 1881. Reminiscences of my Irish Journey in 1849, 1882. Last Words of Thomas Carlyle, 1882 (ed. by J. C. A.). Last Words of Thomas Carlyle, 1892. Rescued Essays (ed. P. Newberry), 1892. Historical Sketches of Notable Persons and Events in the Reign of James I. and Charles I. (ed. A. Carlyle), 1898.

Leslie Stephen's article on Carlyle in the *Dictionary of National Biography* gives a list of his occasional writings which have never been collected or reprinted.

CONTENTS

BOOK I.—PROEM

BOOK II.—THE ANCIENT MONK

BOOK III.—THE MODERN WORKER

BOOK IV.—HOROSCOPE

PAST AND PRESENT

BOOK I.—PROEM

CHAPTER I

MIDAS

THE condition of England, on which many pamphlets are now in the course of publication, and many thoughts unpublished are going on in every reflective head, is justly regarded as one of the most ominous, and withal one of the strangest, ever seen in this world. England is full of wealth, of multifarious produce, supply for human want in every kind; yet England is dying of inanition. With unabated bounty the land of England blooms and grows; waving with yellow harvests; thick-studded with workshops, industrial implements, with fifteen millions of workers, understood to be the strongest, the cunningest and the willingest our Earth ever had; these men are here; the work they have done, the fruit they have realised is here, abundant, exuberant on every hand of us: and behold, some baleful fiat as of Enchantment has gone forth, saying, "Touch it not, ye workers, ye master-workers, ye master-idlers; none of you can touch it, no man of you shall be the better for it; this is enchanted fruit!" On the poor workers such fiat falls first, in its rudest shape; but on the rich master-workers too it falls; neither can the rich master-idlers, nor any richest or highest man escape, but all are like to be brought low with it, and made 'poor' enough, in the money sense or a far fataler one.

Of these successful skilful workers some two millions, it is now counted, sit in Workhouses, Poor-law Prisons; or have 'out-door relief' flung over the wall to them,—

A 608

the workhouse Bastille being filled to bursting, and the
strong Poor-law broken asunder by a stronger.[1] They
sit there, these many months now; their hope of deliverance as yet small. In workhouses, pleasantly so-named,
because work cannot be done in them. Twelve-hundred-
thousand workers in England alone; their cunning right-
hand lamed, lying idle in their sorrowful bosom; their
hopes, outlooks, share of this fair world, shut-in by
narrow walls. They sit there, pent up, as in a kind of
horrid enchantment; glad to be imprisoned and enchanted, that they may not perish starved. The
picturesque Tourist, in a sunny autumn day, through
this bounteous realm of England, descries the Union
Workhouse on his path. ' Passing by the Workhouse of
St. Ives in Huntingdonshire, on a bright day last autumn,'
says the picturesque Tourist, ' I saw sitting on wooden
benches, in front of their Bastille and within their ring-
wall and its railings, some half-hundred or more of these
men. Tall robust figures, young mostly or of middle
age; of honest countenance, many of them thoughtful
and even intelligent-looking men. They sat there, near
by one another; but in a kind of torpor, especially in a
silence, which was very striking. In silence: for, alas,
what word was to be said? An Earth all lying round,
crying, Come and till me, come and reap me;—yet we
here sit enchanted! In the eyes and brows of these men
hung the gloomiest expression, not of anger, but of grief
and shame and manifold inarticulate distress and weariness; they returned my glance with a glance that seemed
to say, " Do not look at us. We sit enchanted here, we
know not why. The Sun shines and the Earth calls;
and, by the governing Powers and Impotences of this
England, we are forbidden to obey. It is impossible,
they tell us!" There was something that reminded me
of Dante's Hell in the look of all this; and I rode swiftly
away.'

So many hundred thousands sit in workhouses: and

[1] The Return of Paupers for England and Wales, at Ladyday
1842, is, ' In-door 221,687, Out-door 1,207,402, Total 1,429,089.'
Official Report.

other hundred thousands have not yet got even work-houses; and in thrifty Scotland itself, in Glasgow or Edinburgh City, in their dark lanes, hidden from all but the eye of God, and of rare Benevolence the minister of God, there are scenes of woe and destitution and desolation, such as, one may hope, the Sun never saw before in the most barbarous regions where men dwelt. Competent witnesses, the brave and humane Dr. Alison, who speaks what he knows, whose noble Healing Art in his charitable hands becomes once more a truly sacred one, report these things for us: these things are not of this year, or of last year, have no reference to our present state of commercial stagnation, but only to the common state. Not in sharp fever-fits, but in chronic gangrene of this kind is Scotland suffering. A Poor-law, any and every Poor-law, it may be observed, is but a temporary measure; an anodyne, not a remedy: Rich and Poor, when once the naked facts of their condition have come into collision, cannot long subsist together on a mere Poor-law. True enough:—and yet, human beings cannot be left to die! Scotland too, till something better come, must have a Poor-law, if Scotland is not to be a byword among the nations. O, what a waste is there; of noble and thrice-noble national virtues; peasant Stoicisms, Heroisms; valiant manful habits, soul of a Nation's worth,—which all the metal of Potosi cannot purchase back; to which the metal of Potosi, and all you can buy with *it*, is dross and dust!

Why dwell on this aspect of the matter? It is too indisputable, not doubtful now to any one. Descend where you will into the lower class, in Town or Country, by what avenue you will, by Factory Inquiries, Agricultural Inquiries, by Revenue Returns, by Mining-Labourer Committees, by opening your own eyes and looking, the same sorrowful result discloses itself: you have to admit that the working body of this rich English Nation has sunk or is fast sinking into a state, to which, all sides of it considered, there was literally never any parallel. At Stockport Assizes,—and this too has no reference to the present state of trade, being of date prior to that,—a Mother and a Father are arraigned and found guilty of poisoning three of their children, to defraud a ' burial-society ' of some £3 8s. due on the death of each child: they are arraigned, found guilty; and the official authorities, it is whispered, hint that perhaps the case is not solitary, that perhaps you had better not probe farther into that department of things. This is in the autumn of 1841; the crime itself is of the previous year or season. " Brutal savages, degraded Irish," mutters the idle reader of Newspapers; hardly lingering on this incident. Yet it is an incident worth lingering on; the depravity, savagery and degraded Irishism being never so well admitted. In the British land, a human Mother and Father, of white skin and professing the Christian religion, had done this thing; they, with their Irishism and necessity and savagery, had been driven to do it. Such instances are like the highest mountain apex emerged into view; under which lies a whole mountain region and land, not yet emerged. A human Mother and Father had said to themselves, What shall we do to escape starvation? We are deep sunk here, in our dark cellar; and help is far.—Yes, in the Ugolino Hunger-tower stern things happen; best-loved little Gaddo fallen dead on his Father's knees!—The Stockport Mother and Father think and hint: Our poor little starveling Tom, who cries all day for victuals, who will see only evil and not good in this world: if he were out of misery at once; he well dead, and the rest of us perhaps kept alive? It is thought. and hinted; at last it is done. And now Tom being killed, and all spent and eaten, Is it poor little starveling Jack that must go, or poor little starveling Will?—What a committee of ways and means!

In starved sieged cities, in the uttermost doomed ruin of old Jerusalem fallen under the wrath of God, it was prophesied and said, ' The hands of the pitiful women have sodden their own children.' The stern Hebrew imagination could conceive no blacker gulf of wretchedness; that was the ultimatum of degraded god-punished man. And we here, in modern England, exuberant with supply of all kinds, besieged by nothing if it be not by invisible Enchantments, are we reaching that?——How come these things? Wherefore are they, wherefore should they be?

Nor are they of the St. Ives workhouses, of the Glasgow lanes, and Stockport cellars, the only unblessed among us. This successful industry of England, with its plethoric wealth, has as yet made nobody rich; it is an enchanted wealth, and belongs yet to nobody. We might ask, Which of us has it enriched? We can spend thousands where we once spent hundreds; but can purchase nothing good with them. In Poor and Rich, instead of noble thrift and plenty, there is idle luxury alternating with mean scarcity and inability. We have sumptuous garnitures for our Life, but have forgotten to *live* in the middle of them. It is an enchanted wealth; no man of us can yet touch it. The class of men who feel that they are truly better off by means of it, let them give us their name!

Many men eat finer cookery, drink dearer liquors,— with what advantage they can report, and their Doctors can: but in the heart of them, if we go out of the dyspeptic stomach, what increase of blessedness is there? Are they better, beautifuler, stronger, braver? Are they even what they call ' happier '? Do they look with satisfaction on more things and human faces in this God's-Earth; do more things and human faces look with satisfaction on them? Not so. Human faces gloom discordantly, disloyally on one another. Things, if it be not mere cotton and iron things, are growing disobedient to man. The Master Worker is enchanted, for the present, like his Workhouse Workman; clamours, in vain hitherto, for a very simple sort of ' Liberty: ' the liberty ' to buy where he finds it cheapest, to sell where he finds it dearest.' With guineas jingling in every pocket, he was no whit richer; but now, the very guineas threatening to vanish, he feels that he is poor indeed. Poor Master Worker! And the Master Unworker, is not he in a still fataler situation? Pausing amid his game-preserves, with awful eye,

—as he well may! Coercing fifty-pound tenants; coercing, bribing, cajoling; ' doing what he likes with his
own.' His mouth full of loud futilities, and arguments
to prove the excellence of his Corn-law; and in his heart
the blackest misgiving, a desperate half-consciousness
that his excellent Corn-law is *in*defensible, that his loud
arguments for it are of a kind to strike men too literally
dumb.

To whom, then, is this wealth of England wealth?
Who is it that it blesses; makes happier, wiser, beautifuler, in any way better? Who has got hold of it, to
make it fetch and carry for him, like a true servant, not
like a false mock-servant; to do him any real service
whatsoever? As yet no one. We have more riches than
any Nation ever had before; we have less good of them
than any Nation ever had before. Our successful industry
is hitherto unsuccessful; a strange success, if we stop
here! In the midst of plethoric plenty, the people perish;
with gold walls, and full barns, no man feels himself safe
or satisfied. Workers, Master Workers, Unworkers, all
men, come to a pause; stand fixed, and cannot farther.
Fatal paralysis spreading inwards, from the extremities,
in St. Ives workhouses, in Stockport cellars, through all
limbs, as if towards the heart itself. Have we actually
got enchanted, then; accursed by some God?—

Midas longed for gold, and insulted the Olympians.
He got gold, so that whatsoever he touched became gold,
—and he, with his long ears, was little the better for it.
Midas had misjudged the ceiestial music-tones; Midas
had insulted Apollo and the gods: the gods gave him his
wish, and a pair of long ears, which also were a good
appendage to it. What a truth in these old Fables!

CHAPTER II

THE SPHINX

How true, for example, is that other old Fable of the Sphinx, who sat by the wayside, propounding her riddle to the passengers, which if they could not answer she destroyed them! Such a Sphinx is this Life of ours, to all men and societies of men. Nature, like the Sphinx, is of womanly celestial loveliness and tenderness; the face and bosom of a goddess, but ending in claws and the body of a lioness. There is in her a celestial beauty,—which means celestial order, pliancy to wisdom; but there is also a darkness, a ferocity, fatality, which are infernal. She is a goddess, but one not yet disimprisoned; one still half-imprisoned,—the articulate, lovely still encased in the inarticulate, chaotic. How true! And does she not propound her riddles to us? Of each man she asks daily, in mild voice, yet with a terrible significance, " Knowest thou the meaning of this Day? What thou canst do Today; wisely attempt to do? " Nature, Universe, Destiny, Existence, howsoever we name this grand un-namable Fact in the midst of which we live and struggle, is as a heavenly bride and conquest to the wise and brave, to them who can discern her behests and do them; a destroying fiend to them who cannot. Answer her riddle, it is well with thee. Answer it not, pass on regarding it not, it will answer itself; the solution for thee is a thing of teeth and claws; Nature is a dumb lioness, deaf to thy pleadings, fiercely devouring. Thou art not now her victorious bridegroom; thou art her mangled victim, scattered on the precipices, as a slave found treacherous, recreant, ought to be and must.

With Nations it is as with individuals: Can they rede the riddle of Destiny? This English Nation, will it get to know the meaning of *its* strange new Today? Is there sense enough extant, discoverable anywhere or anyhow, in our united twenty-seven million heads to discern the same; valour enough in our twenty-seven million hearts to dare and do the bidding thereof? It will be seen!—

The secret of gold Midas, which he with his long ears never could discover, was, That he had offended the Supreme Powers;—that he had parted company with the eternal inner Facts of this Universe, and followed the transient outer Appearances thereof; and so was arrived *here*. Properly it is the secret of all unhappy men and unhappy nations. Had they known Nature's right truth, Nature's right truth would have made them free. They have become enchanted; stagger spell-bound, reeling on the brink of huge peril, because they were not wise enough. They have forgotten the right Inner True, and taken up with the Outer Sham-true. They answer the Sphinx's question *wrong*. Foolish men cannot answer it aright! Foolish men mistake transitory semblance for eternal fact, and go astray more and more.

Foolish men imagine that because judgment for an evil thing is delayed, there is no justice, but an accidental one, here below. Judgment for an evil thing is many times delayed some day or two, some century or two, but it is sure as life, it is sure as death! In the centre of the world-whirlwind, verily now as in the oldest days, dwells and speaks a God. The great soul of the world is *just*. O brother, can it be needful now, at this late epoch of experience, after eighteen centuries of Christian preaching for one thing, to remind thee of such a fact; which all manner of Mahometans, old Pagan Romans, Jews, Scythians and heathen Greeks, and indeed more or less all men that God made, have managed at one time to see into; nay which thou thyself, till 'redtape' strangled the inner life of thee, hadst once some inkling of: That there *is* justice here below; and even, at bottom, that there is nothing else but justice! Forget that, thou hast forgotten all. Success will never more attend thee: how can it now? Thou hast the whole Universe against thee. No more success: mere sham-success, for a day and days; rising ever higher,—towards its Tarpeian Rock. Alas, how, in thy soft-hung Longacre vehicle, of polished leather to the bodily eye, of redtape philosophy, of expediencies, club-room moralities, Parliamentary majorities to the mind's eye thou beautifully rollest: but knowest thou whither-

ward? It is towards the *road's end*. Old use-and-wont;
established methods, habitudes, *once* true and wise;
man's noblest tendency, his perseverance, and man's
ignoblest, his inertia; whatsoever of noble and ignoble
Conservatism there is in men and Nations, strongest
always in the strongest men and Nations: all this is as a
road to thee, paved smooth through the abyss,—till all
this *end*. Till men's bitter necessities can endure thee
no more. Till Nature's patience with thee is done; and
there is no road or footing any farther, and the abyss
yawns sheer!—

Parliament and the Courts of Westminster are venerable
to me; how venerable; gray with a thousand years of
honourable age! For a thousand years and more, Wisdom
and faithful Valour, struggling amid much Folly and
greedy Baseness, not without most sad distortions in the
struggle, have built them up; and they are as we see.
For a thousand years, this English Nation has found them
useful or supportable: they have served this English
Nation's want; *been* a road to it through the abyss of
Time. They are venerable, they are great and strong.
And yet it is good to remember always that they are not
the venerablest, nor the greatest, nor the strongest! Acts
of Parliament are venerable; but if they correspond not
with the writing on the " Adamant Tablet," what are
they? Properly their one element of venerableness, of
strength or greatness, is, that they at all times correspond
therewith as near as by human possibility they can.
They are cherishing destruction in their bosom every
hour that they continue otherwise.

Alas, how many causes that can plead well for themselves in the Courts of Westminster; and yet in the
general Court of the Universe, and free Soul of Man,
have no word to utter! Honourable Gentlemen may
find this worth considering, in times like ours. And truly,
the din of triumphant Law-logic, and all shaking of
horse-hair wigs and learned-serjeant gowns having com-
fortably ended, we shall do well to ask ourselves withal,
What says that high and highest Court to the verdict?
For it is the Court of Courts, that same; where the

universal soul of Fact and very Truth sits President;—
and thitherward, more and more swiftly, with a really
terrible increase of swiftness, all causes do in these days
crowd for revisal,—for confirmation, for modification, for
reversal with costs. Dost thou know that Court; hast
thou had any Law-practice there? What, didst thou
never enter; never file any petition of redress, reclaimer,
disclaimer or demurrer, written as in thy heart's blood,
for thy own behoof or another's; and silently await the
issue? Thou knowest not such a Court? Hast merely
heard of it by faint tradition as a thing that was or had
been? Of thee, I think, we shall get little benefit.

For the gowns of learned-serjeants are good: parchment records, fixed forms, and poor terrestrial Justice,
with or without horse-hair, what sane man will not
reverence these? And yet, behold, the man is not sane
but insane, who considers these alone as venerable. Oceans
of horse-hair, continents of parchment, and learned-
serjeant eloquence, were it continued till the learned
tongue wore itself small in the indefatigable learned
mouth, cannot make unjust just. The grand question
still remains, Was the judgment just? If unjust, it will
not and cannot get harbour for itself, or continue to have
footing in this Universe, which was made by other than
One Unjust. Enforce it by never such statuting, three
readings, royal assents; blow it to the four winds with all
manner of quilted trumpeters and pursuivants, in the
rear of them never so many gibbets and hangmen, it will
not stand, it cannot stand. From all souls of men, from
all ends of Nature, from the Throne of God above, there
are voices bidding it: Away, away! Does it take no
warning; does it stand, strong in its three readings, in its
gibbets and artillery-parks? The more woe is to it, the
frightfuler woe. It will continue standing for its day,
for its year, for its century, doing evil all the while; but
it has One enemy who is Almighty: dissolution, explosion,
and the everlasting Laws of Nature incessantly advance
towards it; and the deeper its rooting, more obstinate its
continuing, the deeper also and huger will its ruin and
overturn be.

In this God's-world, with its wild-whirling eddies and mad foam-oceans, where men and nations perish as if without law, and judgment for an unjust thing is sternly delayed, dost thou think that there is therefore no justice? It is what the fool hath said in his heart. It is what the wise, in all times, were wise because they denied, and knew forever not to be. I tell thee again, there is nothing else but justice. One strong thing I find here below: the just thing, the true thing. My friend, if thou hadst all the artillery of Woolwich trundling at thy back in support of an unjust thing; and infinite bonfires visibly waiting ahead of thee, to blaze centuries long for thy victory on behalf of it,—I would advise thee to call halt, to fling down thy baton, and say, " In God's name, No! " Thy ' success ' ? Poor devil, what will thy success amount to? If the thing is unjust, thou hast not succeeded; no, not though bonfires blazed from North to South, and bells rang, and editors wrote leading-articles, and the just thing lay trampled out of sight, to all mortal eyes an abolished and annihilated thing. Success? In few years thou wilt be dead and dark,—all cold, eyeless, deaf; no blaze of bonfires, ding-dong of bells or leading-articles visible or audible to thee again at all forever: What kind of success is that!—

It is true, all goes by approximation in this world; with any not insupportable approximation we must be patient. There is a noble Conservatism as well as an ignoble. Would to Heaven, for the sake of Conservatism itself, the noble alone were left, and the ignoble, by some kind severe hand, were ruthlessly lopped away, forbidden evermore to show itself! For it is the right and noble alone that will have victory in this struggle; the rest is wholly an obstruction, a postponement and fearful imperilment of the victory. Towards an eternal centre of right and nobleness, and of that only, is all this confusion tending. We already know whither it is all tending; what will have victory, what will have none! The Heaviest will reach the centre. The Heaviest, sinking through complex fluctuating media and vortices, has its

deflexions, its obstructions, nay at times its resiliences,
its reboundings; whereupon some blockhead shall be
heard jubilating, "See, your Heaviest ascends!"—but
at all moments it is moving centreward, fast as is convenient for it; sinking, sinking; and, by laws older than
the World, old as the Maker's first Plan of the World, it
has to arrive there.

Await the issue. In all battles, if you await the issue,
each fighter has prospered according to his right. His
right and his might, at the close of the account, were one
and the same. He has fought with all his might, and in
exact proportion to all his right he has prevailed. His
very death is no victory over him. He dies indeed; but
his work lives, very truly lives. A heroic Wallace,
quartered on the scaffold, cannot hinder that his Scotland
become, one day, a part of England: but he does hinder
that it become, on tyrannous unfair terms, a part of it;
commands still, as with a god's voice, from his old Valhalla
and Temple of the Brave, that there be a just real union
as of brother and brother, not a false and merely semblant
one as of slave and master. If the union with England
be in fact one of Scotland's chief blessings, we thank
Wallace withal that it was not the chief curse. Scotland
is not Ireland: no, because brave men rose there, and
said, "Behold, ye must not tread us down like slaves;
and ye shall not,—and cannot!" Fight on, thou brave
true heart, and falter not, through dark fortune and
through bright. The cause thou fightest for, so far as it is
true, no farther, yet precisely so far, is very sure of
victory. The falsehood alone of it will be conquered,
will be abolished, as it ought to be: but the truth of it
is part of Nature's own Laws, coöperates with the World's
eternal Tendencies, and cannot be conquered.

The _dust_ of controversy, what is it but the _falsehood_
flying off from all manner of conflicting true forces, and
making such a loud dust-whirl-wind,—that so the truths
alone may remain, and embrace brother-like in some true
resulting-force! It is ever so. Savage fighting Heptar-
chies: their fighting is an ascertainment, who has the
right to rule over whom; that out of such waste-bickering

Saxondom a peacefully coöperating England may arise. Seek through this Universe; if with other than owl's eyes, thou wilt find nothing nourished there, nothing kept in life, but what has right to nourishment and life. The rest, look at it with other than owl's eyes, is not living; is all dying, all as good as dead! Justice was ordained from the foundations of the world; and will last with the world and longer. *optimism!*

From which I infer that the inner sphere of Fact, in this present England as elsewhere, differs infinitely from the outer sphere and spheres of Semblance. That the Temporary, here as elsewhere, is too apt to carry it over the Eternal. That he who dwells in the temporary Semblances, and does not penetrate into the eternal Substance, will *not* answer the Sphinx-riddle of Today, or of any Day. For the substance alone is substantial; that *is* the law of Fact; if you discover not that, Fact, who already knows it, will let you also know it by and by.

What is Justice? that, on the whole, is the question of the Sphinx to us. The law of Fact is, that Justice must and will be done. The sooner the better; for the Time grows stringent, frightfully pressing! "What is Justice?" ask many, to whom cruel Fact alone will be able to prove responsive. It is like jesting Pilate asking, What is Truth? Jesting Pilate had not the smallest chance to ascertain what was Truth. He could not have known it, had a god shown it to him. Thick serene opacity, thicker than amaurosis, veiled those smiling eyes of his to Truth; the inner *retina* of them was gone paralytic, dead. He looked at Truth; and discerned her not, there where she stood. "What is Justice?" The clothed embodied Justice that sits in Westminster Hall, with penalties, parchments, tipstaves, is very visible. But the *un*embodied Justice, whereof that other is either an emblem, or else is a fearful indescribability, is not so visible! For the unembodied Justice is of Heaven; a Spirit, and Divinity of Heaven,— invisible to all but the noble and pure of soul. The impure ignoble gaze with eyes, and she is not there. They will prove it to you by logic, by endless Hansard

Debatings, by bursts of Parliamentary eloquence. It is not consolatory to behold! For properly, as many men as there are in a Nation who *can* withal see Heaven's invisible Justice, and know it to be on Earth also omnipotent, so many men are there who stand between a Nation and perdition. So many, and no more. Heavy‑laden England, how many hast thou in this hour? The Supreme Power sends new and ever new, all *born* at least with hearts of flesh and not of stone;—and heavy Misery itself, once heavy enough, will prove didactic!—

CHAPTER III

MANCHESTER INSURRECTION

BLUSTEROWSKI, Colacorde, and other Editorial prophets of the Continental-Democratic Movement, have in their leading-articles shown themselves disposed to vilipend the late Manchester Insurrection, as evincing in the rioters an extreme backwardness to battle; nay as betokening, in the English People itself, perhaps a want of the proper animal courage indispensable in these ages. A million hungry operative men started up, in utmost paroxysm of desperate protest against their lot; and, ask Colacorde and company, How many shots were fired? Very few in comparison! Certain hundreds of drilled soldiers sufficed to suppress this million-headed hydra, and tread it down, without the smallest appeasement or hope of such, into its subterranean settlements again, there to reconsider itself. Compared with our revolts in Lyons, in Warsaw and elsewhere, to say nothing of incomparable Paris City past or present, what a lamblike Insurrection!—

The present Editor is not here, with his readers, to vindicate the character of Insurrections; nor does it matter to us whether Blusterowski and the rest may think the English a courageous people or not courageous. In passing, however, let us mention that, to our view, this was not an unsuccessful Insurrection; that as Insurrections go, we have not heard lately of any that succeeded so well.

A million of hungry operative men, as Blusterowski says, rose all up, came all out into the streets, and—stood there. What other could they do? Their wrongs and griefs were bitter, insupportable, their rage against the same was just: but who are they that cause these wrongs, who that will honestly make effort to redress them? Our enemies are we know not who or what; our friends are we know not where! How shall we attack any one, shoot or be shot by any one? Oh, if the accursed invisible Nightmare, that is crushing out the life of us and ours, would take a shape; approach us like the Hyrcanian tiger, the Behemoth of Chaos, the Archfiend himself; in any shape that we could see, and fasten on!—A man can have himself shot with cheerfulness; but it needs first that he see clearly for what. Show him the divine face of Justice, then the diabolic monster which is eclipsing that: he will fly at the throat of such monster, never so monstrous, and need no bidding to do it. Woolwich grapeshot will sweep clear all streets, blast into invisibility so many thousand men: but if your Woolwich grapeshot be but eclipsing Divine Justice, and the God's-radiance itself gleam recognisable athwart such grapeshot,—then, yes then is the time come for fighting and attacking. All artillery-parks have become weak, and are about to dissipate: in the God's thunder, their poor thunder slackens, ceases; finding that it is, in all senses of the term, a *brute* one!—

That the Manchester Insurrection stood still, on the streets, with an indisposition to fire and bloodshed, was wisdom for it even as an Insurrection. Insurrection, never so necessary, is a most sad necessity; and governors who wait for that to instruct them, are surely getting into the fatalest courses,—proving themselves Sons of Nox and Chaos, of blind Cowardice, not of seeing Valour! How can there be any remedy in insurrection? It is a mere announcement of the disease,—visible now even to Sons of Night. Insurrection usually 'gains' little; usually wastes how much! One of its worst kinds of waste, to say nothing of the rest, is that of irritating and exasperating men against each other, by violence done; which is always sure to be injustice done, for violence does even justice unjustly.

Who shall compute the waste and loss, the obstruction of every sort, that was produced in the Manchester region by Peterloo alone! Some thirteen unarmed men and women cut down,—the number of the slain and maimed is very countable: but the treasury of rage, burning hidden or visible in all hearts ever since, more or less perverting the effort and aim of all hearts ever since, is of unknown extent. "How ye came among us, in your cruel armed blindness, ye unspeakable County Yeomanry, sabres flourishing, hoofs prancing, and slashed us down at your brute pleasure; deaf, blind to all *our* claims and woes and wrongs; of quick sight and sense to your own claims only! There lie poor sallow work-worn weavers, and complain no more now; women themselves are slashed and sabred, howling terror fills the air; and ye ride prosperous, very victorious,—ye unspeakable: give *us* sabres too, and then come-on a little!" Such are Peterloos. In all hearts that witnessed Peterloo, stands written, as in fire-characters, or smoke-characters prompt to become fire again, a legible balance-account of grim vengeance; very unjustly balanced, much exaggerated, as is the way with such accounts: but payable readily at sight, in full with compound interest! Such things should be avoided as the very pestilence! For men's hearts ought not to be set against one another; but set *with* one another, and all against the Evil Thing only. Men's souls ought to be left to see clearly; not jaundiced, blinded, twisted all awry, by revenge, mutual abhorrence, and the like. An Insurrection that can announce the disease, and then retire with no such balance-account opened anywhere, has attained the highest success possible for it.

And this was what these poor Manchester operatives, with all the darkness that was in them and round them, did manage to perform. They put their huge inarticulate question, "What do you mean to do with us?" in a manner audible to every reflective soul in this kingdom; exciting deep pity in all good men, deep anxiety in all men whatever; and no conflagration or outburst of madness came to cloud that feeling anywhere, but everywhere it operates unclouded. All England heard the question: it is the first practical form of *our* Sphinx-riddle. England will answer it; or, on the whole, England will perish;—one does not yet expect the latter result!

For the rest, that the Manchester Insurrection could yet discern no radiance of Heaven on any side of its horizon; but feared that all lights, of the O'Connor or other sorts, hitherto kindled, were but deceptive fish-oil transparencies, or bog will-o'-wisp lights, and no day-spring from on high: for this also we will honour the poor Manchester Insurrection, and augur well of it. A deep unspoken sense lies in these strong men,—inconsiderable, almost stupid, as all they can articulate of it is. Amid all violent stupidity of speech, a right noble instinct of what is doable and what is not doable never forsakes them: the strong inarticulate men and workers, whom *Fact* patronises; of whom, in all difficulty and work whatsoever, there is good augury! This work too is to be done: Governors and Governing Classes that *can* articulate and utter, in any measure, what the law of Fact and Justice is, may calculate that here is a Governed Class who will listen.

And truly this first practical form of the Sphinx-question, inarticulately and so audibly put there, is one of the most impressive ever asked in the world. "Behold us here, so many thousands, millions, and increasing at the rate of fifty every hour. We are right willing and able to work; and on the Planet Earth is plenty of work and wages for a million times as many. We ask, If you mean to lead us towards work; to try to lead us,—by ways new, never yet heard of till this new unheard-of Time? Or if you declare that you cannot lead us? And expect that we are to remain quietly unled, and in a composed manner perish of starvation? What is it you expect of us? What is it you mean to do with us?" This question, I say, has been put in the hearing of all

Britain; and will be again put, and ever again, till some answer be given it.

Unhappy Workers, unhappier Idlers, unhappy men and women of this actual England. We are yet very far from an answer, and there will be no existence for us without finding one. "A fair day's-wages for a fair day's-work:" it is as just a demand as Governed men ever made of Governing. It is the everlasting right of man. Indisputable as Gospels, as arithmetical multiplication-tables: it must and will have itself fulfilled;—and yet, in these times of ours, with what enormous difficulty, next-door to impossibility! For the times are really strange; of a complexity intricate with all the new width of the ever-widening world; times here of half-frantic velocity of impetus, there of the deadest-looking stillness and paralysis; times definable as showing two qualities, Dilettantism and Mammonism;—most intricate obstructed times! Nay, if there were not a Heaven's radiance of Justice, prophetic, clearly of Heaven, discernible behind all these confused world-wide entanglements, of Land-lord interests, Manufacturing interests, Tory - Whig interests, and who knows what other interests, expediencies, vested interests, established possessions, inveterate Dilettantisms, Midas - eared Mammonisms, — it would seem to every one a flat impossibility, which all wise men might as well at once abandon. If you do not know eternal Justice from momentary Expediency, and understand in your heart of hearts how Justice, radiant, beneficent, as the all-victorious Light-element, is also in essence, if need be, an all-victorious *Fire*-element, and melts all manner of vested interests, and the hardest iron cannon, as if they were soft wax, and does ever in the long-run rule and reign, and allows nothing else to rule and reign,—you also would talk of impossibility! But it is only difficult, it is not impossible. Possible? It is, with whatever difficulty, very clearly inevitable.

Fair day's - wages for fair day's-work! exclaims a sarcastic man: Alas, in what corner of this Planet, since Adam first awoke on it, was that ever realised? The day's-wages of John Milton's day's-work, named *Paradise Lost* and *Milton's Works*, were Ten Pounds paid by instalments, and a rather close escape from death on the gallows. Consider that: it is no rhetorical flourish; it is an authentic, altogether quiet fact,— emblematic, quietly documentary of a whole world of such, ever since human history began.   Oliver Cromwell quitted his farming; undertook a Hercules' Labour and lifelong wrestle with that Lernean Hydra-coil, wide as England, hissing heaven-high through its thousand crowned, coroneted, shovel-hatted quack-heads; and he did wrestle with it, the truest and terriblest wrestle I have heard of; and he wrestled it, and mowed and cut it down a good many stages, so that its hissing is ever since pitiful in comparison, and one can walk abroad in comparative peace from it; —and his wages, as I understand, were burial under the gallows-tree near Tyburn Turnpike, with his head on the gable of Westminster Hall, and two centuries now of mixed cursing and ridicule from all manner of men.   His dust lies under the Edgware Road, near Tyburn Turnpike, at this hour; and his memory is—Nay what matters what his memory is?   His memory, at bottom, is or yet shall be as that of a god: a terror and horror to all quacks and cowards and insincere persons; an everlasting encouragement, new memento, battleword, and pledge of victory to all the brave.   It is the natural course and history of the Godlike, in every place, in every time.   What god ever carried it with the Tenpound Franchisers; in Open Vestry, or with any Sanhedrim of considerable standing? When was a god found ' agreeable ' to everybody?   The regular way is to hang, kill, crucify your gods, and execrate and trample them under your stupid hoofs for a century or two; till you discover that they are gods,—and then take to braying over them, still in a very long-eared manner!—So speaks the sarcastic man; in his wild way, very mournful truths.

Carlyle = sarcastic man

Day's-wages for day's-work? continues he: The Progress of Human Society consists even in this same, The better and better apportioning of wages to work. Give me this, you have given me all. Pay to every man accurately what he has worked for, what he has earned and done and deserved,—to this man broad lands and honours, to that man high gibbets and treadmills: what more have I to ask? Heaven's Kingdom, which we daily pray for, *has* come; God's will is done on Earth even as it is in Heaven! This *is* the radiance of celestial Justice; in the light or in the fire of which all impediments, vested interests, and iron cannon, are more and more melting like wax, and disappearing from the pathways of men. A thing ever struggling forward; irrepressible, advancing inevitable; perfecting itself, all days, more and more,—never to be *perfect* till that general Doomsday, the ultimate Consummation, and Last of earthly Days.

True, as to ' perfection ' and so forth, answer we; true enough! And yet withal we have to remark, that imperfect Human Society holds itself together, and finds place under the Sun, in virtue simply of some *approximation* to perfection being actually made and put in practice. We remark farther, that there are supportable approximations, and then likewise insupportable. With some, almost with any, supportable approximation men are apt, perhaps too apt, to rest indolently patient, and say, It will do. Thus these poor Manchester manual workers mean only, by day's-wages for day's-work, certain coins of money adequate to keep them living;—in return for their work, such modicum of food, clothes and fuel as will enable them to continue their work itself! They as yet clamour for no more; the rest, still inarticulate, cannot yet shape itself into a demand at all, and only lies in them as a dumb wish; perhaps only, still more inarticulate, as a dumb, although unconscious want. *This* is the supportable approximation they would rest patient with, That by their work they might be kept alive to work more!— *This* once grown unattainable, I think your approximation may consider itself to have reached the *in*supportable stage; and may prepare, with whatever difficulty, reluctance and astonishment, for one of two things, for changing or perishing! With the millions no longer able to live, how can the units keep living? It is too clear the Nation itself is on the way to suicidal death.

Shall we say then, The world has retrograded in its talent of apportioning wages to work, in late days? The world had always a talent of that sort, better or worse. Time was when the mere *hand*-worker needed not announce his claim to the world by Manchester Insurrections!— The world, with its Wealth of Nations, Supply-and-demand and such-like, has of late days been terribly inattentive to that question of work and wages. We will not say, the poor world has retrograded even here: we will say rather, the world has been rushing on with such fiery animation to get work and ever more work done, it has had no time to think of dividing the wages; and has merely left them to be scrambled for by the Law of the Stronger, law of Supply-and-demand, law of Laissez-faire, and other idle Laws and Un-laws,—saying, in its dire haste to get the work done, That is well enough!

And now the world will have to pause a little, and take up that other side of the problem, and in right earnest strive for some solution of that. For it has become pressing. What is the use of your spun shirts? They hang there by the million unsaleable; and here, by the million, are diligent bare backs that can get no hold of them. Shirts are useful for covering human backs; useless otherwise, an unbearable mockery otherwise. You have fallen terribly behind with that side of the problem! Manchester Insurrections, French Revolutions, and thousandfold phenomena great and small, announce loudly that you must bring it forward a little again. Never till now, in the history of an Earth which to this hour nowhere refuses to grow corn if you will plough it, to yield shirts if you will spin and weave in it, did the mere manual two-handed worker (however it might fare with other workers) cry in vain for such ' wages ' as *he* means by ' fair wages,' namely food and warmth! The Godlike could not and cannot be paid; but the Earthly always could. Gurth, a mere swineherd, born thrall of Cedric the Saxon, tended pigs in the wood, and did get some parings of the pork. Why, the four-footed worker has already *got* all that this two-handed one is clamouring for! How often must I remind you? There is not a

horse in England, able and willing to work, but *has* due
food and lodging; and goes about sleek-coated, satisfied
in heart. And you say, It is impossible. Brothers, I
answer, if for you it be impossible, what is to become of
you? It is impossible for us to believe it to be impossible.
The human brain, looking at these sleek English horses,
refuses to believe in such impossibility for English men.
Do you depart quickly; clear the ways soon, lest worse
befall. We for our share do purpose, with full view of
the enormous difficulty, with total disbelief in the impossibility, to endeavour while life is in us, and to die
endeavouring, we and our sons, till we attain it or have
all died and ended.

Such a Platitude of a World, in which all working
horses could be well fed, and innumerable working men
should die starved, were it not best to end it; to have done
with it, and restore it once for all to the *Jötuns*, Mud-giants,
Frost-giants, and Chaotic Brute-gods of the Beginning?
For the old Anarchic Brute-gods it may be well enough;
but it is a Platitude which Men should be above coun-
tenancing by their presence in it. We pray you, let the
word *impossible* disappear from your vocabulary in this
matter. It is of awful omen; to all of us, and to yourselves first of all.

CHAPTER IV

MORRISON'S PILL

WHAT is to be done, what would you have us do? asks
many a one, with a tone of impatience, almost of reproach;
and then, if you mention some one thing, some two things,
twenty things that might be done, turns round with a
satirical tehee, and "These are your remedies!" The
state of mind indicated by such question, and such
rejoinder, is worth reflecting on.

It seems to be taken for granted, by these interrogative
philosophers, that there is some 'thing,' or handful of
'things,' which could be done; some Act of Parliament,

' remedial measure ' or the like, which could be passed, whereby the social malady were fairly fronted, conquered, put an end to; so that, with your remedial measure in your pocket, you could then go on triumphant, and be troubled no farther. " You tell us the evil," cry such persons, as if justly aggrieved, " and do not tell us how it is to be cured! "

How it is to be cured? Brothers, I am sorry I have got no Morrison's Pill for curing the maladies of Society. It were infinitely handier if we had a Morrison's Pill, Act of Parliament, or remedial measure, which men could swallow, one good time, and then go on in their old courses, cleared from all miseries and mischiefs! Unluckily we have none such; unluckily the Heavens themselves, in their rich pharmacopœia, contain none such. There will no ' thing ' be done that will cure you. There will a radical universal alteration of your regimen and way of life take place; there will a most agonising divorce between you and your chimeras, luxuries and falsities, take place; a most toilsome, all-but ' impossible ' return to Nature, and her veracities and her integrities, take place: that so the inner fountains of life may again begin, like eternal Light-fountains, to irradiate and purify your bloated, swollen, foul existence, drawing nigh, as at present, to nameless death! Either death, or else all this will take place. Judge if, with such diagnosis, any Morrison's Pill is like to be discoverable!

But the Life-fountain within you once again set flowing, what innumerable ' things,' whole sets and classes and continents of ' things," year after year, and decade after decade, and century after century, will then be doable and done! Not Emigration, Education, Corn-Law Abrogation, Sanitary Regulation, Land Property-Tax; not these alone, nor a thousand times as much as these. Good Heavens, there will then be light in the inner heart of here and there a man, to discern what is just, what is commanded by the Most High God, what *must* be done, were it never so ' impossible.' Vain jargon in favour of the palpably unjust will then abridge itself within limits. Vain jargon, on Hustings, in Parliaments or wherever else, when here and there a man has vision for the essential God's-Truth of the things jargoned of, will become very vain indeed. The silence of here and there such a man, how eloquent in answer to such jargon! Such jargon, frightened at its own gaunt echo, will unspeakably abate; nay, for a while, may almost in a manner disappear,—the wise answering it in silence, and even the simple taking cue from them to hoot it down wherever heard. It will be a blessed time; and many ' things ' will become doable, —and when the brains are out, an absurdity will die! Not easily again shall a Corn-Law argue ten years for itself; and still talk and argue, when impartial persons have to say with a sigh that, for so long back, they have heard no ' argument ' advanced for it but such as might make the angels and almost the very jackasses weep!—

Wholly a blessed time: when jargon might abate, and here and there some genuine speech begin. When to the noble opened heart, as to such heart they alone do, all noble things began to grow visible; and the difference between just and unjust, between true and false, between work and sham-work, between speech and jargon, was once more, what to our happier Fathers it used to be, *infinite*,—as between a Heavenly thing and an Infernal: the one a thing which you were *not* to do, which you were wise not to attempt doing; which it were better for you to have a millstone tied round your neck, and be cast into the sea, than concern yourself with doing!—Brothers, it will not be a Morrison's Pill, or remedial measure, that will bring all this about for us.

And yet, very literally, till, in some shape or other, it be brought about, we remain cureless; till it begin to be brought about, the cure does not begin. For Nature and Fact, not Redtape and Semblance, are to this hour the basis of man's life; and on those, through never such strata of these, man and his life and all his interests do, sooner or later, infallibly come to rest,—and to be supported or be swallowed according as they agree with those. The question is asked of them, not, How do you agree with Downing Street and accredited Semblance? but,

How do you agree with God's Universe and the actual Reality of things? This Universe *has* its Laws. If we walk according to the Law, the Law-Maker will befriend us; if not, not. Alas, by no Reform Bill, Ballot-box, Five-point Charter, by no boxes or bills or charters, can you perform this alchemy: ' Given a world of Knaves, to produce an Honesty from their united action!' It is a distillation, once for all, not possible. You pass it through alembic after alembic, it comes out still a Dishonesty, *still* with a new dress on it, a new colour to it. ' While we ourselves continue valets, how *can* any hero come to govern us? ' We are governed, very infallibly, by the ' sham-hero,'—whose name is Quack, whose work and governance is Plausibility, and also is Falsity and Fatuity; to which Nature says, and must say when it comes to *her* to speak, eternally No! Nations cease to be befriended of the Law-Maker, when they walk *not* according to the Law. The Sphinx-question remains unsolved by them, becomes ever more insoluble.

If thou ask again, therefore, on the Morrison's-Pill hypothesis, What is to be done? allow me to reply: By thee, for the present, almost nothing. Thou there, the thing for thee to do is, if possible, to cease to be a hollow sounding-shell of hearsays, egoisms, purblind dilettantisms; and become, were it on the infinitely small scale, a faithful *reform from self* discerning soul. Thou shalt descend into thy inner man, and see if there be any traces of a *soul* there; till then there can be nothing done! O brother, we must if possible resuscitate some soul and conscience in us, exchange our dilettantisms for sincerities, our dead hearts of stone for living hearts of flesh. Then shall we discern, not one thing, but, in clearer or dimmer sequence, a whole endless host of things that can be done. *Do* the first of these; do it; the second will already have become clearer, doabler; the second, third and three-thousandth will then have begun to be possible for us. Not any universal Morrison's Pill shall we then, either as swallowers or as vendors, ask after at all; but a far different sort of remedies: Quacks shall no more have dominion over us, but true Heroes and Healers!

Will not that be a thing worthy of ' doing; ' to deliver ourselves from quacks, sham-heroes; to deliver the whole world more and more from such? They are the one bane of the world. Once clear the world of them, it ceases to be a Devil's-world, in all fibres of it wretched, accursed; and begins to be a God's-world, blessed, and working hourly towards blessedness. Thou for one wilt not again vote for any quack, do honour to any edge-gilt vacuity in man's shape: cant shall be known to thee by the sound of it;—thou wilt fly from cant with a shudder never felt before; as from the opened litany of Sorcerers' Sabbaths, the true Devil-worship of this age, more horrible than any other blasphemy, profanity or genuine blackguardism elsewhere audible among men. It is alarming to witness,—in its present completed state! And Quack and Dupe, as we must ever keep in mind, are upper-side and under of the selfsame substance; convertible personages: turn up your dupe into the proper fostering element, and he himself can become a quack; there is in him the due prurient insincerity, open voracity for profit, and closed sense for truth, whereof quacks too, in all their kinds, are made.

Alas, it is not to the hero, it is to the sham-hero, that, of right and necessity, the valet-world belongs. ' What is to be done? ' The reader sees whether it is like to be the seeking and swallowing of some ' remedial measure '!

CHAPTER V

ARISTOCRACY OF TALENT

WHEN an individual is miserable, what does it most of all behove him to do? To complain of this man or of that, of this thing or of that? To fill the world and the street with lamentation, objurgation? Not so at all; the reverse of so. All moralists advise him not to complain of any person or of anything, but of himself only. He is to know of a truth that being miserable he has been unwise, he.

Had he faithfully followed Nature and her Laws, Nature. ever true to her Laws, would have yielded fruit and increase and felicity to him: but he has followed other than Nature's Laws; and now Nature, her patience with him being ended, leaves him desolate; answers with very emphatic significance to him: No. Not by this road, my son; by another road shalt thou attain well-being: this, thou perceivest, is the road to ill-being; quit this!—So do all moralists advise: that the man penitently say to himself first of all, Behold I was not wise enough; I quitted the laws of Fact, which are also called the Laws of God, and mistook for them the Laws of Sham and Semblance, which are called the Devil's Laws; therefore am I here!

Neither with Nations that become miserable is it fundamentally otherwise. The ancient guides of Nations, Prophets, Priests, or whatever their name, were well aware of this; and, down to a late epoch, impressively taught and inculcated it. The modern guides of Nations, who also go under a great variety of names, Journalists, Political Economists, Politicians, Pamphleteers, have entirely forgotten this, and are ready to deny this. But it nevertheless remains eternally undeniable: nor is there any doubt but we shall all be taught it yet, and made again to confess it; we shall all be striped and scourged till we do learn it; and shall at last either get to know it, or be striped to death in the process. For it is undeniable! When a Nation is unhappy, the old Prophet was right and not wrong in saying to it: Ye have forgotten God, ye have quitted the ways of God, or ye would not have been unhappy. It is not according to the laws of Fact that ye have lived and guided yourselves, but according to the laws of Delusion, Imposture, and wilful and unwilful *Mistake* of Fact; behold therefore the Unveracity is worn out; Nature's long-suffering with you is exhausted; and ye are here!

Surely there is nothing very inconceivable in this, even to the Journalist, to the Political Economist, Modern Pamphleteer, or any two-legged animal without feathers! If a country finds itself wretched, sure enough that country has been *mis*guided: it is with the wretched

Twenty-seven Millions, fallen wretched, as with the Unit
fallen wretched: they, as he, have quitted the course
prescribed by Nature and the Supreme Powers, and so are
fallen into scarcity, disaster, infelicity; and pausing to
consider themselves, have to lament and say: Alas, we
were not wise enough! We took transient superficial
Semblance for everlasting central Substance; we have
departed far away from the *Laws* of this Universe, and
behold now lawless Chaos and inane Chimera is ready to
devour us!—' Nature in late centuries,' says Sauerteig,
' was universally supposed to be dead; an old eight-day
clock, made many thousand years ago, and still ticking,
but dead as brass,—which the Maker, at most, sat looking
at, in a distant, singular and indeed incredible manner:
but now I am happy to observe, she is everywhere asserting herself to be not dead and brass at all, but alive and
miraculous, celestial-infernal, with an emphasis that will
again penetrate the thickest head of this Planet by and
by!'——

Indisputable enough to all mortals now, the guidance
of this country has not been sufficiently wise; men too
foolish have been set to the guiding and governing of it,
and have guided it *hither;* we must find wiser,—wiser, or
else we perish! To this length of insight all England has
now advanced; but as yet no farther. All England stands
wringing its hands, asking itself, nigh desperate, What
farther? Reform Bill proves to be a failure; Benthamee
Radicalism, the gospel of ' Enlightened Selfishness,' dies
out, or dwindles into Five-point Chartism, amid the tears
and hootings of men; what next are we to hope or try?
Five-point Charter, Free-trade, Church-extension, Sliding-
scale; what, in Heaven's name, are we next to attempt,
that we sink not in inane Chimera, and be devoured of
Chaos?—The case is pressing, and one of the most com-
plicated in the world. A God's-message never came to
thicker-skinned people; never had a God's-message to
pierce through thicker integuments, into heavier ears.
It is Fact, speaking once more, in miraculous thunder-
voice, from out of the centre of the world;—how unknown
its language to the deaf and foolish many; how distinct,

undeniable, terrible and yet beneficent, to the hearing
few: Behold, ye shall grow wiser, or ye shall die! Truer
to Nature's Fact, or inane Chimera will swallow you; in
whirlwinds of fire, you and your Mammonisms, Dilettantisms, your Midas-eared philosophies, double-barrelled
Aristocracies, shall disappear!—Such is the God's-message
to *us*, once more, in these modern days.

We must have more Wisdom to govern us, we must be
governed by the Wisest, we must have an Aristocracy of
Talent! cry many. True, most true; but how to get it?
The following extract from our young friend of the *Houndsditch Indicator* is worth perusing: 'At this time,' says he,
' while there is a cry everywhere, articulate or inarticulate,
for an " Aristocracy of Talent," a Governing Class namely
which did govern, not merely which took the wages of
governing, and could not with all our industry be kept
from misgoverning, corn-lawing, and playing the very
deuce with us,—it may not be altogether useless to remind
some of the greener-headed sort what a dreadfully difficult
affair the getting of such an Aristocracy is! Do you
expect, my friends, that your indispensable Aristocracy
of Talent is to be enlisted straightway, by some sort of
recruitment aforethought, out of the general population;
arranged in supreme regimental order; and set to rule
over us? That it will be got sifted, like wheat out of chaff,
from the Twenty-seven Million British subjects; that any
Ballot-box, Reform Bill, or other Political Machine, with
Force of Public Opinion never so active on it, is likely to
perform said process of sifting? Would to Heaven that
we had a sieve; that we could so much as fancy any kind
of sieve, wind-fanners, or ne-plus-ultra of machinery,
devisable by man, that would do it!

' Done nevertheless, sure enough, it must be; it shall
and will be. We are rushing swiftly on the road to
destruction; every hour bringing us nearer, until it be, in
some measure, done. The doing of it is not doubtful;
only the method and the costs! Nay I will even mention
to you an infallible sifting process whereby he that has
ability will be sifted out to rule among us, and that same
blessed Aristocracy of Talent be verily, in an approxi-

mate degree, vouchsafed us by and by: an infallible sifting-process; to which, however, no soul can help his neighbour, but each must, with devout prayer to Heaven, endeavour to help himself. It is, O friends, that all of us, that many of us, should acquire the true *eye* for talent, which is dreadfully wanting at present! The true eye for talent presupposes the true reverence for it,—O Heavens, presupposes so many things!

'For example, you Bobus Higgins, Sausage-maker on the great scale, who are raising such a clamour for this Aristocracy of Talent, what is it that you do, in that big heart of yours, chiefly in very fact pay reverence to? Is it to talent, intrinsic manly worth of any kind, you unfortunate Bobus? The manliest man that you saw going in a ragged coat, did you ever reverence him; did you so much as know that he was a manly man at all, till his coat grew better? Talent! I understand you to be able to worship the fame of talent, the power, cash, celebrity or other success of talent; but the talent itself is a thing you never saw with eyes. Nay what is it in yourself that you are proudest of, that you take most pleasure in surveying meditatively in thoughtful moments? Speak now, is it the bare Bobus stript of his very name and shirt, and turned loose upon society, that you admire and thank Heaven for; or Bobus with his cash-accounts and larders dropping fatness, with his respectabilities, warm garnitures, and pony-chaise, admirable in some measure to certain of the flunky species? Your own degree of worth and talent, is it of *infinite* value to you; or only of finite,— measurable by the degree of currency, and conquest of praise or pudding, it has brought you to? Bobus, you are in a vicious circle, rounder than one of your own sausages; and will never vote for or promote any talent, except what talent or sham-talent has already *got* itself voted for!'—We here cut short the *Indicator ;* all readers perceiving whither he now tends.

'More Wisdom' indeed: but where to find more Wisdom? We have already a Collective Wisdom, after its kind,—though 'class-legislation,' and another thing

or two, affect it somewhat! On the whole, as they say,
Like people like priest; so we may say, Like people like
king. The man gets himself appointed and elected who
is ablest—to be appointed and elected. What can the
incorruptiblest *Bobuses* elect, if it be not some *Bobissimus*,
should they find such?

Or again, perhaps there is not, in the whole Nation,
Wisdom enough, 'collect' it as we may, to make an
adequate Collective! That too is a case which may befall:
a ruined man staggers down to ruin because there was
not wisdom enough in him; so, clearly also, may Twenty-
seven Million collective men!—But indeed one of the
infalliblest fruits of Unwisdom in a Nation is that it
cannot get the use of what Wisdom is actually in it: that
it is not governed by the wisest it has, who alone have a
divine right to govern in all Nations; but by the sham-
wisest, or even by the openly not-so-wise, if they are
handiest otherwise! This is the infalliblest result of Unwisdom; and also the balefulest, immeasurablest,—not
so much what we can call a poison-*fruit*, as a universal
death-disease, and poisoning of the whole tree. For
hereby are fostered, fed into gigantic bulk, all manner of
Unwisdoms, poison-fruits; till, as we say, the life-tree
everywhere is made a upas-tree, deadly Unwisdom over-
shadowing all things; and there is done what lies in
human skill to stifle all Wisdom everywhere in the birth,
to smite our poor world barren of Wisdom,—and make
your utmost Collective Wisdom, were it collected and
elected by Rhadamanthus, Æacus and Minos, not to
speak of drunken Tenpound Franchisers with their ballot-
boxes, an inadequate Collective! The Wisdom is not
now there: how will you 'collect' it? As well wash
Thames mud, by improved methods, to find more gold
in it.

Truly, the first condition is indispensable, That Wisdom
be there: but the second is like unto it, is properly one
with it; these two conditions act and react through every
fibre of them, and go inseparably together. If you have
much Wisdom in your Nation, you will get it faithfully
collected; for the wise love Wisdom, and will search for

it as for life and salvation. If you have little Wisdom, you will get even that little ill-collected, trampled under foot, reduced as near as possible to annihilation; for fools do not love Wisdom; they are foolish, first of all, because they have never loved Wisdom,—but have loved their own appetites, ambitions, their coroneted coaches, tankards of heavy-wet. Thus is your candle lighted at both ends, and the progress towards consummation is swift. Thus is fulfilled that saying in the Gospel: To him that hath shall be given; and from him that hath not shall be taken away even that which he hath. Very literally, in a very fatal manner, that saying is here fulfilled.

Our 'Aristocracy of Talent' seems at a considerable distance yet; does it not, O Bobus?

CHAPTER VI

HERO-WORSHIP

To the present Editor, not less than to Bobus, a Government of the Wisest, what Bobus calls an Aristocracy of Talent, seems the one healing remedy: but he is not so sanguine as Bobus with respect to the means of realising it. He thinks that we have at once missed realising it, and come to need it so pressingly, by departing far from the inner eternal Laws, and taking-up with the temporary outer semblances of Laws. He thinks that 'enlightened Egoism,' never so luminous, is not the rule by which man's life can be led. That 'Laissez-faire,' 'Supply-and-demand,' 'Cash-payment for the sole nexus,' and so forth, were not, are not and will never be, a practicable Law of Union for a Society of Men. That Poor and Rich, that Governed and Governing, cannot long live together on any such Law of Union. Alas, he thinks that man has a soul in him, *different* from the stomach in any sense of this word; that if said soul be asphyxied, and lie quietly forgotten, the man and his affairs are in a bad way. He

thinks that said soul will have to be resuscitated from its
asphyxia; that if it prove irresuscitable, the man is not
long for this world. In brief, that Midas-eared Mammonism, double-barrelled Dilettantism, and their thousand
adjuncts and corollaries, are *not* the Law by which God
Almighty has appointed this his Universe to go. That,
once for all, these are not the Law: and then farther that
we shall have to return to what *is* the Law,—not by
smooth flowery paths, it is like, and with ' tremendous
cheers ' in our throat; but over steep untrodden places,
through stormclad chasms, waste oceans, and the bosom
of tornadoes; thank Heaven, if not through very Chaos
and the Abyss! The resuscitating of a soul that has
gone to asphyxia is no momentary or pleasant process,
but a long and terrible one.

To the present Editor, ' Hero-worship,' as he has elsewhere named it, means much more than an elected
Parliament, or stated Aristocracy of the Wisest; for in
his dialect it is the summary, ultimate essence, and
supreme practical perfection of all manner of ' worship,'
and true worthships and noblenesses whatsoever. Such
blessed Parliament and, were it once in perfection,
blessed Aristocracy of the Wisest, god-honoured and man-
honoured, he does look for, more and more perfected,—
as the topmost blessed practical apex of a whole world
reformed from sham-worship, informed anew with
worship, with truth and blessedness! He thinks that
Hero-worship, done differently in every different epoch
of the world, is the soul of all social business among men;
that the doing of it well, or the doing of it ill, measures
accurately what degree of well-being or of ill-being there
is in the world's affairs. He thinks that we, on the whole,
do our Hero-worship worse than any Nation in this world
ever did it before: that the Burns an Exciseman, the
Byron a Literary Lion, are intrinsically, all things considered, a baser and falser phenomenon than the Odin a
God, the Mahomet a Prophet of God. It is this Editor's
clear opinion, accordingly, that we must learn to do our
Hero-worship better; that to do it better and better,

means the awakening of the Nation's soul from its asphyxia, and the return of blessed life to us,—Heaven's blessed life, not Mammon's galvanic accursed one. To resuscitate the Asphyxied, apparently now moribund and in the last agony if not resuscitated: such and no other seems the consummation.

'Hero-worship,' if you will,—yes, friends; but, first of all, by being ourselves of heroic mind. A whole world of Heroes; a world not of Flunkies, where no Hero-King *can* reign: that is what we aim at! We, for our share, will put away all Flunkyism, Baseness, Unveracity from us; we shall then hope to have Noblenesses and Veracities set over us; never till then. Let Bobus and Company sneer, "That is your Reform!" Yes, Bobus, that is our Reform; and except in that, and what will follow out of that, we have no hope at all. Reform, like Charity, O Bobus, must begin at home. Once well at home, how will it radiate outwards, irrepressible, into all that we touch and handle, speak and work; kindling ever new light, by incalculable contagion, spreading in geometric ratio, far and wide,—doing good only, wheresoever it spreads, and not evil.

By Reform Bills, Anti-Corn-Law Bills, and thousand other bills and methods, we will demand of our Governors, with emphasis, and for the first time not without effect, that they cease to be quacks, or else depart; that they set no quackeries and blockheadisms anywhere to rule over us, that they utter or act no cant to us,—it will be better if they do not. For we shall now know quacks when we see them; cant, when we hear it, shall be horrible to us! We will say, with the poor Frenchman at the Bar of the Convention, though in wiser style than he, and 'for the space' not 'of an hour' but of a lifetime: " *Je demande l'arrestation des coquins et des lâches.*" 'Arrestment of the knaves and dastards:' ah, we know what a work that is; how long it will be before *they* are all or mostly got ' arrested: '—but here is one; arrest him, in God's name; it is one fewer! We will, in all practicable ways, by word and silence, by act and refusal to act, energetically demand that arrestment,—" *je demande cette arrestation-*

là !"—and by degrees infallibly attain it. Infallibly: for light spreads; all human souls, never so bedarkened, love light; light once kindled spreads, till all is luminous; —till the cry, "*Arrest* your knaves and dastards" rises imperative from millions of hearts, and rings and reigns from sea to sea. Nay how many of them may we not 'arrest' with our own hands, even now; we! Do not countenance them, thou there: turn away from their lacquered sumptuosities, their belauded sophistries, their serpent graciosities, their spoken and acted cant, with a sacred horror, with an *Apage Satanas.*—Bobus and Company, and all men will gradually join us. We demand arrestment of the knaves and dastards, and begin by arresting our own poor selves out of that fraternity. There is no other reform conceivable. Thou and I, my friend, can, in the most flunky world, make, each of us, *one* non-flunky, one hero, if we like: that will be two heroes to begin with:—Courage! even that is a whole world of heroes to end with, or what we poor Two can do in furtherance thereof!

Yes, friends: Hero-kings, and a whole world not unheroic,—there lies the port and happy haven, towards which, through all these stormtost seas, French Revolutions, Chartisms, Manchester Insurrections, that make the heart sick in these bad days, the Supreme Powers are driving us. On the whole, blessed be the Supreme Powers, stern as they are! Towards that haven will we, O friends; let all true men, with what of faculty is in them, bend valiantly, incessantly, with thousandfold endeavour, thither, thither! There, or else in the Ocean-abysses, it is very clear to me, we shall arrive.

Well; here truly is no answer to the Sphinx-question; not the answer a disconsolate public, inquiring at the College of Health, was in hopes of! A total change of regimen, change of constitution and existence from the very centre of it; a new body to be got, with resuscitated soul,—not without convulsive travail-throes; as all birth and new-birth presupposes travail! This is sad news to a disconsolate discerning Public, hoping to have got off by some Morrison's Pill, some Saint-John's corrosive mixture and perhaps a little blistery friction on the back!—We were prepared to part with our Corn-Law, with various Laws and Unlaws: but this, what is this?

Nor has the Editor forgotten how it fares with your ill-boding Cassandras in Sieges of Troy. Imminent perdition is not usually driven away by words of warning. Didactic Destiny has other methods in store; or these would fail always. Such words should, nevertheless, be uttered, when they dwell truly in the soul of any man. Words are hard, are importunate; but how much harder the importunate events they foreshadow! Here and there a human soul may listen to the words,—who knows how many human souls?—whereby the importunate events, if not diverted and prevented, will be rendered *less* hard. The present Editor's purpose is to himself full of hope.

For though fierce travails, though wide seas and roaring gulfs lie before us, is it not something if a Loadstar, in the eternal sky, do once more disclose itself; an everlasting light, shining through all cloud-tempests and roaring billows, ever as we emerge from the trough of the sea: the blessed beacon, far off on the edge of far horizons, towards which we are to steer incessantly for life? Is it not something; O Heavens, is it not all? There lies the Heroic Promised Land; under that Heaven's-light, my brethren, bloom the Happy Isles,—there, O there! Thither will we;

'There dwells the great Achilles whom we knew.' [1]

There dwell all Heroes, and will dwell: thither, all ye heroic-minded!—The Heaven's Loadstar once clearly in our eye, how will each true man stand truly to *his* work in the ship; how, with undying hope, will all things be fronted, all be conquered. Nay, with the ship's prow once turned in that direction, is not all, as it were, already well? Sick wasting misery has become noble manful effort with a goal in our eye. 'The choking Nightmare

[1] Tennyson's *Poems* (Ulysses).

chokes us no longer; for we *stir* under it; the Nightmare
has already fled.'—

Certainly, could the present Editor instruct men how
to know Wisdom, Heroism, when they see it, that they
might do reverence to *it* only, and loyally make it ruler
over them,—yes, he were the living epitome of all Editors,
Teachers, Prophets, that now teach and prophesy; he
were an *Apollo*-Morrison, a Trismegistus and *effective*
Cassandra! Let no Able Editor hope such things. It
is to be expected the present laws of copyright, rate of
reward per sheet, and other considerations, will save him
from that peril. Let no Editor hope such things: no;—
and yet let all Editors aim towards such things, and even
towards such alone! One knows not what the meaning
of editing and writing is, if even this be not it.

Enough, to the present Editor it has seemed possible
some glimmering of light, for here and there a human
soul, might lie in these confused Paper-Masses now in-
trusted to him; wherefore he determines to edit the same.
Out of old Books, new Writings, and much Meditation
not of yesterday, he will endeavour to select a thing or
two; and from the Past, in a circuitous way, illustrate
the Present and the Future. The Past is a dim indubitable
fact: the Future too is one, only dimmer; nay properly
it is the *same* fact in new dress and development. For
the Present holds it in both the whole Past and the whole
Future;—as the Life-tree Igdrasil, wide-waving, many-
toned, has its roots down deep in the Death-kingdoms,
among the oldest dead dust of men, and with its boughs
reaches always beyond the stars; and in all times and
places is one and the same Life-tree!

BOOK II.—THE ANCIENT MONK

CHAPTER I

JOCELIN OF BRAKELOND

WE will, in this Second Portion of our Work, strive to penetrate a little, by means of certain confused Papers, printed and other, into a somewhat remote Century; and to look face to face on it, in hope of perhaps illustrating our own poor Century thereby. It seems a circuitous way; but it may prove a way nevertheless. For man has ever been a striving, struggling, and, in spite of widespread calumnies to the contrary, a veracious creature: the Centuries too are all lineal children of one another; and often, in the portrait of early grandfathers, this and the other enigmatic feature of the newest grandson shall disclose itself, to mutual elucidation. This Editor will venture on such a thing.

Besides, in Editors' Books, and indeed everywhere else in the world of Today, a certain latitude of movement grows more and more becoming for the practical man. Salvation lies not in tight lacing, in these times;—how far from that, in any province whatsoever! Readers and men generally are getting into strange habits of asking all persons and things, from poor Editors' Books up to Church Bishops and State Potentates, not, By what designation art thou called; in what wig and black triangle dost thou walk abroad? Heavens, I know thy designation and black triangle well enough! But, in God's name, what *art* thou? Not Nothing, sayest thou! Then, How much and what? This is the thing I would know; and even *must* soon know, such a pass am I come to!—— What weather-symptoms, — not for the poor Editor of Books alone! The Editor of Books may understand withal that if, as is said, 'many kinds are permissible,' there is one kind not permissible, 'the kind that has nothing in it, *le genre ennuyeux ;* ' and go on his way accordingly.

A certain Jocelinus de Brakelonda, a natural-born Englishman, has left us an extremely foreign Book,[1] which the labours of the Camden Society have brought to light in these days. Jocelin's Book, the 'Chronicle,' or private Boswellean Notebook, of Jocelin, a certain old St. Edmundsbury Monk and Boswell, now seven centuries old, how remote is it from us; exotic, extraneous; in all ways, coming from far abroad! The language of it is not foreign only but dead: Monk-Latin lies across not the British Channel, but the ninefold Stygian Marshes, Stream of Lethe, and one knows not where! Roman Latin itself, still alive for us in the Elysian Fields of Memory, is domestic in comparison. And then the ideas, life-furniture, whole workings and ways of this worthy Jocelin; covered deeper than Pompeii with the lava-ashes and inarticulate wreck of seven hundred years!

Jocelin of Brakelond cannot be called a conspicuous literary character; indeed few mortals that have left so visible a work, or footmark, behind them can be more obscure. One other of those vanished Existences, whose work has not yet vanished;—almost a pathetic phenomenon, were not the whole world full of such! The builders of Stonehenge, for example:—or, alas, what say we, Stonehenge and builders? The writers of the *Universal Review* and *Homer's Iliad;* the paviors of London streets;—sooner or later, the entire Posterity of Adam! It is a pathetic phenomenon; but an irremediable, nay, if well meditated, a consoling one.

By his dialect of Monk-Latin, and indeed by his name, this Jocelin seems to have been a Norman Englishman; the surname *de Brakelonda* indicates a native of St. Edmundsbury itself, *Brakelond* being the known old name of a street or quarter in that venerable Town. Then

[1] *Chronica* JOCELINI DE BRAKELONDA, *de rebus gestis Samsonis Abbatis Monasterii Sancti Edmundi : nunc primum typis mandata, curante Johanne Gage Rokewood.* (Camden Society, London, 1840.)

farther, sure enough, our Jocelin was a Monk of St.
Edmundsbury Convent; held some ' *obedientia*,' subaltern
officiality there, or rather, in succession several; was, for
one thing, ' chaplain to my Lord Abbot, living beside him
night and day for the space of six years;'—which last,
indeed, is the grand fact of Jocelin's existence, and properly
the origin of this present Book, and of the chief meaning
it has for us now. He was, as we have hinted, a kind of
born *Boswell*, though an infinitesimally small one; neither
did he altogether want his *Johnson* even there and then.
Johnsons are rare; yet, as has been asserted, Boswells
perhaps still rarer,—the more is the pity on both sides!
This Jocelin, as we can discern well, was an ingenious and
ingenuous, a cheery-hearted, innocent, yet withal shrewd,
noticing, quick-witted man; and from under his monk's
cowl has looked out on that narrow section of the world
in a really *human* manner; not in any *simial*, canine,
ovine, or otherwise *in*human manner,—afflictive to all
that have humanity! The man is of patient, peaceable,
loving, clear-smiling nature; open for this and that. A
wise simplicity is in him; much natural sense; a *veracity*
that goes deeper than words. Veracity: it is the basis of
all; and, some say, means genius itself; the prime essence
of all genius whatsoever. Our Jocelin, for the rest, has
read his classical manuscripts, his Virgilius, his Flaccus,
Ovidius Naso; of course still more, his Homilies and
Breviaries, and if not the Bible, considerable extracts of
the Bible. Then also he has a pleasant wit; and loves a
timely joke, though in mild subdued manner; very
amiable to see. A learned grown man, yet with the heart
as of a good child; whose whole life indeed has been that
of a child,—St. Edmundsbury Monastery a larger kind of
cradle for him, in which his whole prescribed duty was to
sleep kindly, and love his mother well! This is the
Biography of Jocelin; ' a man of excellent religion,' says
one of his contemporary Brother monks, '*eximiæ religionis,
potens sermone et opere.*'

For one thing, he had learned to write a kind of Monk
or Dog-Latin, still readable to mankind; and, by good
luck for us, had bethought him of noting down thereby

what things seemed notablest to him. Hence gradually
resulted a *Chronica Jocelini ;* new Manuscript in the *Liber
Albus* of St. Edmundsbury. Which Chronicle, once
written in its childlike transparency, in its innocent good-
humour, not without touches of ready pleasant wit and
many kinds of worth, other men liked naturally to read:
whereby it failed not to be copied, to be multiplied, to be
inserted in the *Liber Albus ;* and so surviving Henry the
Eighth, Putney Cromwell, the Dissolution of Monasteries,
and all accidents of malice and neglect for six centuries or
so, it got into the *Harleian Collection,*—and has now therefrom, by Mr. Rokewood of the Camden Society, been
deciphered into clear print; and lies before us, a dainty
thin quarto, to interest for a few minutes whomsoever it
can.

Here too it will behove a just Historian gratefully to
say that Mr. Rokewood, Jocelin's Editor, has done his
editorial function well. Not only has he deciphered his
crabbed Manuscript into clear print; but he has attended,
what his fellow editors are not always in the habit of doing,
to the important truth that the Manuscript so deciphered
ought to have a meaning for the reader. Standing faithfully by his text, and printing its very errors in spelling, in
grammar or otherwise, he has taken care by some note to
indicate that they are errors, and what the correction of
them ought to be. Jocelin's Monk-Latin is generally
transparent, as shallow limpid water. But at any stop
that may occur, of which there are a few, and only a very
few, we have the comfortable assurance that a meaning
does lie in the passage, and may by industry be got at;
that a faithful editor's industry had already got at it
before passing on. A compendious useful Glossary is
given; nearly adequate to help the uninitiated through:
sometimes one wishes it had been a trifle larger; but, with
a Spelman and Ducange at your elbow, how easy to have
made it far too large! Notes are added, generally brief;
sufficiently explanatory of most points. Lastly, a copious
correct Index; which no such Book should want, and
which unluckily very few possess. And so, in a word, the
Chronicle of Jocelin is, as it professes to be, unwrapped

from its thick cerements, and fairly brought forth into
the common daylight, so that he who runs, and has a
smattering of grammar, may read.

We have heard so much of Monks; everywhere, in real
and fictitious History, from Muratori Annals to Radcliffe
Romances, these singular two legged animals, with their
rosaries and breviaries, with their shaven crowns, hair-
cilices, and vows of poverty, masquerade so strangely
through our fancy; and they are in fact so very strange
an extinct species of the human family,—a veritable Monk
of Bury St. Edmunds is worth attending to, if by chance
made visible and audible. Here he is; and in his hand
a magical speculum, much gone to rust indeed, yet in
fragments still clear; wherein the marvellous image of his
existence does still shadow itself, though fitfully, and as
with an intermittent light! Will not the reader peep
with us into this singular *camera lucida*, where an extinct
species, though fitfully, can still be seen alive? Extinct
species, we say; for the live specimens which still go about
under that character are too evidently to be classed as
spurious in Natural History: the Gospel of Richard Arkwright once promulgated, no Monk of the old sort is any
longer possible in this world. But fancy a deep-buried
Mastodon, some fossil Megatherion, Ichthyosaurus, were
to begin to *speak* from amid its rock-swathings, never so
indistinctly! The most extinct fossil species of Men or
Monks can do, and does, this miracle,—thanks to the
Letters of the Alphabet, good for so many things.

Jocelin, we said, was somewhat of a Boswell; but
unfortunately, by Nature, he is none of the largest, and
distance has now dwarfed him to an extreme degree.
His light is most feeble, intermittent, and requires the
intensest kindest inspection; otherwise, it will disclose
mere vacant haze. It must be owned, the good Jocelin,
spite of his beautiful child-like character, is but an altogether imperfect ' mirror ' of these old-world things! The
good man, he looks on us so clear and cheery, and in his
neighbourly soft-smiling eyes we see so well our *own*
shadow,—we have a longing always to cross-question him,

to force from him an explanation of much. But no; Jocelin, though he talks with such clear familiarity, like a next-door neighbour, will not answer any question: that is the peculiarity of him, dead these six hundred and fifty years, and quite deaf to us, though still so audible! The good man, he cannot help it, nor can we.

But truly it is a strange consideration this simple one, as we go on with him, or indeed with any lucid simple-hearted soul like him: Behold therefore, this England of the Year 1200 was no chimerical vacuity or dreamland, peopled with mere vaporous Fantasms, Rymer's Fœdera, and Doctrines of the Constitution; but a green solid place, that grew corn and several other things. The Sun shone on it; the vicissitude of seasons and human fortunes. Cloth was woven and worn; ditches were dug, furrow-fields ploughed, and houses built. Day by day all men and cattle rose to labour, and night by night returned home weary to their several lairs. In wondrous Dualism, then as now, lived nations of breathing men; alternating, in all ways, between Light and Dark; between joy and sorrow, between rest and toil,—between hope, hope reaching high as Heaven, and fear deep as very Hell. Not vapour Fantasms, Rymer's Fœdera at all! Cœur-de-Lion was not a theatrical popinjay with greaves and steel-cap on it, but a man living upon victuals,—*not* imported by Peel's Tariff. Cœur-de-Lion came palpably athwart this Jocelin at St. Edmundsbury; and had almost peeled the sacred gold ' *Feretrum*,' or St. Edmund Shrine itself, to ransom him out of the Danube Jail.

These clear eyes of neighbour Jocelin looked on the bodily presence of King John; the very John *Sansterre*, or Lackland, who signed *Magna Charta* afterwards in Runnymead. Lackland, with a great retinue, boarded once, for the matter of a fortnight, in St. Edmundsbury Convent; daily in the very eyesight, palpable to the very fingers of our Jocelin: O Jocelin, what did he say, what did he do; how looked he, lived he;—at the very lowest, what coat or breeches had he on? Jocelin is obstinately silent. Jocelin marks down what interests *him;* entirely deaf to *us*. With Jocelin's eyes we discern almost nothing

of John Lackland. As through a glass darkly, we with
our own eyes and appliances, intensely looking, discern
at most: A blustering, dissipated human figure, with a
kind of blackguard quality air, in cramoisy velvet, or other
uncertain texture, uncertain cut, with much plumage and
fringing; amid numerous other human figures of the like;
riding abroad with hawks; talking noisy nonsense;—tear-
out the bowels of St. Edmundsbury Convent (its larders
namely and cellars) in the most ruinous way, by living at
rack and manger there. Jocelin notes only, with a slight
subacidity of manner, that the King's Majesty, *Dominus
Rex*, did leave, as gift for our St. Edmund Shrine, a handsome enough silk cloak,—or rather pretended to leave,
for one of his retinue borrowed it of us, and *we* never got
sight of it again; and, on the whole, that the *Dominus Rex*,
at departing, gave us ' thirteen *sterlingii*,' one shilling and
one penny, to say a mass for him; and so departed,—like
a shabby Lackland as he was! 'Thirteen pence sterling,'
this was what the Convent got from Lackland, for all the
victuals he and his had made away with. We of course
said our mass for him, having covenanted to do it,—but
let impartial posterity judge with what degree of fervour!

And in this manner vanishes King Lackland; traverses
swiftly our strange intermittent magic-mirror, jingling
the shabby thirteen pence merely; and rides with his
hawks into Egyptian night again. It is Jocelin's manner
with all things; and it is men's manner and men's necessity.
How intermittent is our good Jocelin; marking down,
without eye to *us*, what *he* finds interesting! How much
in Jocelin, as in all History, and indeed in all Nature, is
at once inscrutable and certain; so dim, yet so indubitable; exciting us to endless considerations. For King
Lackland *was* there, verily he; and did leave these
tredecim sterlingii, if nothing more, and did live and look
in one way or the other, and a whole world was living and
looking along with him! There, we say, is the grand
peculiarity; the immeasurable one; distinguishing, to a
really infinite degree, the poorest historical Fact from all
Fiction whatsoever. Fiction, ' Imagination,' ' Imaginative Poetry,' etc. etc., except as the vehicle for truth, or

act of some sort,—which surely a man should first try various other ways of vehiculating, and conveying safe, —what is it? Let the Minerva and other Presses respond!—

But it is time we were in St. Edmundsbury Monastery and Seven good Centuries off. If indeed it be possible, by any aid of Jocelin, by any human art, to get thither, with a reader or two still following us?

CHAPTER II

ST. EDMUNDSBURY

THE *Burg*, Bury, or ' Berry ' as they call it, of St. Edmund is still a prosperous brisk Town; beautifully diversifying, with its clear brick houses, ancient clean streets, and twenty or fifteen thousand busy souls, the general grassy face of Suffolk; looking out right pleasantly, from its hill-slope, towards the rising Sun: and on the eastern edge of it, still runs, long, black and massive, a range of monastic ruins; into the wide internal spaces of which the stranger is admitted on payment of one shilling. Internal spaces laid out, at present, as a botanic garden. Here stranger or townsman, sauntering at his leisure amid these vast grim venerable ruins, may persuade himself that an Abbey of St. Edmundsbury did once exist; nay there is no doubt of it: see here the ancient massive Gateway, of architecture interesting to the eye of Dilettantism; and farther on, that other ancient Gateway, now about to tumble, unless Dilettantism, in these very months, can subscribe money to cramp it and prop it !

Here, sure enough, is an Abbey; beautiful in the eye of Dilettantism. Giant Pedantry also will step in, with its huge *Dugdale* and other enormous *Monasticons* under its arm, and cheerfully apprise you, That this was a very great Abbey, owner and indeed creator of St. Edmund's Town itself, owner of wide lands and revenues; nay that its land were once a county of themselves; that indeed King Canute or Knut was very kind to it, and gave St.

Edmund his own gold crown off his head, on one occasion:
for the rest, that the Monks were of such and such a
genus, such and such a number; that they had so many
carucates of land in this hundred, and so many in that;
and then farther that the large Tower or Belfry was built
by such a one, and the smaller Belfry was built by etc. etc.
—Till human nature can stand no more of it; till human
nature desperately take refuge in forgetfulness, almost in
flat disbelief of the whole business, Monks, Monastery,
Belfries, Carucates and all! Alas, what mountains of
dead ashes, wreck and burnt bones, does assiduous
Pedantry dig up from the Past Time, and name it History,
and Philosophy of History; till, as we say, the human
soul sinks wearied and bewildered; till the Past Time
seems all one infinite incredible gray void, without sun,
stars, hearth-fires, or candle-light; dim offensive dust-
whirlwinds filling universal Nature; and over your
Historical Library, it is as if all the Titans had written for
themselves: DRY RUBBISH SHOT HERE!

And yet these grim old walls are not a dilettantism and
dubiety; they are an earnest fact. It was a most real
and serious purpose they were built for! Yes, another
world it was, when these black ruins, white in their new
mortar and fresh chiselling, first saw the sun as walls,
long ago. Gauge not, with thy dilettante compasses,
with that placid dilettante simper, the Heaven's-Watch-
tower of our Fathers, the fallen God's-Houses, the
Golgotha of true Souls departed!

Their architecture, belfries, land-carucates? Yes,—
and that is but a small item of the matter. Does it never
give thee pause, this other strange item of it, that men
then had a *soul*,—not by hearsay alone, and as a figure of
speech; but as a truth that they *knew*, and practically
went upon! Verily it was another world then. Their
Missals have become incredible, a sheer platitude, sayest
thou? Yes, a most poor platitude; and even, if thou
wilt, an idolatry and blasphemy, should any one persuade
thee to believe them, to pretend praying by them. But
yet it is pity we had lost tidings of our souls:—actually
we shall have to go in quest of them again, or worse in all

ways will befall! A certain degree of soul, as Ben Jonson reminds us, is indispensable to keep the very body from destruction of the frightfulest sort; to ' save us,' says he. ' the expense of *salt*.' Ben has known men who had soul enough to keep their body and five senses from becoming carrion, and save salt:—men, and also Nations. You may look in Manchester Hunger-mobs and Corn-law Commons Houses, and various other quarters, and say whether either soul or else salt is not somewhat wanted at present!—

Another world, truly: and this present poor distressed world might get some profit by looking wisely into it, instead of foolishly. But at lowest, O dilettante friend, let us know always that it *was* a world, and not a void infinite of gray haze with fantasms swimming in it. These old St. Edmundsbury walls, I say, were not peopled with fantasms; but with men of flesh and blood, made altogether as we are. Had thou and I then been, who knows but we ourselves had taken refuge from an evil Time, and fled to dwell here, and meditate on an Eternity, in such fashion as we could? Alas, how like an old osseous fragment, a broken blackened shin-bone of the old dead Ages, this black ruin looks out, not yet covered by the soil; still indicating what a once gigantic Life lies buried there! It is dead now, and dumb; but was alive once, and spake. For twenty generations, here was the earthly arena where painful living men worked out their life-wrestle,—looked at by Earth, by Heaven and Hell. Bells tolled to prayers; and men, of many humours, various thoughts, chanted vespers, matins;—and round the little islet of their life rolled forever (as round ours still rolls, though we are blind and deaf) the illimitable Ocean, tinting all things with *its* eternal hues and reflexes; making strange prophetic music! How silent now; all departed, clean gone. The World-Dramaturgist has written: *Exeunt*. The devouring Time-Demons have made away with it all: and in its stead, there is either nothing; or what is worse, offensive universal dust-clouds, and gray eclipse of Earth and Heaven, from ' dry rubbish shot here!'—

Truly it is no easy matter to get across the chasm of Seven Centuries, filled with such material. But here, of all helps, is not a Boswell the welcomest; even a small Boswell? Veracity, true simplicity of heart, how valuable are these always! He that speaks what *is* really in him, will find men to listen, though under never such impediments. Even gossip, springing free and cheery from a human heart, this too is a kind of veracity and *speech;* —much preferable to pedantry and inane gray haze! Jocelin is weak and garrulous, but he is human. Through the thin watery gossip of our Jocelin, we do get some glimpses of that deep-buried Time; discern veritably, though in a fitful intermittent manner, these antique figures and their life-method, face to face! Beautifully, in our earnest loving glance, the old centuries melt from opaque to partially translucent, transparent here and there; and the void black Night, one finds, is but the summing-up of innumerable peopled luminous *Days.* Not parchment Chartularies, Doctrines of the Constitution, O Dryasdust; not altogether, my erudite friend!—

Readers who please to go along with us into this poor *Jocelini Chronica* shall wander inconveniently enough, as in wintry twilight, through some poor stript hazel-grove, rustling with foolish noises, and perpetually hindering the eyesight; but across which, here and there, some real human figure is seen moving: very strange; whom we could hail if he would answer;—and we look into a pair of eyes deep as our own, *imaging* our own, but all unconscious of us; to whom we, for the time, are become as spirits and invisible!

CHAPTER III

LANDLORD EDMUND

SOME three centuries or so had elapsed since *Beodric's-worth* [1] became St. Edmund's *Stow*, St. Edmund's *Town* and Monastery, before Jocelin entered himself a Novice there. ' It was,' says he, ' the year after the Flemings were defeated at Fornham St. Genevieve.'

Much passes away into oblivion: this glorious victory over the Flemings at Fornham has, at the present date, greatly dimmed itself out of the minds of men. A victory and battle nevertheless it was, in its time: some thrice-renowned Earl of Leicester, not of the De Montfort breed (as may be read in Philosophical and other Histories, could any human memory retain such things), had quarrelled with his sovereign, Henry Second of the name; had been worsted, it is like, and maltreated, and obliged to fly to foreign parts; but had rallied there into new vigour; and so, in the year 1173, returns across the German Sea with a vengeful army of Flemings. Returns, to the coast of Suffolk; to Framlingham Castle, where he is welcomed; westward towards St. Edmundsbury and Fornham Church, where he is met by the constituted authorities with *posse comitatus ;* and swiftly cut in pieces, he and his, or laid by the heels; on the right bank of the obscure river Lark,—as traces still existing will verify.

¹ Dryasdust puzzles and pokes for some biography of this Beodric; and repugns to consider him a mere East-Anglian Person of Condition, not in need of a biography,—whose Þeopð, *weorth* or *worth*, that is to say, *Growth*, Increase, or as we should now name it, *Estate*, that same Hamlet and wood Mansion, now St. Edmund's Bury, originally was. For, adds our erudite Friend, the Saxon Þeopðan, equivalent to the German *werden*, means to *grow*, to *become ;* traces of which old vocable are still found in the North-country dialects; as, ' What is *word* of him? ' meaning, ' What is *become* of him? ' and the like. Nay we in modern English still say, ' Woe *worth* the hour ' (Woe *befall* the hour), and speak of the ' *Weird* Sisters;' not to mention the innumerable other names of places still ending in *weorth* or *worth*. And indeed, our common noun *worth*, in the sense of *value*, does not this mean simply, What a thing has *grown* to, What a man has *grown* to, How much he amounts to,—by the Threadneedle-street standard or another!

For the river Lark, though not very discoverably, still runs or stagnates in that country; and the battle-ground is there; serving at present as a pleasure-ground to his Grace of Northumberland. Copper pennies of Henry II. are still found there;—rotted out from the pouches of poor slain soldiers, who had not had *time* to buy liquor with them. In the river Lark itself was fished up, within man's memory, an antique gold ring; which fond Dilettantism can almost believe may have been the very ring Countess Leicester threw away, in her flight, into that same Lark river or ditch.[1] Nay, few years ago, in tearing out an enormous superannuated ash-tree, now grown quite corpulent, bursten, superfluous, but long a fixture in the soil, and not to be dislodged without revolution,— there was laid bare, under its roots, 'a circular mound of skeletons wonderfully complete,' all radiating from a centre, faces upwards, feet inwards; a 'radiation' not of Light, but of the Nether Darkness rather; and evidently the fruit of battle; for 'many of the heads were cleft, or had arrow-holes in them.' The Battle of Fornham, therefore, is a fact, though a forgotten one; no less obscure than undeniable,—like so many other facts.

Like the St. Edmund's Monastery itself! Who can doubt, after what we have said, that there was a Monastery here at one time? No doubt at all there was a Monastery here; no doubt, some three centuries prior to this Fornham Battle, there dwelt a man in these parts of the name of Edmund, King, Landlord, Duke or whatever his title was, of the Eastern Counties;—and a very singular man and landlord he must have been.

For his tenants, it would appear, did not in the least complain of him; his labourers did not think of burning his wheat stacks, breaking into his game-preserves; very far the reverse of all that. Clear evidence, satisfactory even to my friend Dryasdust, exists that, on the contrary, they honoured, loved, admired this ancient Landlord to a quite astonishing degree,—and indeed at last to an immeasurable and inexpressible degree; for, finding no

---

[1] Lyttelton's *History of Henry II*. (2nd edition), v. 169, etc.

limits or utterable words for their sense of his worth, they
took to beatifying and adoring him! ' Infinite admiration,' we are taught, ' means worship.'

Very singular,—could we discover it! What Edmund's
specific duties were; above all, what his method of dis-
charging them with such results was, would surely be
interesting to know; but are *not* very discoverable now.
His life has become a poetic, nay a religious *Mythus;*
though, undeniably enough, it was once a prose Fact, as
our poor lives are; and even a very rugged unmanageable
one. This landlord Edmund did go about in leather
shoes, with *femoralia* and bodycoat of some sort on him;
and daily had his breakfast to procure; and daily had
contradictory speeches, and most contradictory facts not
a few, to reconcile with himself. No man becomes a
Saint in his sleep. Edmund, for instance, instead of
reconciling those same contradictory facts and speeches to
himself,—which means *subduing,* and in a manlike and
godlike manner conquering them to himself,—might have
merely thrown new contention into them, new unwisdom
into them, and so been conquered *by* them; much the
commoner case! In that way he had proved no ' Saint,'
or Divine-looking Man, but a mere Sinner, and unfortunate,
blameable, more or less Diabolic-looking man! No landlord Edmund becomes infinitely admirable in his sleep.

With what degree of wholesome rigour his rents were
collected, we hear not. Still less by what methods he
preserved his game, whether by ' bushing ' or how,—and
if the partridge-seasons were ' excellent,' or were indifferent. Neither do we ascertain what kind of Corn-
bill he passed, or wisely-adjusted Sliding-scale:—but
indeed there were few spinners in those days; and the
nuisance of spinning, and other dusty labour, was not
yet so glaring a one.

How then, it may be asked, did this Edmund rise into
favour; become to such astonishing extent a recognised
Farmer's Friend? Really, except it were by doing justly
and loving mercy to an unprecedented extent, one does
not know. The man, it would seem ' had walked,' as
they say, ' humbly with God;' humbly and valiantly with

God; struggling to make the Earth heavenly as he could: instead of walking sumptuously and pridefully with Mammon, leaving the Earth to grow hellish as it liked. Not sumptuously with Mammon? How then could he 'encourage trade,'—cause Howel and James, and many wine-merchants, to bless him, and the tailor's heart (though in a very short-sighted manner) to sing for joy? Much in this Edmund's Life is mysterious.

That he could, on occasion, do what he liked with his own, is meanwhile evident enough. Certain Heathen Physical-Force Ultra-Chartists, 'Danes' as they were then called, coming into his territory with their 'five points,' or rather with their five-and-twenty thousand *points* and edges too, of pikes namely and battle-axes; and proposing mere Heathenism, confiscation, spoliation, and fire and sword,—Edmund answered that he would oppose to the utmost such savagery. They took him prisoner; again required his sanction to said proposals. Edmund again refused. Cannot we kill you? cried they. —Cannot I die? answered he. My life, I think, is my own to do what I like with! And he died, under barbarous tortures, refusing to the last breath; and the Ultra-Chartist Danes *lost* their propositions;—and went with their 'points' and other apparatus, as is supposed, to the Devil, the Father of them. Some say, indeed, these Danes were not Ultra-Chartists, but Ultra-Tories, demanding to reap where they had not sown, and live in this world without working, though all the world should starve for it; which likewise seems a possible hypothesis. Be what they might, they went, as we say, to the Devil: and Edmund doing what he liked with his own, the Earth was got cleared of them.

Another version is, that Edmund on this and the like occasions stood by his order; the oldest, and indeed only true order of Nobility known under the stars, that of Just Men and Sons of God, in opposition to Unjust and Sons of Belial,—which latter indeed are *second*-oldest, but yet a very unvenerable order. This, truly, seems the likeliest hypothesis of all. Names and appearances alter so strangely, in some half - score centuries; and all

fluctuates chameleon-like, taking now this hue, now that.
Thus much is very plain, and does not change hue; Landlord Edmund was seen and felt by all men to have done
verily a man's part in this life-pilgrimage of his; and
benedictions, and outflowing love and admiration from
the universal heart, were his meed. Well-done! Well-
done! cried the hearts of all men. They raised his slain
and martyred body; washed its wounds with fast-flowing
universal tears; tears of endless pity, and yet of a sacred
joy and triumph. The beautifulest kind of tears,—
indeed perhaps the beautifulest kind of thing: like a sky
all flashing diamonds and prismatic radiance; all weeping,
yet shone on by the everlasting Sun:—and *this* is not a
sky, it is a Soul and living Face! Nothing liker the
Temple of the Highest, bright with some real effulgence of
the Highest, is seen in this world.

Oh, if all Yankee-land follow a small good ' Schnüspel
the distinguished Novelist ' with blazing torches, dinner-
invitations, universal hep-hep-hurrah, feeling that he,
though small, *is* something; how might all Angle-land
once follow a hero-martyr and great true Son of Heaven!
It is the very joy of man's heart to admire, where he can;
nothing so lifts him from all his mean imprisonments,
were it but for moments, as true admiration. Thus it has
been said, ' all men, especially all women, are born wor-
shippers; ' and will worship, if it be but possible. Possible
to worship a Something, even a small one; not so possible
a mere loud-blaring Nothing! What sight is more
pathetic than that of poor multitudes of persons met to
gaze at Kings' Progresses, Lord Mayors' Shows, and other
gilt-gingerbread phenomena of the worshipful sort, in
these times; each so eager to worship; each, with a dim
fatal sense of disappointment, finding that he cannot
rightly here! There be thy gods, O Israel? And thou
art so *willing* to worship,—poor Israel!

In this manner, however, did the men of the Eastern
Counties take up the slain body of their Edmund, where
it lay cast forth in the village of Hoxne; seek out the
severed head, and reverently reunite the same. They
embalmed him with myrrh and sweet spices, with love,

pity, and all high and awful thoughts; consecrating him
with a very storm of melodious adoring admiration, and
sun-dyed showers of tears;—joyfully, yet with awe (as
all deep joy has something of the awful in it), com-
memorating his noble deeds and godlike walk and conversation while on Earth. Till, at length, the very Pope
and Cardinals at Rome were forced to hear of it; and
they, summing up as correctly as they well could, with
Advocatus-Diaboli pleadings and their other forms of
process, the general verdict of mankind, declared: That
he had, in very fact, led a hero's life in this world; and
being now *gone,* was gone, as they conceived, to God
above, and reaping his reward *there.* Such, they said, was
the best judgment they could form of the case;—and
truly not a bad judgment. Acquiesced in, zealously
adopted, with full assent of 'private judgment,' by all
mortals.

The rest of St. Edmund's history, for the reader sees
he has now become a *Saint,* is easily conceivable. Pious
munificence provided him a *loculus,* a *feretrum* or shrine;
built for him a wooden chapel, a stone temple, ever
widening and growing by new pious gifts;—such the
overflowing heart feels it a blessedness to solace itself by
giving. St. Edmund's Shrine glitters now with diamond
flowerages, with a plating of wrought gold. The wooden
chapel, as we say, has become a stone temple. Stately
masonries, long-drawn arches, cloisters, sounding aisles
buttress it, begirdle it far and wide. Regimented com-
panies of men, of whom our Jocelin is one, devote themselves, in every generation, to meditate here on man's
Nobleness and Awfulness, and celebrate and show forth
the same, as they best can,—thinking they will do it
better here, in presence of God the Maker, and of the so
Awful and so Noble made by Him. In one word, St.
Edmund's Body has raised a Monastery round it. To
such length, in such manner, has the Spirit of the Time
visibly taken body, and crystallised itself here. New
gifts, houses, farms, *katalla* [1]—come ever in. King Knut,

[1] Goods, properties; what we now call *chattels,* and still more
singularly *cattle,* says my erudite friend.

whom men call Canute, whom the Oceantide would not be
forbidden to wet,—we heard already of this wise King,
with his crown and gifts; but of many others, Kings,
Queens, wise men and noble loyal women, let Dryasdust
and divine Silence be the record! Beodric's-Worth has
become St. Edmund's *Bury ;*—and lasts visible to this
hour. All this that thou now seest, and namest Bury
Town, is properly the Funeral Monument of Saint or
Landlord Edmund. The present respectable Mayor of
Bury may be said, like a Fakeer (little as he thinks of it),
to have his dwelling in the extensive, many-sculptured
Tombstone of St. Edmund; in one of the brick niches
thereof dwells the present respectable Mayor of Bury.

Certain Times do crystallise themselves in a magnificent
manner; and others, perhaps, are like to do it in rather
a shabby one!—But Richard Arkwright too will have his
Monument, a thousand years hence: all Lancashire and
Yorkshire, and how many other shires and countries,
with their machineries and industries, for his monument!
A true *pyr*amid or '*flame*-mountain,' flaming with steam
fires and useful labour over wide continents, usefully
towards the Stars, to a certain height;—how much
grander than your foolish Cheops Pyramids or Sakhara
clay ones! Let us withal be hopeful, be content or
patient.

CHAPTER IV

ABBOT HUGO

It is true all things have two faces, a light one and a
dark. It is true, in three centuries much imperfection
accumulates; many an Ideal, monastic or other, shooting
forth into practice as it can, grows to a strange enough
Reality; and we have to ask with amazement, Is this
your Ideal! For, alas, the Ideal always has to grow in
the Real, and to seek out its bed and board there, often
in a very sorry way. No beautifulest Poet is a Bird-of-
Paradise, living on perfumes; sleeping in the æther with

outspread wings. The Heroic, *independent* of bed and board, is found in Drury-Lane Theatre only; to avoid disappointments, let us bear this in mind.

By the law of Nature, too, all manner of Ideals have their fatal limits and lot; their appointed periods, of youth, of maturity or perfection, of decline, degradation, and final death and disappearance. There is nothing born but has to die. Ideal monasteries, once grown real, do seek bed and board in this world; do find it more and more successfully; do get at length too intent on finding it, exclusively intent on that. They are then like diseased corpulent bodies fallen idiotic, which merely eat and sleep; *ready* for ' dissolution,' by a Henry the Eighth or some other. Jocelin's St. Edmundsbury is still far from this last dreadful state; but here too the reader will prepare himself to see an Ideal not sleeping in the æther like a bird-of-paradise, but roosting as the common wood-fowl do, in an imperfect, uncomfortable, more or less contemptible manner!—

Abbot Hugo, as Jocelin, breaking at once into the heart of the business, apprises us, had in those days grown old, grown rather blind, and his eyes were somewhat darkened, *aliquantulum caligaverunt oculi ejus.* He dwelt apart very much, in his *Talamus* or peculiar Chamber; got into the hands of flatterers, a set of mealy-mouthed persons who strove to make the passing hour easy for him,—for him easy, and for themselves profitable; accumulating in the distance mere mountains of confusion. Old Dominus Hugo sat inaccessible in this way, far in the interior, wrapt in his warm flannels and delusions; inaccessible to all voice of Fact; and bad grew ever worse with us. Not that our worthy old *Dominus Abbas* was inattentive to the divine offices, or to the maintenance of a devout spirit in us or in himself; but the Account-Books of the Convent fell into the frightfulest state, and Hugo's annual Budget grew yearly emptier, or filled with futile expectations, fatal deficit, wind and debts!

His one worldly care was to raise ready money; sufficient for the day is the evil thereof. And how he raised it: From usurious insatiable Jews; every fresh Jew sticking on him like a fresh horseleech, sucking his and our life out; crying continually, Give, give! Take one example instead of scores. Our *Camera* having fallen into ruin, William the Sacristan received charge to repair it; strict charge, but no money; Abbot Hugo would, and indeed could, give him no fraction of money. The *Camera* in ruins, and Hugo penniless and inaccessible, Willelmus Sacrista borrowed Forty Marcs (some Seven-and-twenty Pounds) of Benedict the Jew, and patched-up our Camera again. But the means of repaying him? There were no means. Hardly could *Sacrista, Cellerarius,* or any public officer, get ends to meet, on the indispensablest scale, with their shrunk allowances: ready money had vanished.

Benedict's Twenty-seven pounds grew rapidly at compound-interest; and at length, when it had amounted to a Hundred pounds, he, on a day of settlement, presents the account to Hugo himself. Hugo already owed him another Hundred of his own; and so here it has become Two Hundred! Hugo, in a fine frenzy, threatens to depose the Sacristan, to do this and do that; but, in the meanwhile, How to quiet your insatiable Jew? Hugo, for this couple of hundreds, grants the Jew his bond for Four hundred payable at the end of four years. At the end of four years there is, of course, still no money; and the Jew now gets a bond for Eight hundred and eighty pounds, to be paid by instalments, Fourscore pounds every year. Here was a way of doing business!

Neither yet is this insatiable Jew satisfied or settled with: he had papers against us of ' small debts fourteen years old; ' his modest claim amounts finally to ' Twelve hundred pounds besides interest; '—and one hopes he never got satisfied in this world; one almost hopes he was one of those beleaguered Jews who hanged themselves in York Castle shortly afterwards, and had his usances and quittances and horseleech papers summarily set fire to! For approximate justice will strive to accomplish itself; if not in one way, then in another. Jews, and also Christians and Heathens, who accumulate in this manner, though furnished with never so many parchments, do, at times, ' get their grinder-teeth successively pulled out of their head, each day a new grinder,' till they consent to disgorge again. A sad fact,—worth reflecting on.

Jocelin, we see, is not without secularity: Our *Dominus Abbas* was intent enough on the divine offices; but then his Account-Books—?—One of the things that strike us most, throughout, in Jocelin's *Chronicle*, and indeed in Eadmer's *Anselm*, and other old monastic Books, written evidently by pious men, is this, That there is almost no mention whatever of ' personal religion ' in them; that the whole gist of their thinking and speculation seems to be the ' privileges of our order,' ' strict exaction of our dues,' ' God's honour ' (meaning the honour of our Saint), and so forth. Is not this singular? A body of men, set apart for perfecting and purifying their own souls, do not seem disturbed about that in any measure: the ' Ideal ' says nothing about its idea; says much about finding bed and board for itself! How is this?

Why, for one thing, bed and board are a matter very apt to come to speech: it is much easier to *speak* of them than of ideas; and they are sometimes much more pressing with some! Nay, for another thing, may not this religious reticence, in these devout good souls, be perhaps a merit, and sign of health in them? Jocelin, Eadmer, and such religious men, have as yet nothing of ' Methodism;' no Doubt or even root of Doubt. Religion is not a diseased self-introspection, an agonising inquiry: their duties are clear to them, the way of supreme good plain, indisputable, and they are travelling on it. Religion lies over them like an all-embracing heavenly canopy, like an atmosphere and life-element, which is not spoken of, which in all things is pre-supposed without speech. Is not serene or complete Religion the highest aspect of human nature; as serene Cant, or complete No-religion, is the lowest and miserablest? Between which two, all manner of earnest Methodisms, introspections, agonising inquiries, never so morbid, shall play their respective parts, not without approbation.

But let any reader fancy himself one of the Brethren in St. Edmundsbury Monastery under such circumstances! How can a Lord Abbot, all stuck-over with horseleeches of this nature, front the world? He is fast losing his life-blood, and the Convent will be as one of Pharaoh's lean kine. Old monks of experience draw their hoods deeper down; careful what they say: the monk's first duty is obedience. Our Lord the King, hearing of such work, sends down his Almoner to make investigations: but what boots it? Abbot Hugo assembles us in Chapter; asks, " If there is any complaint? " Not a soul of us dare answer, " Yes, thousands! " but we all stand silent, and the Prior even says that things are in a very comfortable condition. Whereupon old Abbot Hugo, turning to the royal messenger, says, " You see! "—and the business terminates in that way. I, as a brisk-eyed noticing youth and novice, could not help asking of the elders, asking of Magister Samson in particular: Why he, well-instructed and a knowing-man, had not spoken out, and brought matters to a bearing? Magister Samson was Teacher of the Novices, appointed to breed us up to the rules, and I loved him well. " *Fili mi,*" answered Samson, " the burnt child shuns the fire. Dost thou not know, our Lord the Abbot sent me once to Acre in Norfolk, to solitary confinement and bread-and-water, already? The Hinghams, Hugo and Robert, have just got home from banishment for speaking. This is the hour of darkness: the hour when flatterers rule and are believed. *Videat Dominus,* let the Lord see, and judge."

In very truth, what could poor old Abbot Hugo do? A frail old man, and the Philistines were upon him,—that is to say, the Hebrews. He had nothing for it but to shrink away from them; get back into his warm flannels, into his warm delusions again. Happily, before it was quite too late, he bethought him of pilgriming to St. Thomas of Canterbury. He set out, with a fit train, in the autumn days of the year 1180; near Rochester City, his mule threw him, dislocated his poor kneepan, raised incurable inflammatory fever; and the poor old man got his dismissal from the whole coil at once. St. Thomas à Becket, though in a circuitous way, had *brought* deliverance! Neither Jew usurers, nor grumbling monks, nor other importunate despicability of men or mud-elements afflicted Abbot Hugo any more; but he dropt his rosaries, closed his account-books, closed his old eyes, and lay down into the long sleep. Heavy-laden hoary old Dominus Hugo, fare thee well.

One thing we cannot mention without a due thrill of horror: namely, that, in the empty exchequer of Dominus Hugo, there was not found one penny to distribute to the Poor that they might pray for his soul! By a kind of godsend, Fifty shillings did, in the very nick of time, fall due, or seem to fall due, from one of his Farmers (the *Firmarius* de Palegrava), and he paid it, and the Poor had it; though, alas, this too only *seemed* to fall due, and we had it to pay again afterwards. Dominus Hugo's apartments were plundered by his servants, to the last portable stool, in a few minutes after the breath was out of his body. Forlorn old Hugo, fare thee well forever.

CHAPTER V

TWELFTH CENTURY

Our Abbot, being dead, the *Dominus Rex* Henry II., or Ranulf de Glanvill *Justiciarius* of England for him, set Inspectors or Custodians over us;—not in any breathless haste to appoint a new Abbot, our revenues coming into his own *Scaccarium*, or royal Exchequer, in the mean while. They proceeded with some rigour, these Custodiars; took written inventories, clapt-on seals, exacted everywhere strict tale and measure: but wherefore should a living monk complain? The living monk has to do his devotional drill-exercise; consume his allotted *pitantia*, what we call *pittance*, or ration of victual; and possess his soul in patience.

Dim, as through a long vista of Seven Centuries, dim

and very strange looks that monk-life to us; the ever-surprising circumstance this, That it is a *fact* and no dream, that we see it there, and gaze into the very eyes of it! Smoke rises daily from those culinary chimney-throats; there are living human beings there, who chant, loud-braying, their matins, nones, vespers; awakening *echoes*, not to the bodily ear alone. St. Edmund's Shrine, perpetually illuminated, glows ruddy through the Night, and through the Night of Centuries withal; St. Edmundsbury Town paying yearly Forty pounds for that express end. Bells clang out; on great occasions, all the bells. We have Processions, Preachings, Festivals, Christmas Plays, *Mysteries* shown in the Churchyard, at which latter the Townsfolk sometimes quarrel. Time was, Time is, as Friar Bacon's Brass Head remarked; and withal Time will be. There are three Tenses, *Tempora*, or Times; and there is one Eternity; and as for us,

'We are such stuff as Dreams are made of!'

Indisputable, though very dim to modern vision, rests on its hill-slope that same *Bury*, *Stow*, or Town of St. Edmund; already a considerable place, not without traffic, nay manufactures, would Jocelin only tell us what. Jocelin is totally careless of telling: but, through dim fitful apertures, we can see *Fu'lones*, 'Fullers,' see cloth-making; looms dimly going, dye-vats, and old women spinning yarn. We have Fairs too, *Nundinæ*, in due course; and the Londoners give us much trouble, pretending that they, as a metropolitan people, are exempt from toll. Besides there is Field-husbandry, with perplexed settlement of Convent rents: corn-ricks pile themselves within burgh, in their season; and cattle depart and enter; and even the poor weaver has his cow,—'dung-heaps' lying quiet at most doors (*ante foras*, says the incidental Jocelin), for the Town has yet no improved police. Watch and ward nevertheless we do keep, and have Gates,—as what Town must not; thieves so abounding; war, *werra*, such a frequent thing! Our thieves, at the Abbot's judgment bar, deny; claim wager of battle; fight, are beaten, and *then* hanged. 'Ketel, the thief,' took this course; and it did nothing for him,—merely brought us, and indeed himself, new trouble!

Everyway a most foreign Time. What difficulty, for example, has our *Cellerarius* to collect the *repselver,* 'reaping silver,' or penny, which each householder is by law bound to pay for cutting down the Convent grain! Richer people pretend that it is commuted, that it is this and the other; that, in short, they will not pay it. Our *Cellerarius* gives up calling on the rich. In the houses of the poor, our *Cellerarius* finding, in like manner, neither penny nor good promise, snatches, without ceremony, what *vadium* (pledge, *wad*) he can come at: a joint-stool, kettle, nay the very house-door, '*hostium ;*' and old women, thus exposed to the unfeeling gaze of the public, rush out after him with their distaffs and the angriest shrieks: '*vetulæ exibant cum colis suis,*' says Jocelin, '*minantes et exprobrantes.*'

What a historical picture, glowing visible, as St. Edmund's Shrine by night, after Seven long Centuries or so! *Vetulæ cum colis :* My venerable ancient spinning grandmothers,—ah, and ye too have to shriek, and rush out with your distaffs; and become Female Chartists, and scold all evening with void doorway;—and in old Saxon, as we in modern, would fain demand some Five-point Charter, could it be fallen-in with, the Earth being too tyrannous!—Wise Lord Abbots, hearing of such phenomena, did in time abolish or commute the reap-penny, and one nuisance was abated. But the image of these justly offended old women, in their old wool costumes, with their angry features, and spindles brandished, lives forever in the historical memory. Thanks to thee, Jocelin Boswell. Jerusalem was taken by the Crusaders, and again lost by them; and Richard Cœur-de-Lion ' veiled his face ' as he passed in sight of it; but how many other things went on, the while!

Thus, too, our trouble with the Lakenheath eels is very great. King Knut namely, or rather his Queen who also did herself honour by honouring St. Edmund, decreed by authentic deed yet extant on parchment, that the Holders of the Town Fields, once Beodric's, should, for one thing, go yearly and catch us four thousand eels in the marsh-pools of Lakenheath. Well, they went, they continued to go; but, in later times, got into the way of returning with a most short account of eels. Not the due six-score apiece; no, Here are two-score, Here are twenty, ten,—sometimes, Here are none at all; Heaven help us, we *could* catch no more, they were not there! What is a distressed *Cellerarius* to do? We agree that each Holder of so many acres shall pay one penny yearly, and let-go the eels as too slippery. But, alas, neither is this quite effectual: the Fields, in my time, have got divided among so many hands, there is no catching of *them* either; I have known our Cellerar get seven-and-twenty pence formerly, and now it is much if he get ten pence farthing (*vix decem denarios et obolum*). And then their sheep, which they are bound to fold nightly in our pens, for the manure's sake; and, I fear, do not always fold: and their *aver-pennies*, and their *avragiums*, and their *fodercorns*, and mill-and-market dues! Thus, in its un-deniable but dim manner, does old St. Edmundsbury spin and till, and laboriously keep its pot boiling, and St. Edmund's Shrine lighted, under such conditions and averages as it can.

How much is still alive in England; how much has not yet come into life! A Feudal Aristocracy is still alive, in the prime of life; superintending the cultivation of the land, and less consciously the distribution of the produce of the land, the adjustment of the quarrels of the land; judging, soldiering, adjusting; everywhere governing the people,—so that even a Gurth, born thrall of Cedric, lacks not his due parings of the pigs he tends. Governing;—and, alas, also game-preserving; so that a Robert Hood, a William Scarlet and others have, in these days, put on Lincoln coats, and taken to living, in some universal-suffrage manner, under the greenwood-tree!

How silent, on the other hand, lie all Cotton-trades and suchlike; not a steeple-chimney yet got on end from sea to sea! North of the Humber, a stern Willelmus Conquæstor burnt the Country, finding it unruly, into very stern repose. Wild fowl scream in those ancient silences, wild cattle roam in those ancient solitudes; the scanty sulky Norse-bred population all coerced into silence, —feeling that, under these new Norman Governors, their history has probably as good as *ended*. Men and North-umbrian Norse populations know little what has ended, what is but beginning! The Ribble and the Aire roll down, as yet unpolluted by dyers' chemistry; tenanted by merry trouts and piscatory otters; the sunbeam and the vacant wind's-blast alone traversing those moors. Side by side sleep the coal-strata and the iron-strata for so many ages; no Steam-Demon has yet risen smoking into being. Saint Mungo rules in Glasgow; James Watt still slumbering in the deep of Time. *Mancunium*, Manceaster, what we now call Manchester, spins no cotton,—if it be not *wool* ' cottons,' clipped from the backs of mountain sheep. The Creek of the Mersey gurgles, twice in the four-and-twenty hours, with eddying brine, clangorous with sea-fowl; and is a *Lither*-Pool, a *lazy* or sullen Pool, no monstrous pitchy City, and Seahaven of the world! The Centuries are big; and the birth-hour is coming, not yet come. *Tempus ferax, tempus edax rerum.*

CHAPTER VI

MONK SAMSON

WITHIN doors, down at the hill-foot, in our Convent here, we are a peculiar people,—hardly conceivable in the Arkwright Corn-Law ages, of mere Spinning-Mills and Joe-Mantons! There is yet no Methodism among us, and we speak much of Secularities: no Methodism; our Religion is not yet a horrible restless Doubt, still less a far horribler composed Cant; but a great heaven-high Unquestionability, encompassing, interpenetrating the whole of Life. Imperfect as we may be, we are here, with our litanies, shaven crowns, vows of poverty, to testify incessantly and indisputably to every heart,

That this Earthly Life and *its* riches and possessions, and good and evil hap, are not intrinsically a reality at all, but *are* a shadow of realities eternal, infinite; that this Time-world, as an air-image, fearfully *emblematic*, plays and flickers in the grand still mirror of Eternity; and man's little Life has Duties that are great, that are alone great, and go up to Heaven and down to Hell. This, with our poor litanies, we testify, and struggle to testify.

Which, testified or not, remembered by all men or forgotten by all men, does verily remain the fact, even in Arkwright Joe-Manton ages! But it is incalculable, when litanies have grown obsolete; when *fodercorns*, *avragiums*, and all human dues and reciprocities have been fully changed into one great due of *cash payment;* and man's duty to man reduces itself to handing him certain metal coins, or covenanted money-wages, and then shoving him out of doors; and man's duty to God becomes a cant, a doubt, a dim inanity, a 'pleasure of virtue' or suchlike; and the thing a man does infinitely fear (the real *Hell* of a man) is, 'that he do not make money and advance himself,'—I say, it is incalculable what a change has introduced itself everywhere into human affairs! How human affairs shall now circulate everywhere not healthy life-blood in them, but, as it were, a detestable copperas banker's ink; and all is grown acrid, divisive, threatening dissolution; and the huge tumultuous Life of Society is galvanic, devil-ridden, too truly possessed by a devil! For, in short, Mammon *is* not a god at all; but a devil, and even a very despicable devil. Follow the Devil faithfully, you are sure enough to *go* to the Devil: whither else can you go?—In such situations, men look back with a kind of mournful recognition even on poor limited Monk-figures, with their poor litanies; and reflect, with Ben Jonson, that soul is indispensable, some degree of soul, even to save you the expense of salt!—

For the rest, it must be owned, we Monks of St. Edmundsbury are but a limited class of creatures, and seem to have a somewhat dull life of it. Much given to

E 608

idle gossip; having indeed no other work, when our chanting is over. Listless gossip, for most part, and a mitigated
slander; the fruit of idleness, not of spleen. We are dull,
insipid men, many of us; easy-minded; whom prayer and
digestion of food will avail for a life. We have to receive
all strangers in our Convent, and lodge them gratis; such
and such sorts go by rule to the Lord Abbot and his
special revenues; such and such to us and our poor
Cellarer, however straitened. Jews themselves send
their wives and little ones hither in war-time, into our
Pitanceria ; where they abide safe, with due *pittances,—*
for a consideration. We have the fairest chances for
collecting news. Some of us have a turn for reading
Books; for meditation, silence; at times we even write
Books. Some of us can preach, in English-Saxon, in
Norman-French, and even in Monk-Latin; others cannot
in any language or jargon, being stupid.

Failing all else, what gossip about one another! This
is a perennial resource. How one hooded head applies
itself to the ear of another, and whispers—*tacenda.* Willelmus Sacrista, for instance, what does he nightly, over
in that Sacristy of his? Frequent bibations, '*frequentes
bibationes et quædam tacenda,*'—eheu! We have '*tempora
minutionis,*' stated seasons of blood-letting, when we are
all let blood together; and then there is a general free-
conference, a sanhedrim of clatter. Notwithstanding our
vow of poverty, we can by rule amass to the extent of
'two shillings;' but it is to be given to our necessitous
kindred, or in charity. Poor Monks! Thus too a certain
Canterbury Monk was in the habit of 'slipping, *clanculo,*
from his sleeve,' five shillings into the hand of his mother,
when she came to see him, at the divine offices, every
two months. Once, slipping the money clandestinely,
just in the act of taking leave, he slipt it not into her
hand but on the floor, and another had it; whereupon the
poor Monk, coming to know it, looked mere despair for
some days; till Lanfranc the noble Archbishop, questioning his secret from him, nobly made the sum *seven*
shillings,[1] and said, Never mind!

[1] *Eadmeri Hist.* p. 8.

One Monk, of a taciturn nature, distinguishes himself among these babbling ones: the name of him Samson; he that answered Jocelin, "*Fili mi*, a burnt child shuns the fire." They call him 'Norfolk *Barrator*,' or litigious person; for indeed, being of grave taciturn ways, he is not universally a favourite; he has been in trouble more than once. The reader is desired to mark this Monk. A personable man of seven-and-forty; stout-made, stands erect as a pillar; with bushy eyebrows, the eyes of him beaming into you in a really strange way; the face massive, grave, with 'a very eminent nose;' his head almost bald, its auburn remnants of hair, and the copious ruddy beard, getting slightly streaked with gray. This is Brother Samson; a man worth looking at.

He is from Norfolk, as the nickname indicates; from Tottington in Norfolk, as we guess; the son of poor parents there. He has told me Jocelin, for I loved him much, That once in his ninth year he had an alarming dream;—as indeed we are all somewhat given to dreaming here. Little Samson, lying uneasily in his crib at Tottington, dreamed that he saw the Arch Enemy in person, just alighted in front of some grand building, with outspread bat-wings, and stretching forth detestable clawed hands to grip him, little Samson, and fly-off with him: whereupon the little dreamer shrieked desperate to St. Edmund for help, shrieked and again shrieked; and St. Edmund, a reverend heavenly figure, did come,—and indeed poor little Samson's mother, awakened by his shrieking, did come; and the Devil and the Dream both fled away fruitless. On the morrow, his mother, pondering such an awful dream, thought it were good to take him over to St. Edmund's own Shrine, and pray with him there. See, said little Samson at sight of the Abbey-Gate; see, mother, this is the building I dreamed of! His poor mother dedicated him to St. Edmund,—left him there with prayers and tears: what better could she do? The exposition of the dream, Brother Samson used to say, was this: *Diabolus* with outspread bat-wings shadowed forth the pleasures of this world, *voluptates hujus sæculi*, which were about to snatch and fly away

with me, had not St. Edmund flung his arms round me,
that is to say, made me a monk of his.   A monk, accordingly, Brother Samson is; and here to this day where his
mother left him.   A learned man, of devout grave nature;
has studied at Paris, has taught in the Town Schools here,
and done much else; can preach in three languages, and,
like Dr. Caius, ' has had losses ' in his time.   A thoughtful, firm-standing man; much loved by some, not loved
by all; his clear eyes flashing into you, in an almost
inconvenient way!

Abbot Hugo, as we said, had his own difficulties with
him; Abbot Hugo had him in prison once, to teach him
what authority was, and how to dread the fire in future.
For Brother Samson, in the time of the Antipopes, had
been sent to Rome on business; and, returning successful,
was too late,—the business had all misgone in the interim!
As tours to Rome are still frequent with us English,
perhaps the reader will not grudge to look at the method
of travelling thither in those remote ages.   We happily
have, in small compass, a personal narrative of it.
Through the clear eyes and memory of Brother Samson
one peeps direct into the very bosom of that Twelfth
Century, and finds it rather curious.   The actual *Papa*,
Father, or universal President of Christendom, as yet not
grown chimerical, sat there; think of that only!   Brother
Samson went to Rome as to the real Light-fountain of
this lower world; we now—!—But let us hear Brother
Samson, as to his mode of travelling:

' You know what trouble I had for that Church of
Woolpit; how I was despatched to Rome in the time of
the Schism between Pope Alexander and Octavian; and
passed through Italy at that season, when all clergy
carrying letters for our Lord Pope Alexander were laid
hold of, and some were clapt in prison, some hanged; and
some, with nose and lips cut off, were sent forward to our
Lord the Pope, for the disgrace and confusion of him (*in
dedecus et confusionem ejus*).   I, however, pretended to be
Scotch, and putting on the garb of a Scotchman, and
taking the gesture of one, walked along; and when anybody mocked at me, I would brandish my staff in the

manner of that weapon they call *gaveloc*,[1] uttering comminatory words after the way of the Scotch. To those that met and questioned me who I was, I made no answer but: *Ride, ride Rome ; turne Cantwereberei*.[2] Thus did I, to conceal myself and my errand, and get safer to Rome under the guise of a Scotchman.

'Having at last obtained a Letter from our Lord the Pope according to my wishes, I turned homewards again. I had to pass through a certain strong town on my road; and lo, the soldiers thereof surrounded me, seizing me, and saying: "This vagabond (*iste solivagus*), who pretends to be Scotch, is either a spy, or has Letters from the false Pope Alexander." And whilst they examined every stitch and rag of me, my leggings (*caligas*), breeches, and even the old shoes that I carried over my shoulder in the way of the Scotch,—I put my hand into the leather scrip I wore, wherein our Lord the Pope's Letter lay, close by a little jug (*ciffus*) I had for drinking out of; and the Lord God so pleasing, and St. Edmund, I got out both the Letter and the jug together; in such a way that, extending my arm aloft, I held the Letter hidden between jug and hand: they saw the jug, but the Letter they saw not. And thus I escaped out of their hands in the name of the Lord. Whatever money I had, they took from me; wherefore I had to beg from door to door, without any payment (*sine omni expensa*) till I came to England again. But hearing that the Woolpit Church was already given to Geoffry Ridell, my soul was struck with sorrow because I had laboured in vain. Coming home, therefore, I sat me down secretly under the Shrine of St. Edmund, fearing lest our Lord Abbot should seize and imprison me, though I had done no mischief; nor was there a monk who durst speak to me, nor a laic who durst bring me food except by stealth.'[3]

---

[1] Javelin, missile pike. *Gaveloc* is still the Scotch name for *crowbar*.

[2] Does this mean, " Rome forever, Canterbury *not* " (which claims an unjust Supremacy over us)! Mr. Rokewood is silent. Dryasdust would perhaps explain it,—in the course of a week or two of talking; did one dare to question him!

[3] *Jocelini Chronica*, p. 36.

Such resting and welcoming found Brother Samson, with his worn soles, and strong heart! He sits silent, revolving many thoughts, at the foot of St. Edmund's Shrine. In the wide Earth, if it be not Saint Edmund, what friend or refuge has he? Our Lord Abbot, hearing of him, sent the proper officer to lead him down to prison, and clap 'foot-gyves on him' there. Another poor official furtively brought him a cup of wine; bade him "be comforted in the Lord." Samson utters no complaint; obeys in silence. 'Our Lord Abbot, taking counsel of it, banished me to Acre, and there I had to stay long.'

Our Lord Abbot next tried Samson with promotions; made him Subsacristan; made him Librarian, which he liked best of all, being passionately fond of Books: Samson, with many thoughts in him, again obeyed in silence; discharged his offices to perfection, but never thanked our Lord Abbot,—seemed rather as if looking into him, with those clear eyes of his. Whereupon Abbot Hugo said, *Se nunquam vidisse*, He had never seen such a man; whom no severity would break to complain, and no kindness soften into smiles or thanks:—a questionable kind of man!

In this way, not without troubles, but still in an erect clear-standing manner, has Brother Samson reached his forty-seventh year; and his ruddy beard is getting slightly grizzled. He is endeavouring, in these days, to have various broken things thatched in; nay perhaps to have the Choir itself completed, for he can bear nothing ruinous. He has gathered 'heaps of lime and sand;' has masons, slaters working, he and *Warinus monachus noster*, who are joint keepers of the Shrine; paying out the money duly,—furnished by charitable burghers of St. Edmundsbury, they say. Charitable burghers of St. Edmundsbury? To me Jocelin it seems rather, Samson, and Warinus whom he leads, have privily hoarded the oblations at the Shrine itself, in these late years of indolent dilapidation, while Abbot Hugo sat wrapt inaccessible; and are struggling, in this prudent way, to have the rain kept out![1]—Under what conditions, sometimes, has Wisdom

[1] *Jocelini Chronica*, p. 7.

to struggle with Folly; get Folly persuaded to so much as thatch out the rain from itself! For, indeed, if the Infant govern the Nurse, what dextrous practice on the Nurse's part will not be necessary!

It is a new regret to us that, in these circumstances, our Lord the King's Custodiars, interfering, prohibited all building or thatching from whatever source; and no Choir shall be completed, and Rain and Time, for the present, shall have their way. Willelmus Sacrista, he of 'the frequent bibations and some things not to be spoken of;' he, with his red nose, I am of opinion, had made complaint to the Custodiars; wishing to do Samson an ill turn:— Samson his *Sub*-sacristan, with those clear eyes, could not be a prime favourite of his! Samson again obeys in silence.

CHAPTER VII

THE CANVASSING

Now, however, come great news to St. Edmundsbury: That there is to be an Abbot elected; that our interlunar obscuration is to cease; St. Edmund's Convent no more to be a doleful widow, but joyous and once again a bride! Often in our widowed state had we prayed to the Lord and St. Edmund, singing weekly a matter of ' one-and-twenty penitential Psalms, on our knees in the Choir,' that a fit Pastor might be vouchsafed us. And, says Jocelin, had some known what Abbot we were to get, they had not been so devout, I believe!—Bozzy Jocelin opens to mankind the floodgates of authentic Convent gossip; we listen, as in a Dionysius' Ear, to the inanest hubbub, like the voices at Virgil's Horn-Gate of Dreams. Even gossip, seven centuries off, has significance. List, list, how like men are to one another in all centuries.

' *Dixit quidam de quodam*, A certain person said of a certain person, " He, that *Frater*, is a good monk, *pro babilis persona ;* knows much of the order and customs of the church; and, though not so perfect a philosopher as some others, would make a very good Abbot. Old Abbot Ording, still famed among us, knew little of letters. Besides, as we read in Fables, it is better to choose a log for king, than a serpent never so wise, that will venomously hiss and bite his subjects."—" Impossible! " answered the other: " How can such a man make a sermon in the Chapter, or to the people on festival-days, when he is without letters? How can he have the skill to bind and to loose, he who does not understand the Scriptures? How—? " '

And then ' another said of another, *alius de alio*, " That *Frater* is a *homo literatus*, eloquent, sagacious; vigorous in discipline; loves the Convent much, has suffered much for its sake." To which a third party answers, " From all your great clerks, good Lord deliver us! From Norfolk barrators and surly persons, That it would please thee to preserve us, We beseech thee to hear us, good Lord! " Then another *quidam* said of another *quodam*, " That *Frater* is a good manager (*husebondus*); " but was swiftly answered, " God forbid that a man who can neither read nor chant, nor celebrate the divine offices, an unjust person withal, and grinder of the faces of the poor, should ever be Abbot! " ' One man, it appears, is nice in his victuals. Another is indeed wise, but apt to slight inferiors; hardly at the pains to answer, if they argue with him too foolishly. And so each *aliquis* concerning his *aliquo*,—through whole pages of electioneering babble. ' For,' says Jocelin, ' So many men, as many minds.' Our Monks ' at time of blood-letting, *tempore minutionis*,' holding their sanhedrim of babble, would talk in this manner: Brother Samson, I remarked, never said anything; sat silent, sometimes smiling; but he took good note of what others said, and would bring it up, on occasion, twenty years after. As for me Jocelin, I was of opinion that ' some skill in Dialectics, to distinguish true from false,' would be good in an Abbot. I spake, as a rash Novice in those days, some conscientious words of a certain benefactor of mine; ' and behold, one of those sons of Belial ' ran and reported them to him, so that he never after looked at me with the same face again! Poor Bozzy!—

Such is the buzz and frothy simmering ferment of the general mind and no-mind; struggling to 'make itself up,' as the phrase is, or ascertain what *it* does really want: no easy matter, in most cases. St. Edmundsbury, in that Candlemas season of the year 1182, is a busily fermenting place. The very clothmakers sit meditative at their looms; asking, Who shall be Abbot? The *sochemanni* speak of it, driving their ox-teams afield; the old women with their spindles: and none yet knows what the days will bring forth.

The Prior, however, as our interim chief, must proceed to work; get ready 'Twelve Monks,' and set off with them to his Majesty at Waltham, there shall the election be made. An election, whether managed directly by ballot-box on public hustings, or indirectly by force of public opinion, or were it even by open alehouses, land-lords' coercion, popular club-law, or whatever electoral methods, is always an interesting phenomenon. A mountain tumbling in great travail, throwing up dust-clouds and absurd noises, is visibly there; uncertain yet what mouse or monster it will give birth to.

Besides, it is a most important social act; nay, at bottom, the one important social act. Given the men a People choose, the People itself, in its exact worth and worthlessness, is given. A heroic people chooses heroes, and is happy; a valet or flunky people chooses sham-heroes, what are called quacks, thinking them heroes, and is not happy. The grand summary of a man's spiritual condition, what brings out all his herohood and insight, or all his flunkyhood and horn-eyed dimness, is this question put to him, What man dost thou honour? Which is thy ideal of a man; or nearest that? So too of a People: for a People too, every People, *speaks* its choice,—were it only by silently obeying, and not revolt-ing,—in the course of a century or so. Nor are electoral methods, Reform Bills and such-like, unimportant. A People's electoral methods are, in the long-run, the express image of its electoral *talent;* tending and gravitating perpetually, irresistibly, to a conformity with that: and are, at all stages, very significant of the People. Judicious readers, of these times, are not disinclined to see how Monks elect their Abbot in the Twelfth Century: how the St. Edmundsbury mountain manages its midwifery; and what mouse or man the outcome is.

CHAPTER VIII

THE ELECTION

ACCORDINGLY our Prior assembles us in Chapter; and we adjuring him before God to do justly, nominates, not by our selection, yet with our assent, Twelve Monks, moderately satisfactory.   Of whom are Hugo Third-Prior, Brother Dennis a venerable man, Walter the *Medicus,* Samson *Subsacrista,* and other esteemed characters,— though Willelmus *Sacrista,* of the red nose, too is one. These shall proceed straightway to Waltham; and there elect the Abbot as they may and can.   Monks are sworn to obedience; must not speak too loud, under penalty of foot-gyves, limbo, and bread-and-water: yet monks too would know what it is they are obeying.   The St. Edmundsbury Community has no hustings, ballot-box, indeed no open voting: yet by various vague manipulations, pulse-feelings, we struggle to ascertain what its virtual aim is, and succeed better or worse.

This question, however, rises; alas, a quite preliminary question: Will the *Dominus Rex* allow us to choose freely? It is to be hoped!   Well, if so, we agree to choose one of our own Convent.   If not, if the *Dominus Rex* will force a stranger on us, we decide on demurring, the Prior and his Twelve shall demur: we can appeal, plead, remonstrate; appeal even to the Pope, but trust it will not be necessary. Then there is this other question, raised by Brother Samson: What if the Thirteen should not themselves be able to agree?   Brother Samson *Subsacrista,* one remarks, is ready oftenest with some question, some suggestion, that has wisdom in it. Though a servant of servants, and saying little, his words all tell, having sense in them; it seems by his light mainly that we steer ourselves in this great dimness.

What if the Thirteen should not themselves be able to agree? Speak, Samson, and advise.—Could not, hints Samson, Six of our venerablest elders be chosen by us, a kind of electoral committee, here and now: of these, ' with their hand on the Gospels, with their eye on the *Sacrosancta*,' we take oath that they will do faithfully; let these, in secret and as before God, agree on Three whom they reckon fittest; write their names in a Paper, and deliver the same sealed, forthwith, to the Thirteen: one of those Three the Thirteen shall fix on, if permitted. If not permitted, that is to say, if the *Dominus Rex* force us to demur,—the paper shall be brought back unopened, and publicly burned, that no man's secret bring him into trouble.

So Samson advises, so we act; wisely, in this and in other crises of the business. Our electoral committee, its eye on the Sacrosancta, is soon named, soon sworn; and we, striking-up the Fifth Psalm, ' *Verba mea,*

' Give ear unto my words, O Lord,
My meditation weigh,'

march out chanting, and leave the Six to their work in the Chapter here. Their work, before long, they announce as finished: they, with their eye on the Sacrosancta, imprecating the Lord to weigh and witness their meditation, have fixed on Three Names, and written them in this Sealed Paper. Let Samson Subsacrista, general servant of the party, take charge of it. On the morrow morning, our Prior and his Twelve will be ready to get under way.

This, then, is the ballot-box and electoral winnowing-machine they have at St. Edmundsbury: a mind fixed on the Thrice Holy, an appeal to God on high to witness their meditation: by far the best, and indeed the only good electoral winnowing-machine,—if men have souls in them. Totally worthless, it is true, and even hideous and poisonous, if men have no souls. But without soul, alas, what winnowing-machine in human elections can be of avail? We cannot get along without soul; we stick fast, the mournfulest spectacle; and salt itself will not save us!

On the morrow morning, accordingly, our Thirteen set forth; or rather our Prior and Eleven; for Samson, as general servant of the party, has to linger, settling many things. At length he too gets upon the road; and, · carrying the sealed Paper in a leather pouch hung round his neck; and *froccum bajulans in ulnis* ' (thanks to thee, Bozzy Jocelin), ' his frock-skirts looped over his elbow,' showing substantial stern-works, tramps stoutly along. Away across the Heath, not yet of Newmarket and horse-jockeying; across your Fleam-dike and Devil's-dike, no longer useful as a Mercian East-Anglian boundary or bulwark: continually towards Waltham, and the Bishop of Winchester's House there, for his Majesty is in that. Brother Samson, as purse-bearer, has the reckoning always, when there is one, to pay; ' delays are numerous,' progress none of the swiftest.

But, in the solitude of the Convent, Destiny thus big and in her birthtime, what gossiping, what babbling, what dreaming of dreams! The secret of the Three our electoral elders alone know: some Abbot we shall have to govern us; but which Abbot, oh, which! One Monk discerns in a vision of the night-watches, that we shall get an Abbot of our own body, without needing to demur: a prophet appeared to him clad all in white, and said, " Ye shall have one of yours, and he will rage among you like a wolf, *sæviet ut lupus.*" Verily! — then which of ours? Another Monk now dreams: he has seen clearly which; a certain Figure taller by head and shoulders than the other two, dressed in alb and *pallium*, and with the attitude of one about to fight;—which tall Figure a wise Editor would rather not name at this stage of the business! Enough that the vision is true: that Saint Edmund himself, pale and awful, seemed to rise from his Shrine, with naked feet, and say audibly, " He, *ille*, shall veil my feet;" which part of the vision also proves true. Such guessing, visioning, dim perscrutation of the momentous future: the very clothmakers, old women, all townsfolk speak of it, ' and more than once it is reported in St. Edmundsbury, This one is elected; and then, This one, and That other.' Who knows?

But now, sure enough, at Waltham ' on the second Sunday of Quadragesima,' which Dryasdust declares to mean the 22d day of February, year 1182, Thirteen St. Edmundsbury Monks are, at last, seen processioning towards the Winchester Manorhouse; and, in some high Presence-chamber and Hall of State, get access to Henry II. in all his glory. What a Hall,—not imaginary in the least, but entirely real and indisputable, though so extremely dim to us; sunk in the deep distances of Night! The Winchester Manorhouse has fled bodily, like a Dream of the old Night; not Dryasdust himself can show a wreck of it. House and people, royal and episcopal, lords and varlets, where are they? Why *there*, I say, Seven Centuries off; sunk *so* far in the Night, there they *are;* peep through the blankets of the old Night, and thou wilt see! King Henry himself is visibly there; a vivid, noble-looking man, with grizzled beard, in glittering uncertain costume; with earls round him, and bishops, and digni-taries, in the like. The Hall is large, and has for one thing an altar near it,—chapel and altar adjoining it; but what gilt seats, carved tables, carpeting of rush-cloth, what arras-hangings, and huge fire of logs:—alas, it has Human Life in it; and is not that the grand miracle, in what hangings or costume soever?—

The *Dominus Rex*, benignantly receiving our Thirteen with their obeisance, and graciously declaring that he will strive to act for God's honour and the Church's good, commands, ' by the Bishop of Winchester and Geoffrey the Chancellor,'—*Galfridus Cancellarius*, Henry's and the Fair Rosamond's authentic Son present here!—com-mands, " That they, the said Thirteen, do now withdraw, and fix upon Three from their own Monastery." A work soon done; the Three hanging ready round Samson's neck, in that leather pouch of his. Breaking the seal, we find the names,—what think *ye* of it, ye higher dignitaries, thou indolent Prior, thou Willelmus *Sacrista* with the red bottle-nose?—the names, in this order: of Samson *Subsacrista*, of Roger the distressed Cellarer, of Hugo *Tertius-Prior*.

The higher dignitaries, all omitted here, ' flush suddenly red in the face; ' but have nothing to say. One curious fact and question certainly is, How Hugo Third-Prior, who was of the electoral committee, came to nominate *himself* as one of the Three? A curious fact, which Hugo Third-Prior has never yet entirely explained, that I know of!—However, we return, and report to the King our Three names; merely altering the order; putting Samson last, as lowest of all. The King, at recitation of our Three, asks us: "Who are they? Were they born in my domain? Totally unknown to me! You must nominate three others." Whereupon Willelmus Sacrista says, "Our Prior must be named, *quia caput nostrum est*, being already our head." And the Prior responds, "Willelmus Sacrista is a fit man, *bonus vir est*,"—for all his red nose. Tickle me, Toby, and I'll tickle thee! Venerable Dennis too is named; none in his conscience can say nay. There are now Six on our List. "Well," said the King, "they have done it swiftly, they! *Deus est cum eis.*" The Monks withdraw again; and Majesty revolves, for a little, with his *Pares* and *Episcopi*, Lords or ' *Law-wards* ' and Soul-Overseers, the thoughts of the royal breast. The Monks wait silent in an outer room.

In short while, they are next ordered, To add yet another three; but not from their own Convent; from other Convents, "for the honour of my kingdom." Here, —what is to be done here? We will demur, if need be! We do name three, however, for the nonce: the Prior of St. Faith's, a good Monk of St. Neot's, a good Monk of St. Alban's; good men all; all made abbots and dignitaries since, at this hour. There are now Nine upon our List. What the thoughts of the Dominus Rex may be farther? The Dominus Rex, thanking graciously, sends out word that we shall now strike off three. The three strangers are instantly struck off. Willelmus Sacrista adds, that he will of his own accord decline,—a touch of grace and respect for the *Sacrosancta*, even in Willelmus! The King then orders us to strike off a couple more; then yet one more: Hugo Third-Prior goes, and Roger *Cellerarius*, and venerable Monk Dennis;—and now there remain on our List two only, Samson Subsacrista and the Prior.

Which of these two? It were hard to say,—by Monks who may get themselves foot-gyved and thrown into limbo for speaking! We humbly request that the Bishop of Winchester and Geoffrey the Chancellor may again enter, and help us to decide. "Which do you want?" asks the Bishop. Venerable Dennis made a speech, 'commending the persons of the Prior and Samson; but always in the corner of his discourse, *in angulo sui sermonis*, brought Samson in.' "I see!" said the Bishop: "We are to understand that your Prior is somewhat remiss; that you want to have him you call Samson for Abbot." "Either of them is good," said venerable Dennis, almost trembling; "but we would have the better, if it pleased God." "Which of the two *do* you want?" inquires the Bishop pointedly. "Samson!" answered Dennis; "Samson!" echoed all of the rest that durst speak or echo anything: and Samson is reported to the King accordingly. His Majesty, advising of it for a moment, orders that Samson be brought in with the other Twelve.

The King's Majesty, looking at us somewhat sternly, then says: "You present to me Samson; I do not know him: had it been your Prior, whom I do know, I should have accepted him: however, I will now do as you wish. But have a care of yourselves. By the true eyes of God, *per veros oculos Dei*, if you manage badly, I will be upon you!" Samson, therefore, steps forward, kisses the King's feet; but swiftly rises erect again, swiftly turns towards the altar, uplifting with the other Twelve, in clear tenor-note, the Fifty-first Psalm, '*Miserere mei Deus*,

> 'After thy loving-kindness, Lord,
> Have mercy upon *me*;'

with firm voice, firm step and head, no change in his countenance whatever. "By God's eyes," said the King,

" that one, I think, will govern the Abbey well." By the
same oath (charged to your Majesty's account), I too am
precisely of that opinion! It is some while since I fell in
with a likelier man anywhere than this new Abbot Samson.
Long life to him, and may the Lord *have* mercy on him as
Abbot!

Thus, then, have the St. Edmundsbury Monks, without
express ballot-box or other good winnowing-machine,
contrived to accomplish the most important social feat
a body of men can do, to winnow-out the man that is to
govern them: and truly one sees not that, by any winnowing-machine whatever, they could have done it better.
O ye kind Heavens, there is in every Nation and Community a *fittest*, a wisest, bravest, best; whom could we
find and make King over us, all were in very truth well;—
the best that God and Nature had permitted *us* to make
it! By what art discover him? Will the Heavens in
their pity teach us no art; for our need of him is great!
Ballot-boxes, Reform Bills, winnowing-machines: all
these are good, or are not so good;—alas, brethren, how
can these, I say, be other than inadequate, be other than
failures, melancholy to behold? Dim all souls of men to
the divine, the high and awful meaning of Human Worth
and Truth, we shall never, by all the machinery in Birming-
ham, discover the True and Worthy. It is written, ' if we
are ourselves valets, there shall exist no hero for us; we
shall not know the hero when we see him; '—we shall take
the quack for a hero; and cry, audibly through all ballot-
boxes and machinery whatsoever, Thou art he; be thou
King over us!

What boots it? Seek only deceitful Speciosity, money
with gilt carriages, ' fame ' with newspaper-paragraphs,
whatever name it bear, you will find only deceitful
Speciosity; godlike Reality will be forever far from you.
The Quack shall be legitimate inevitable King of you;
no earthly machinery able to exclude the Quack. Ye shall
be born thralls of the Quack, and suffer under him, till
your hearts are near broken, and no French Revolution
or Manchester Insurrection, or partial or universal

volcanic combustions and explosions, never so many, can do more than ' change the *figure* of your Quack;' the essence of him remaining, for a time and times.—" How long, O Prophet?" say some, with a rather melancholy sneer. Alas, ye *un*prophetic, ever till this come about: Till deep misery, if nothing softer will, have driven you out of your Speciosities *into* your Sincerities; and you find that there either is a Godlike in the world, or else ye are an unintelligible madness; that there is a God, as well as a Mammon and a Devil, and a Genius of Luxuries and canting Dilettantisms and Vain Shows! How long that will be, compute for yourselves. My unhappy brothers!—

CHAPTER IX

ABBOT SAMSON

So, then, the bells of St. Edmundsbury clang out one and all, and in church and chapel the organs go: Convent and Town, and all the west side of Suffolk, are in gala; knights, viscounts, weavers, spinners, the entire population, male and female, young and old, the very sockmen with their chubby infants,—out to have a holiday, and see the Lord Abbot arrive! And there is ' stripping barefoot' of the Lord Abbot at the Gate, and solemn leading of him in to the High Altar and Shrine; with sudden ' silence of all the bells and organs,' as we kneel in deep prayer there; and again with outburst of all the bells and organs, and loud *Te Deum* from the general human windpipe; and speeches by the leading viscount, and giving of the kiss of brotherhood; the whole wound-up with popular games, and dinner within doors of more than a thousand strong, *plus quam mille comedentibus in gaudio magno*.

In such manner is the selfsame Samson once again returning to us, welcomed on *this* occasion. He that went away with his frock-skirts looped over his arm, comes back riding high; suddenly made one of the

dignitaries of this world. Reflective readers will admit
that here was a trial for a man. Yesterday a poor
mendicant, allowed to possess not above two shillings of
money, and without authority to bid a dog run for him,
—this man today finds himself a *Dominus Abbas*, mitred
Peer of Parliament, Lord of manorhouses, farms, manors,
and wide lands; a man with ' Fifty Knights under him,'
and dependent, swiftly obedient multitudes of men. It
is a change greater than Napoleon's; so sudden withal.
As if one of the Chandos day-drudges had, on awakening
some morning, found that *he* overnight was become Duke!
Let Samson with his clear-beaming eyes see into that,
and discern it if he can. We shall now get the measure
of him by a new scale of inches, considerably more rigorous
than the former was. For if a noble soul is rendered
tenfold beautifuler by victory and prosperity, springing
now radiant as into his own due element and sun-throne;
an ignoble one is rendered tenfold and hundredfold uglier,
pitifuler. Whatsoever vices, whatsoever weaknesses were
in the man, the parvenu will show us them enlarged, as
in the solar microscope, into frightful distortion. Nay,
how many mere seminal principles of vice, hitherto all
wholesomely kept latent, may we now see unfolded, as
in the solar hothouse, into growth, into huge universally-
conspicuous luxuriance and development!

But is not this, at any rate, a singular aspect of what
political and social capabilities, nay, let us say, what
depth and opulence of true social vitality, lay in those
old barbarous ages, That the fit Governor could be met
with under such disguises, could be recognised and laid
hold of under such? Here he is discovered with a maximum
of two shillings in his pocket, and a leather scrip round
his neck; trudging along the highway, his frock-skirts
looped over his arm. They think this is he nevertheless,
the true Governor; and he proves to be so. Brethren,
have we no need of discovering true Governors, but will
sham ones forever do for us? These were absurd superstitious blockheads of Monks; and we are enlightened
Tenpound Franchisers, without taxes on knowledge!

Where, I say, are our superior, are our similar or at all
comparable discoveries? We also have eyes, or ought
to have; we have hustings, telescopes; we have lights,
link-lights and rush-lights of an enlightened free Press,
burning and dancing everywhere, as in a universal torch-
dance; singeing your whiskers as you traverse the public
thoroughfares in town and country. Great souls, true
Governors, go about under all manner of disguises now
as then. Such telescopes, such enlightenment,—and
such discovery! How comes it, I say; how comes it?
Is it not lamentable; is it not even, in some sense,
amazing?

Alas, the defect, as we must often urge and again urge,
is less a defect of telescopes than of some eyesight. Those
superstitious blockheads of the Twelfth Century had no
telescopes, but they had still an eye; not ballot-boxes;
only reverence for Worth, abhorrence of Unworth. It is
the way with all barbarians. Thus Mr. Sale informs me,
the old Arab Tribes would gather in liveliest *gaudeamus*,
and sing, and kindle bonfires, and wreathe crowns of
honour, and solemnly thank the gods that, in their Tribe
too, a Poet had shown himself. As indeed they well
might: for what usefuler, I say not nobler and heavenlier
thing could the gods, doing their very kindest, send to
any Tribe or Nation, in any time or circumstances? I
declare to thee, my afflicted quack-ridden brother, in
spite of thy astonishment, it is very lamentable! We
English find a Poet, as brave a man as has been made
for a hundred years or so anywhere under the Sun; and
do we kindle bonfires, or thank the gods? Not at all.
We, taking due counsel of it, set the man to gauge ale-
barrels in the Burgh of Dumfries; and pique ourselves
on our ' patronage of genius.'

Genius, Poet: do we know what these words mean?
An inspired Soul once more vouchsafed us, direct from
Nature's own great fire-heart, to see the Truth, and speak
it, and do it; Nature's own sacred voice heard once more
athwart the dreary boundless element of hearsaying and
canting, of twaddle and poltroonery, in which the bewildered Earth, nigh perishing, has *lost its way*. Hear

once more, ye bewildered benighted mortals; listen once
again to a voice from the inner Light-sea and Flame-sea,
Nature's and Truth's own heart; know the Fact of your
Existence what it is, put away the Cant of it which it is
not; and knowing, do, and let it be well with you!—

George the Third is Defender of something we call ' the
Faith ' in those years; George the Third is head charioteer
of the Destinies of England, to guide them through the
gulf of French Revolutions, American Independences; and
Robert Burns is Gauger of ale in Dumfries. It is an Iliad
in a nutshell. The physiognomy of a world now verging
towards dissolution, reduced now to spasms and death-
throes, lies pictured in that one fact,—which astonishes
nobody, except at me for being astonished at it. The
fruit of long ages of confirmed Valethood, entirely confirmed as into a Law of Nature; cloth-worship and quack-
worship: entirely *confirmed* Valethood,—which will have
to *unc*onfirm itself again; God knows, with difficulty
enough!—

Abbot Samson had found a Convent all in dilapidation;
rain beating through it, material rain and metaphorical,
from all quarters of the compass. Willelmus Sacrista sits
drinking nightly, and doing mere *tacenda*. Our larders
are reduced to leanness, Jew harpies and unclean creatures
our purveyors; in our basket is no bread. Old women
with their distaffs rush out on a distressed Cellarer in
shrill Chartism. ' You cannot stir abroad but Jews and
Christians pounce upon you with unsettled bonds; ' debts
boundless seemingly as the National Debt of England.
For four years our new Lord Abbot never went abroad
but Jew creditors and Christian, and all manner of
creditors, were about him; driving him to very despair.
Our Prior is remiss; our Cellarers, officials are remiss;
our monks are remiss; what man is not remiss? Front
this, Samson, thou alone art there to front it; it is thy
task to front and fight this, and to die or kill it. May
the Lord have mercy on thee!

To our antiquarian interest in poor Jocelin and his
Convent, where the whole aspect of existence, the whole

dialect, of thought, of speech, of activity, is so obsolete,
strange, long-vanished, there now superadds itself a mild
glow of human interest for Abbot Samson; a real pleasure,
as at sight of man's work, especially of governing, which is
man's highest work, done *well*. Abbot Samson had no
experience in governing; had served no apprenticeship
to the trade of governing,—alas, only the hardest apprenticeship to that of obeying. He had never in any
court given *vadium* or *plegium*, says Jocelin; hardly ever
seen a court, when he was set to preside in one. But it
is astonishing, continues Jocelin, how soon he learned the
ways of business; and, in all sorts of affairs, became
expert beyond others. Of the many persons offering him
their service, ' he retained one Knight skilled in taking
vadia and *plegia* ; ' and within the year was himself well
skilled. Nay, by and by, the Pope appoints him Justiciary
in certain causes; the King one of his new Circuit Judges:
official Osbert is heard saying, " That Abbot is one of
your shrewd ones, *disputator est ;* if he go on as he begins,
he will cut out every lawyer of us! " [1]

Why not? What is to hinder this Samson from
governing? There is in him what far transcends all
apprenticeships; in the man himself there exists a model
of governing, something to govern by! There exists in
him a heart-abhorrence of whatever is incoherent, pusillani-
mous, unveracious,—that is to say, chaotic, *ungoverned ;* of
the Devil, not of God. A man of this kind cannot help
governing! He has the living ideal of a governor in him;
and the incessant necessity of struggling to unfold the
same out of him. Not the Devil or Chaos, for any wages,
will he serve; no, this man is the born servant of Another
than them. Alas, how little avail all apprenticeships,
when there is in your governor himself what we may
well call *nothing* to govern by: nothing; — a general
gray twilight, looming with shapes of expediencies,
parliamentary traditions, division-lists, election-funds,
leading-articles; this, with what of vulpine alertness and
adroitness soever, is not much!

But indeed what say we, apprenticeship? Had not

this Samson served, in his way, a right good apprentice-ship to governing; namely, the harshest slave-apprentice-ship to obeying! Walk this world with no friend in it but God and St. Edmund, you will either fall into the ditch, or learn a good many things. To learn obeying is the fundamental art of governing. How much would many a Serene Highness have learned, had he travelled through the world with water-jug and empty wallet, *sine omni expensa ;* and, at his victorious return, sat down not to newspaper-paragraphs and city-illuminations, but at the foot of St. Edmund's Shrine to shackles and bread-and-water! He that cannot be servant of many, will never be master, true guide and deliverer of many;—that is the meaning of true mastership. Had not the Monk-life extraordinary 'political capabilities' in it; if not imitable by us, yet enviable? Heavens, had a Duke of Logwood, now rolling sumptuously to his place in the Collective Wisdom, but himself happened to plough daily, at one time, on seven-and-sixpence a week, with no out-door relief,—what a light, unquenchable by logic and statistic and arithmetic, would it have thrown on several things for him!

In all cases, therefore, we will agree with the judicious Mrs. Glass: 'First catch your hare!' First get your man; all is got: he can learn to do all things, from making boots, to decreeing judgments, governing communities; and will do them like a man. Catch your no-man,—alas, have you not caught the terriblest Tartar in the world! Perhaps all the terribler, the quieter and gentler he looks. For the mischief that one blockhead, that every blockhead does, in a world so feracious, teeming with endless results as ours, no ciphering will sum up. The quack bootmaker is considerable; as corn-cutters can testify, and desperate men reduced to buckskin and list-shoes. But the quack priest, quack high-priest, the quack king! Why do not all just citizens rush, half-frantic, to stop him, as they would a conflagration? Surely a just citizen *is* admonished by God and his own Soul, by all silent and articulate voices of this Universe, to do what in *him* lies towards relief of this poor blockhead-quack, and of a world that

groans under him. Run swiftly; relieve him,—were it
even by extinguishing him! For all things have grown so
old, tinder-dry, combustible; and he is more ruinous than
conflagration. Sweep him *down*, at least; keep him
strictly within the hearth: he will then cease to be conflagration; he will then become useful, more or less, as
culinary fire. Fire is the best of servants; but what a
master! This poor blockhead too is born for uses: why,
elevating him to mastership, will you make a conflagration,
a parish-curse or world-curse of him?

CHAPTER X

GOVERNMENT

How Abbot Samson, giving his new subjects seriatim
the kiss of fatherhood in the St. Edmundsbury chapter-
house, proceeded with cautious energy to set about reforming their disjointed distracted way of life; how he managed
with his Fifty rough *Milites* (Feudal Knights), with his
lazy Farmers, remiss refractory Monks, with Pope's
Legates, Viscounts, Bishops, Kings; how on all sides he
laid about him like a man, and putting consequence on
premiss, and everywhere the saddle on the right horse,
struggled incessantly to educe organic method out of
lazily fermenting wreck,—the careful reader will discern,
not without true interest, in these pages of Jocelin Boswell.
In most antiquarian quaint costume, not of garments
alone, but of thought, word, action, outlook and position,
the substantial figure of a man with eminent nose, bushy
brows and clear-flashing eyes, his russet beard growing
daily grayer, is visible, engaged in true governing of men.
It is beautiful how the chrysalis governing-soul, shaking
off its dusty slough and prison, starts forth winged, a true
royal soul! Our new Abbot has a right honest unconscious feeling, without insolence as without fear or flutter,
of what he is and what others are. A courage to quell
the proudest, an honest pity to encourage the humblest.

Withal there is a noble reticence in this Lord Abbot:
much vain unreason he hears; lays up without response.
He is not there to expect reason and nobleness of others;
he is there to give them of his own reason and nobleness.
Is he not their servant, as we said, who can suffer from
them, and for them; bear the burden their poor spindle-
limbs totter and stagger under; and, in virtue of *being*
their servant, govern them, lead them out of weakness
into strength, out of defeat into victory!

One of the first Herculean Labours Abbot Samson
undertook, or the very first, was to institute a strenuous
review and radical reform of his economics. It is the first
labour of every governing man, from *Paterfamilias* to
Dominus Rex. To get the rain thatched out from you is
the preliminary of whatever farther, in the way of speculation or of action, you may mean to do. Old Abbot
Hugo's budget, as we saw, had become empty, filled with
deficit and wind. To see his account-books clear, be
delivered from those ravening flights of Jew and Christian
creditors, pouncing on him like obscene harpies wherever
he showed face, was a necessity for Abbot Samson.
On the morrow after his instalment he brings in a load
of money-bonds, all duly stamped, sealed with this or the
other Convent Seal: frightful, unmanageable, a bottomless
confusion of Convent finance. There they are;—but there
at least they all are; all that shall be of them. Our Lord
Abbot demands that all the official seals in use among
us be now produced and delivered to him. Three-and-
thirty seals turn up; are straightway broken, and shall
seal no more: the Abbot only, and those duly authorised
by him shall seal any bond. There are but two ways of
paying debt: increase of industry in raising income,
increase of thrift in laying it out. With iron energy, in
slow but steady undeviating perseverance, Abbot Samson
sets to work in both directions. His troubles are manifold: cunning *milites*, unjust bailiffs, lazy sockmen, he
an inexperienced Abbot; relaxed lazy monks, not disinclined to mutiny in mass: but continued vigilance,
rigorous method, what we call 'the eye of the master,'

work wonders. The clear-beaming eyesight of Abbot Samson, steadfast, severe, all-penetrating,—it is like *Fiat lux* in that inorganic waste whirlpool; penetrates gradually to all nooks, and of the chaos makes a *kosmos* or ordered world!

He arranges everywhere, struggles unweariedly to arrange, and place on some intelligible footing, the ' affairs and dues, *res ac redditus*,' of his dominion. The Lakenheath eels cease to breed squabbles between human beings; the penny of *reap-silver* to explode into the streets the Female Chartism of St. Edmundsbury. These and innumerable greater things. Wheresoever Disorder may stand or lie, let it have a care; here is the man that has declared war with it, that never will make peace with it. Man is the Missionary of Order; he is the servant not of the Devil and Chaos, but of God and the Universe! Let all sluggards and cowards, remiss, false-spoken, unjust, and otherwise diabolic persons have a care: this is a dangerous man for them. He has a mild grave face; a thoughtful sternness, a sorrowful pity: but there is a terrible flash of anger in him too; lazy monks often have to murmur, " *Sævit ut lupus*, He rages like a wolf; was not our Dream true! " ' To repress and hold-in such sudden anger he was continually careful,' and succeeded well:—right, Samson; that it may become in thee as noble central heat, fruitful, strong, beneficent; not blaze out, or the seldomest possible blaze out, as wasteful volcanoism to scorch and consume!

" We must first creep, and gradually learn to walk," had Abbot Samson said of himself, at starting. In four years he has become a great walker; striding prosperously along; driving much before him. In less than four years, says Jocelin, the Convent Debts were all liquidated: the harpy Jews not only settled with, but banished, bag and baggage, out of the *Bannaleuca* (Liberties, *Banlieue*) of St. Edmundsbury,—so has the King's Majesty been persuaded to permit. Farewell to *you*, at any rate; let us, in no extremity, apply again to you! Armed men march them over the borders, dismiss them under stern penalties,

—sentence of excommunication on all that shall again
harbour them here: there were many dry eyes at their
departure.

New life enters everywhere, springs up beneficent, the
Incubus of Debt once rolled away. Samson hastes not;
but neither does he pause to rest. This of the Finance
is a lifelong business with him;—Jocelin's anecdotes are
filled to weariness with it. As indeed to Jocelin it was
of very primary interest.

But we have to record also, with a lively satisfaction,
that spiritual rubbish is as little tolerated in Samson's
Monastery as material. With due rigour, Willelmus
Sacrista, and his bibations and *tacenda* are, at the earliest
opportunity, softly yet irrevocably put an end to. The
bibations, namely, had to end; even the building where
they used to be carried on was razed from the soil of
St. Edmundsbury, and ' on its place grow rows of beans: '
Willelmus himself, deposed from the Sacristy and all
offices, retires into obscurity, into absolute taciturnity
unbroken thenceforth to this hour. Whether the poor
Willelmus did not still, by secret channels, occasionally
get some slight wetting of vinous or alcoholic liquor,—
now grown, in a manner, indispensable to the poor man?
Jocelin hints not; one knows not how to hope, what to
hope! But if he did, it was in silence and darkness;
with an ever-present feeling that teetotalism was his only
true course. Drunken dissolute Monks are a class of
persons who had better keep out of Abbot Samson's way.
Sævit ut lupus ; was not the Dream true! murmured many
a Monk. Nay Ranulf de Glanvill, Justiciary in Chief, took
umbrage at him, seeing these strict ways; and watched
farther with suspicion: but discerned gradually that
there was nothing wrong, that there was much the
opposite of wrong.

CHAPTER XI

THE ABBOT'S WAYS

ABBOT Samson showed no extraordinary favour to the Monks who had been his familiars of old; did not promote them to offices,—*nisi essent idonei,* unless they chanced to be fit men! Whence great discontent among certain of these, who had contributed to make him Abbot: reproaches, open and secret, of his being ' ungrateful, hard-tempered, unsocial, a Norfolk *barrator* and *paltenerius.*'

Indeed, except it were for *idonei,* ' fit men,' in all kinds, it was hard to say for whom Abbot Samson had much favour. He loved his kindred well, and tenderly enough acknowledged the poor part of them; with the rich part, who in old days had never acknowledged him, he totally refused to have any business. But even the former he did not promote into offices; finding none of them *idonei.* ' Some whom he thought suitable he put into situations in his own household, or made keepers of his country places: if they behaved ill, he dismissed them without hope of return.' In his promotions, nay almost in his benefits, you would have said there was a certain impartiality. ' The official person who had, by Abbot Hugo's order, put the fetters on him at his return from Italy, was now supported with food and clothes to the end of his days at Abbot Samson's expense.'

Yet he did not forget benefits; far the reverse, when an opportunity occurred of paying them at his own cost. How pay them at the public cost;—how, above all, by *setting fire* to the public, as we said; clapping ' conflagrations ' on the public, which the services of blockheads, *non-idonei,* intrinsically are! He was right willing to remember friends, when it could be done. Take these instances: ' A certain chaplain who had maintained him at the Schools of Paris by the sale of holy water, *quæstu aquæ benedictæ ;*—to this good chaplain he did give a vicarage, adequate to the comfortable sustenance of him.'

' The Son of Elias too, that is, of old Abbot Hugo's Cup-
bearer, coming to do homage for his Father's land, our
Lord Abbot said to him in full Court: " I have, for these
seven years, put off taking thy homage for the land which
Abbot Hugo gave thy Father, because that gift was to
the damage of Elmswell, and a questionable one: but
now I must profess myself overcome; mindful of the
kindness thy Father did me when I was in bonds; because
he sent me a cup of the very wine his master had been
drinking, and bade me be comforted in God." '

' To Magister Walter, son of Magister William de Dice,
who wanted the vicarage of Chevington, he answered:
" Thy Father was Master of the Schools; and when I was
an indigent *clericus*, he granted me freely and in charity
an entrance to his School, and opportunity of learning;
wherefore I now, for the sake of God, grant to thee what
thou askest." ' Or lastly, take this good instance,—and
a glimpse along with it, into long-obsolete times: ' Two
Milites of Risby, Willelm and Norman, being adjudged in
Court to come under his mercy, *in misericordia ejus*,' for
a certain very considerable fine of twenty shillings, ' he
thus addressed them publicly on the spot: " When I was
a Cloister-monk, I was once sent to Durham on business
of our Church; and coming home again, the dark night
caught me at Risby, and I had to beg a lodging there.
I went to Dominus Norman's, and he gave me a flat
refusal. Going then to Dominus Willelm's, and begging
hospitality, I was by him honourably received. The
twenty shillings therefore of *mercy*, I, without mercy, will
exact from Dominus Norman; to Dominus Willelm, on
the other hand, I, with thanks, will wholly remit the said
sum." ' Men know not always to whom they refuse
lodgings; men have lodged Angels unawares!—

It is clear Abbot Samson had a talent; he had learned
to judge better than Lawyers, to manage better than
bred Bailiffs:—a talent shining out indisputable, on whatever side you took him. ' An eloquent man he was,' says
Jocelin, ' both in French and Latin; but intent more on
the substance and method of what was to be said, than

on the ornamental way of saying it. He could read
English Manuscripts very elegantly, *elegantissime :* he
was wont to preach to the people in the English tongue,
though according to the dialect of Norfolk, where he had
been brought up; wherefore indeed he had caused a
Pulpit to be erected in our Church both for ornament of
the same, and for the use of his audiences.' There
preached he, according to the dialect of Norfolk; a man
worth going to hear.

That he was a just clear-hearted man, this, as the
basis of all true talent, is presupposed. How can a man,
without clear vision in his heart first of all, have any
clear vision in the head? It is impossible! Abbot
Samson was one of the justest of judges; insisted on
understanding the case to the bottom, and then swiftly
decided without feud or favour. For which reason,
indeed, the Dominus Rex, searching for such men, as
for hidden treasure and healing to his distressed realm,
had made him one of the new Itinerant Judges,—such as
continue to this day. " My curse on that Abbot's court,"
a suitor was heard imprecating, " *Maledicta sit curia istius
Abbatis,* where neither gold nor silver can help me to
confound my enemy!" And old friendships and all
connections forgotten, when you go to seek an office
from him! " A kinless loon," as the Scotch said of
Cromwell's new judges,—intent on mere indifferent fair-
play!

Eloquence in three languages is good; but it is not
the best. To us, as already hinted, the Lord Abbot's
eloquence is less admirable than his *in*eloquence, his great
invaluable ' talent of silence' ! ' " *Deus, Deus,*" said the
Lord Abbot to me once, when he heard the Convent were
murmuring at some act of his, " I have much need to
remember that Dream they had of me, that I was to rage
among them like a wolf. Above all earthly things I dread
their driving me to do it. How much do I hold in, and
wink at; raging and shuddering in my own secret mind,
and not outwardly at all!" He would boast to me at
other times: " This and that I have seen, this and that
I have heard; yet patiently stood it." He had this way,

too, which I have never seen in any other man, that he affectionately loved many persons to whom he never or hardly ever showed a countenance of love. Once on my venturing to expostulate with him on the subject, he reminded me of Solomon: " Many sons I have; it is not fit that I should smile on them." He would suffer faults, damage from his servants, and know what he suffered, and not speak of it; but I think the reason was, he waited a good time for speaking of it, and in a wise way amending it. He intimated, openly in chapter to us all, that he would have no eavesdropping: " Let none," said he, " come to me secretly accusing another, unless he will publicly stand to the same; if he come otherwise, I will openly proclaim the name of him. I wish, too, that every Monk of you have free access to me, to speak of your needs or grievances when you will." '

The kinds of people Abbot Samson liked worst were these three: ' *Mendaces, ebriosi, verbosi*, Liars, drunkards and wordy or windy persons;' — not good kinds, any of them! He also much condemned ' persons given to murmur at their meat or drink, especially Monks of that disposition.' We remark, from the very first, his strict anxious order to his servants to provide handsomely for hospitality, to guard ' above all things that there be no shabbiness in the matter of meat and drink; no look of mean parsimony, *in novitate meâ*, at the beginning of my Abbotship;' and to the last he maintains a due opulence of table and equipment for others; but he is himself in the highest degree indifferent to all such things.

' Sweet milk, honey and other naturally sweet kinds of food, were what he preferred to eat: but he had this virtue,' says Jocelin, ' he never changed the dish (*ferculum*) you set before him, be what it might. Once when I, still a novice, happened to be waiting table in the refectory, it came into my head ' (rogue that I was!) ' to try if this were true; and I thought I would place before him a *ferculum* that would have displeased any other person, the very platter being black and broken. But he, seeing it, was as one that saw it not: and now some little delay taking place, my heart smote me that I had done this;

and so, snatching up the platter (*discus*), I changed both
it and its contents for a better, and put down that instead;
which emendation he was angry at, and rebuked me for,'
—the stoical monastic man! ' For the first seven years
he had commonly four sorts of dishes on his table; afterwards only three, except it might be presents, or venison
from his own parks, or fishes from his ponds. And if, at
any time, he had guests living in his house at the request
of some great person, or of some friend, or had public
messengers, or had harpers (*citharœdos*), or any one of
that sort, he took the first opportunity of shifting to
another of his Manor-houses, and so got rid of such superfluous individuals,' [1]—very prudently, I think.

As to his parks, of these, in the general repair of buildings, general improvement and adornment of the St.
Edmund Domains, ' he had laid out several, and stocked
them with animals, retaining a proper huntsman with
hounds: and, if any guest of great quality were there, our
Lord Abbot with his Monks would sit in some opening
of the woods, and see the dogs run; but he himself never
meddled with hunting, that I saw.' [2]

' In an opening of the woods;'—for the country was
still dark with wood in those days; and Scotland itself
still rustled shaggy and leafy, like a damp black American
Forest, with cleared spots and spaces here and there.
Dryasdust advances several absurd hypotheses as to the
insensible but almost total disappearance of these woods;
the thick wreck of which now lies as *peat*, sometimes with
huge heart-of-oak timber-logs imbedded in it, on many
a height and hollow. The simplest reason doubtless is,
that by increase of husbandry, there was increase of cattle;
increase of hunger for green spring food; and so, more
and more, the new seedlings got yearly eaten out in April;
and the old trees, having only a certain length of life in
them, died gradually, no man heeding it, and disappeared
into *peat*.

A sorrowful waste of noble wood and umbrage! Yes,
—but a very common one; the course of most things in

[1] *Jocelini Chronica*, p. 31.   [2] *Ibid.* p. 21.

this world. Monachism itself, so rich and fruitful once, is now all rotted into *peat;* lies sleek and buried,—and a most feeble bog-grass of Dilettantism all the crop we reap from it! That also was frightful waste; perhaps among the saddest our England ever saw. Why will men destroy noble Forests, even when in part a nuisance, in such reckless manner; turning loose four-footed cattle and Henry-the-Eighths into them! The fifth part of our English soil, Dryasdust computes, lay consecrated to 'spiritual uses,' better or worse; solemnly set apart to foster spiritual growth and culture of the soul, by the methods then known: and now—it too, like the four-fifths, fosters what? Gentle shepherd, tell me what!

CHAPTER XII

THE ABBOT'S TROUBLES

THE troubles of Abbot Samson, as he went along in this abstemious, reticent, rigorous way, were more than tongue can tell. The Abbot's mitre once set on his head, he knew rest no more. Double, double toil and trouble; that is the life of all governors that really govern: not the spoil of victory, only the glorious toil of battle can be theirs. Abbot Samson found all men more or less head-strong, irrational, prone to disorder; continually threatening to prove *un*governable.

His lazy Monks gave him most trouble. 'My heart is tortured,' said he, 'till we get out of debt, *cor meum cruciatum est.*' Your heart, indeed;—but not altogether ours! By no devisable method, or none of three or four that he devised, could Abbot Samson get these Monks of his to keep their accounts straight; but always, do as he might, the Cellerarius at the end of the term is in a coil, in a flat deficit,—verging again towards debt and Jews. The Lord Abbot at last declares sternly he will keep our accounts too himself; will appoint an officer of his own to see our Cellerarius keep them. Murmurs

thereupon among us: Was the like ever heard? Our
Cellerarius a cipher; the very Townsfolk know it: *sub-
sannatio et derisio sumus*, we have become a laughing-
stock to mankind. The Norfolk barrator and paltener!

And consider, if the Abbot found such difficulty in the
mere economic department, how much in more complex
ones, in spiritual ones perhaps! He wears a stern calm
face; raging and gnashing teeth, *fremens* and *frendens*,
many times, in the secret of his mind. Withal, however,
there is a noble slow perseverance in him; a strength of
'subdued rage' calculated to subdue most things: always,
in the long-run, he contrives to gain his point.

Murmurs from the Monks, meanwhile, cannot fail;
ever deeper murmurs, new grudges accumulating. At
one time, on slight cause, some drop making the cup run
over, they burst into open mutiny: the Cellarer will not
obey, prefers arrest on bread-and-water to obeying; the
Monks thereupon strike work; refuse to do the regular
chanting of the day, at least the younger part of them
with loud clamour and uproar refuse:—Abbot Samson
has withdrawn to another residence, acting only by
messengers: the awful report circulates through St.
Edmundsbury that the Abbot is in danger of being
murdered by the Monks with their knives! How wilt
thou appease this, Abbot Samson! Return; for the
Monastery seems near catching fire!

Abbot Samson returns; sits in his *Talamus*, or inner
room, hurls out a bolt or two of excommunication: lo,
one disobedient Monk sits in limbo, excommunicated, with
foot-shackles on him, all day; and three more our Abbot
has gyved 'with the lesser sentence, to strike fear into the
others!' Let the others think with whom they have to
do. The others think; and fear enters into them. 'On
the morrow morning we decide on humbling ourselves
before the Abbot, by word and gesture, in order to mitigate
his mind. And so accordingly was done. He, on the
other side, replying with much humility, yet always
alleging his own justice and turning the blame on us,
when he saw that we were conquered, became himself

conquered. And bursting into tears, *perfusus lachrymis,* he swore that he had never grieved so much for anything in the world as for this, first on his own account, and then secondly and chiefly for the public scandal which had gone abroad, that St. Edmund's Monks were going to kill their Abbot. And when he had narrated how he went away on purpose till his anger should cool, repeating this word of the philosopher, " I would have taken vengeance on thee, had not I been angry," he arose weeping, and embraced each and all of us with the kiss of peace. He wept; we all wept: '[1]—what a picture! Behave better, ye remiss Monks, and thank Heaven for such an Abbot; or know at least that ye must and shall obey him.

Worn down in this manner, with incessant toil and tribulation, Abbot Samson had a sore time of it; his grizzled hair and beard grew daily grayer. Those Jews, in the first four years, had ' visibly emaciated him: ' Time, Jews, and the task of Governing, will make a man's beard very gray! ' In twelve years,' says Jocelin, ' our Lord Abbot had grown wholly white as snow, *totus efficitur albus sicut nix.*' White atop, like the granite mountains: —but his clear-beaming eyes still look out, in their stern clearness, in their sorrow and pity; the heart within him remains unconquered.

Nay sometimes there are gleams of hilarity too; little snatches of encouragement granted even to a Governor. ' Once my Lord Abbot and I, coming down from London through the Forest, I inquired of an old woman whom we came up to, Whose wood this was, and of what manor; who the master, who the keeper? '—All this I knew very well beforehand, and my Lord Abbot too, Bozzy that I was! But ' the old woman answered, The wood belonged to the new Abbot of St. Edmund's, was of the manor of Harlow, and the keeper of it was one Arnald. How did he behave to the people of the manor? I asked farther. She answered that he used to be a devil incarnate, *dæmon vivus,* an enemy of God, and flayer of the peasants' skins,' —skinning them like live eels, as the manner of some is: ' but that now he dreads the new Abbot, knowing him to

[1] *Jocelini Chronica,* p. 85.

be a wise and sharp man, and so treats the people reasonably, *tractat homines pacifice.*' Whereat the Lord Abbot *factus est hilaris,*—could not but take a triumphant laugh for himself; and determines to leave that Harlow manor yet unmeddled with, for a while.[1]

A brave man, strenuously fighting, fails not of a little triumph now and then, to keep him in heart. Everywhere we try at least to give the adversary as good as he brings; and, with swift force or slow watchful manœuvre, extinguish this and the other solecism, leave one solecism less in God's Creation; and so *proceed* with our battle, not slacken or surrender it! The Fifty feudal Knights, for example, were of unjust greedy temper, and cheated us, in the Installation-day, of ten knights'-fees; —but they know now whether that has profited them aught, and I Jocelin know. Our Lord Abbot for the moment had to endure it, and say nothing; but he watched his time.

Look also how my Lord of Clare, coming to claim his *un*due ' debt ' in the Court of Witham, with barons and apparatus, gets a Roland for his Oliver! Jocelin shall report: ' The Earl, crowded round (*constipatus*) with many barons and men-at-arms, Earl Alberic and others standing by him, said, " That his bailiffs had given him to understand they were wont annually to receive for his behoof, from the Hundred of Risebridge and the bailiffs thereof, a sum of five shillings, which sum was now unjustly held back; " and he alleged farther that his predecessors had been infeft, at the Conquest, in the lands of Alfric son of Wisgar, who was Lord of that Hundred, as may be read in Doomsday Book by all persons.—The Abbot, reflecting for a moment, without stirring from his place, made answer: " A wonderful deficit, my Lord Earl, this that thou mentionest! King Edward gave to St. Edmund that entire Hundred, and confirmed the same with his Charter; nor is there any mention there of those five shillings. It will behove thee to say, for what service, or on what ground, thou exactest those five shillings." Whereupon the Earl, consulting with his followers, replied,

[1] *Jocelini Chronica,* p. 24.

That he had to carry the Banner of St. Edmund in war-time, and for this duty the five shillings were his. To which the Abbot: " Certainly, it seems inglorious, if so great a man, Earl of Clare no less, receive so small a gift for such a service. To the Abbot of St. Edmund's it is no unbearable burden to give five shillings. But Roger Earl Bigot holds himself duly seised, and asserts that he by such seisin has the office of carrying St. Edmund's Banner; and he did carry it when the Earl of Leicester and his Flemings were beaten at Fornham. Then again Thomas de Mendham says that the right is his. When you have made out with one another, that this right is thine, come then and claim the five shillings, and I will promptly pay them! " Whereupon the Earl said, He would speak with Earl Roger his relative; and so the matter *cepit dilationem*,' and lies undecided to the end of the world. Abbot Samson answers by word or act, in this or the like pregnant manner, having justice on his side, innumerable persons: Pope's Legates, King's Viscounts, Canterbury Archbishops, Cellarers, *Sochemanni ;* —and leaves many a solecism extinguished.

On the whole, however, it is and remains sore work. ' One time, during my chaplaincy, I ventured to say to him: " *Domine*, I heard thee, this night after matins, wakeful, and sighing deeply, *valde suspirantem*, contrary to thy usual wont." He answered: " No wonder. Thou, son Jocelin, sharest in my good things, in food and drink, in riding and suchlike; but thou little thinkest concerning the management of House and Family, the various and arduous businesses of the Pastoral Care, which harass me, and make my soul to sigh and be anxious." Whereto I, lifting up my hands to Heaven: " From such anxiety, Omnipotent merciful Lord deliver me! "—I have heard the Abbot say, If he had been as he was before he became a Monk, and could have anywhere got five or six marcs of income,' some three-pound ten of yearly revenue, ' whereby to support himself in the schools, he would never have been Monk nor Abbot. Another time he said with an oath, If he had known what a business it was to govern the Abbey, he would rather have been Almoner,

how much rather Keeper of the Books, than Abbot and
Lord. That latter office he said he had always longed
for, beyond any other. *Quis talia crederet?*' concludes
Jocelin, 'Who can believe such things?'

Three-pound ten, and a life of Literature, especially of
quiet Literature, without copyright, or world-celebrity
of literary-gazettes,—yes, thou brave Abbot Samson, for
thyself it had been better, easier, perhaps also nobler!
But then, for thy disobedient Monks, unjust Viscounts;
for a Domain of St. Edmund overgrown with Solecisms,
human and other, it had not been so well. Nay neither
could *thy* Literature, never so quiet, have been easy.
Literature, when noble, is not easy; but only when
ignoble. Literature too is a quarrel, and internecine
duel, with the whole World of Darkness that lies without
one and within one;—rather a hard fight at times, even
with the three-pound ten secure. Thou, there where thou
art, wrestle and duel along, cheerfully to the end; and
make no remarks!

CHAPTER XIII

IN PARLIAMENT

OF Abbot Samson's public business we say little, though
that also was great. He had to judge the people as
Justice Errant, to decide in weighty arbitrations and
public controversies; to equip his *milites*, send them duly
in war-time to the King;—strive every way that the
Commonweal, in his quarter of it, take no damage.

Once, in the confused days of Lackland's usurpation,
while Cœur-de-Lion was away, our brave Abbot took
helmet himself, having first excommunicated all that
should favour Lackland; and led his men in person to
the siege of *Windleshora*, what we now call Windsor;
where Lackland had entrenched himself, the centre of
infinite confusions; some Reform Bill, then as now, being
greatly needed. There did Abbot Samson 'fight the

battle of reform,'—with other ammunition, one hopes,
than 'tremendous cheering' and suchlike! For these
things he was called 'the magnanimous Abbot.'

He also attended duly in his place in Parliament *de
arduis regni*; attended especially, as in *arduissimo*, when
'the news reached London that King Richard was a
captive in Germany.' Here 'while all the barons sat to
consult,' and many of them looked blank enough, 'the
Abbot started forth, *prosiliit coram omnibus*, in his place
in Parliament, and said, That *he* was ready to go and seek
his Lord the King, either clandestinely by subterfuge (*in
tapinagio*), or by any other method; and search till he
found him, and got certain notice of him; he for one!
By which word,' says Jocelin, 'he acquired great praise
for himself,'—unfeigned commendation from the Able
Editors of that age.

By which word;—and also by which *deed:* for the
Abbot actually went 'with rich gifts to the King in
Germany;'[1] Usurper Lackland being first rooted out
from Windsor, and the King's peace somewhat settled.

As to these 'rich gifts,' however, we have to note one
thing: In all England, as appeared to the Collective
Wisdom, there was not like to be treasure enough for
ransoming King Richard; in which extremity certain
Lords of the Treasury, *Justiciarii ad Scaccarium*, suggested
that St. Edmund's Shrine, covered with thick gold, was
still untouched. Could not it, in this extremity, be
peeled off, at least in part; under condition, of course,
of its being replaced when times mended? The Abbot,
starting plumb up, *se erigens*, answered: "Know ye for
certain, that I will in nowise do this thing; nor is there
any man who could force me to consent thereto. But I
will open the doors of the Church: Let him that likes
enter; let him that dares come forward!" Emphatic
words, which created a sensation round the woolsack.
For the Justiciaries of the *Scaccarium* answered, 'with
oaths, each for himself: "I won't come forward, for my
share; nor will I, nor I! The distant and absent who

_____
[1] *Jocelini Chronica*, pp. 39, 40.

offended him, Saint Edmund has been known to punish fearfully; much more will he those close by, who lay violent hands on his coat, and would strip it off!" These things being said, the Shrine was not meddled with, nor any ransom levied for it.' [1]

For Lords of the Treasury have in all times their impassable limits, be it by 'force of public opinion' or otherwise; and in those days a heavenly Awe overshadowed and encompassed, as it still ought and must, all earthly Business whatsoever.

CHAPTER XIV

HENRY OF ESSEX

Of St. Edmund's fearful avengements have they not the remarkablest instance still before their eyes? He that will go to Reading Monastery may find there, now tonsured into a mournful penitent Monk, the once proud Henry Earl of Essex; and discern how St. Edmund punishes terribly, yet with mercy! This Narrative is too significant to be omitted as a document of the Time. Our Lord Abbot, once on a visit at Reading, heard the particulars from Henry's own mouth; and thereupon charged one of his monks to write it down;—as accordingly the Monk has done, in ambitious rhetorical Latin; inserting the same, as episode, among Jocelin's garrulous leaves. Read it here; with ancient yet with modern eyes.

Henry Earl of Essex, standard-bearer of England, had high places and emoluments; had a haughty high soul, yet with various flaws, or rather with one many-branched flaw and crack, running through the texture of it. For example, did he not treat Gilbert de Cereville in the most shocking manner? He cast Gilbert into prison; and, with chains and slow torments, wore the life out of him there. And Gilbert's crime was understood to be only that of innocent Joseph: the Lady Essex was a Potiphar's

[1] *Jocelini Chronica*, p. 71.

Wife, and had accused poor Gilbert! Other cracks, and branches of that widespread flaw in the Standard-bearer's soul we could point out: but indeed the main stem and trunk of all is too visible in this, That he had no right reverence for the Heavenly in Man,—that far from showing due reverence to St. Edmund, he did not even show him common justice. While others in the Eastern Counties were adorning and enlarging with rich gifts St. Edmund's resting-place, which had become a city of refuge for many things, this Earl of Essex flatly defrauded him, by violence or quirk of law, of five shillings yearly, and converted said sum to his own poor uses! Nay, in another case of litigation, the unjust Standard-bearer, for his own profit, asserting that the cause belonged not to St. Edmund's Court, but to *his* in Lailand Hundred, 'involved us in travellings and innumerable expenses, vexing the servants of St. Edmund for a long tract of time.' In short, he is without reverence for the Heavenly, this Standard-bearer; reveres only the Earthly, Gold-coined; and has a most morbid lamentable flaw in the texture of him. It cannot come to good.

Accordingly, the same flaw, or St.-Vitus' *tic*, manifests itself ere long in another way. In the year 1157, he went with his Standard to attend King Henry, our blessed Sovereign (whom *we* saw afterwards at Waltham), in his War with the Welsh. A somewhat disastrous War; in which while King Henry and his force were struggling to retreat Parthian-like, endless clouds of exasperated Welshmen hemming them in, and now we had come to the 'difficult pass of Coleshill,' and as it were to the nick of destruction,—Henry Earl of Essex shrieks out on a sudden (blinded doubtless by his inner flaw, or 'evil genius' as some name it), That King Henry is killed, That all is lost,—and flings down his Standard to shift for itself there! And, certainly enough, all *had* been lost, had all men been as he;—had not brave men, without such miserable jerking *tic-douloureux* in the souls of them, come dashing up, with blazing swords, and looks, and asserted, That nothing was lost yet, that all must be regained yet. In this manner King Henry and his force

got safely retreated, Parthian-like, from the pass of Coleshill and the Welsh War.[1] But, once home again, Earl
Robert de Montfort, a kinsman of this Standard-bearer's,
rises up in the King's Assembly to declare openly that
such a man is unfit for bearing English Standards, being
in fact either a special traitor, or something almost worse,
a coward namely, or universal traitor. Wager of Battle
in consequence; solemn Duel, by the King's appointment,
'in a certain Island of the Thames-stream at Reading,
apud Radingas, short way from the Abbey there.' King,
Peers, and an immense multitude of people, on such
scaffoldings and heights as they can come at, are gathered
round, to see what issue the business will take. The
business takes this bad issue, in our Monk's own words
faithfully rendered:

'And it came to pass, while Robert de Montfort
thundered on him manfully (*viriliter intonâsset*) with
hard and frequent strokes, and a valiant beginning
promised the fruit of victory, Henry of Essex, rather
giving way, glanced round on all sides; and lo, at the rim
of the horizon, on the confines of the River and land, he
discerned the glorious King and Martyr Edmund, in
shining armour, and as if hovering in the air; looking
towards him with severe countenance, nodding his head
with a mien and motion of austere anger. At St.
Edmund's hand there stood also another Knight, Gilbert
de Cereville, whose armour was not so splendid, whose
stature was less gigantic; casting vengeful looks at him.
This he seeing with his eyes, remembered that old crime
brings new shame. And now wholly desperate, and
changing reason into violence, he took the part of one
blindly attacking, not skilfully defending. Who while he
struck fiercely was more fiercely struck; and so, in short,
fell down vanquished, and it was thought slain. As he
lay there for dead, his kinsmen, Magnates of England,
besought the King, that the Monks of Reading might
have leave to bury him. However, he proved not to be
dead, but got well again among them; and now, with
recovered health, assuming the Regular Habit, he strove

[1] See Lyttelton's *Henry II.* ii. 384.

to wipe out the stain of his former life, to cleanse the long
week of his dissolute history by at least a purifying sabbath,
and cultivate the studies of Virtue into fruits of eternal
Felicity.' [1]

Thus does the Conscience of man project itself athwart
whatsoever of knowledge or surmise, of imagination,
understanding, faculty, acquirement, or natural disposition, he has in him; and, like light through coloured glass,
paint strange pictures ' on the rim of the horizon ' and
elsewhere! Truly, this same ' sense of the Infinite nature
of Duty ' is the central part of all with us; a ray as of
Eternity and Immortality, immured in dusky many-
coloured Time, and its deaths and births. Your ' coloured
glass ' varies so much from century to century;—and, in
certain money-making, game-preserving centuries, it gets
so terrible opaque! Not a Heaven with cherubim surrounds you then, but a kind of vacant leaden-coloured
Hell. One day it will again cease to be *opaque*, this
' coloured glass.' Nay, may it not become at once
transculent and *un*coloured? Painting no Pictures more
for us, but only the everlasting Azure itself? That will
be a right glorious consummation!—

Saint Edmund from the horizon's edge, in shining
armour, threatening the misdoer in his hour of extreme
need: it is beautiful, it is great and true. So old, yet so
modern, actual; true yet for every one of us, as for
Henry the Earl and Monk! A glimpse as of the Deepest
in Man's Destiny, which is the same for all times and
ages. Yes, Henry my brother, there in thy extreme need,
thy soul is *lamed ;* and behold thou canst not so much as
fight! For Justice and Reverence *are* the everlasting
central Law of this Universe; and to forget them, and
have all the Universe against one, God and one's own
Self for enemies, and only the Devil and the Dragons for
friends, is not that a ' lameness ' like few? That some
shining armed St. Edmund hang minatory on thy horizon,
that infinite sulphur-lakes hang minatory, or do not now
hang,—this alters no whit the eternal fact of the thing.
I say, thy soul is lamed, and the God and all Godlike

in it marred: lamed, paralytic, tending towards baleful eternal death, whether thou know it or not;—nay hadst thou never known it, that surely had been worst of all!—

Thus, at any rate, by the heavenly Awe that over-shadows earthly Business, does Samson, readily in those days, save St. Edmund's Shrine, and innumerable still more precious things.

CHAPTER XV

PRACTICAL-DEVOTIONAL

HERE indeed, by rule of antagonisms, may be the place to mention that, after King Richard's return, there was a liberty of tourneying given to the fighting-men of England: that a Tournament was proclaimed in the Abbot's domain, ' between Thetford and St. Edmunds-bury,'—perhaps in the Euston region, on Fakenham Heights, midway between these two localities: that it was publicly prohibited by our Lord Abbot; and never-theless was held in spite of him,—and by the parties, as would seem, considered ' a gentle and free passage of arms.'

Nay, next year, there came to the same spot four-and-twenty young men, sons of Nobles, for another passage of arms; who, having completed the same, all rode into St. Edmundsbury to lodge for the night. Here is modesty! Our Lord Abbot, being instructed of it, ordered the Gates to be closed; the whole party shut in. The morrow was the Vigil of the Apostles Peter and Paul; no outgate on the morrow. Giving their promise not to depart without permission, those four-and-twenty young bloods dieted all that day (*manducaverunt*) with the Lord Abbot, wait-ing for trial on the morrow. ' But after dinner,'—mark it, posterity!—' the Lord Abbot retiring into his *Talamus*, they all started up, and began carolling and singing (*carolare et cantare*); sending into the Town for wine; drinking, and afterwards howling (*ululantes*); — totally

depriving the Abbot and Convent of their afternoon's nap;
doing all this in derision of the Lord Abbot, and spending
in such fashion the whole day till evening, nor would they
desist at the Lord Abbot's order! Night coming on, they
broke the bolts of the Town-Gates, and went off by
violence!'[1] Was the like ever heard of? The roysterous
young dogs; carolling, howling, breaking the Lord Abbot's
sleep,—after that sinful chivalry cockfight of theirs! They
too are a feature of distant centuries, as of near ones.
St. Edmund on the edge of your horizon, or whatever else
there, young scamps, in the dandy state, whether cased
in iron or in whalebone, begin to caper and carol on the
green Earth! Our Lord Abbot excommunicated most of
them; and they gradually came in for repentance.

Excommunication is a great recipe with our Lord
Abbot; the prevailing purifier in those ages. Thus when
the Townsfolk and Monks' menials quarrelled once at the
Christmas Mysteries in St. Edmund's Churchyard, and
'from words it came to cuffs, and from cuffs to cutting
and the effusion of blood,'—our Lord Abbot excom-
municates sixty of the rioters, with bell, book and candle
(*accensis candelis*), at one stroke.[2] Whereupon they all
come suppliant, indeed nearly naked, 'nothing on but
their breeches, *omnino nudi præter femoralia*, and prostrate
themselves at the Church-door.' Figure that!

In fact, by excommunication or persuasion, by im-
petuosity of driving or adroitness in leading, this Abbot,
it is now becoming plain everywhere, is a man that
generally remains master at last. He tempers his medicine
to the malady, now hot, now cool; prudent though fiery,
an eminently practical man. Nay sometimes in his
adroit practice there are swift turns almost of a surprising
nature; Once, for example, it chanced that Geoffrey
Riddell Bishop of Ely, a Prelate rather troublesome to
our Abbot, made a request of him for timber from his
woods towards certain edifices going on at Glemsford.
The Abbot, a great builder himself, disliked the request;
could not, however, give it a negative. While he lay,
therefore, at his Manor-house of Melford not long after,

[1] *Jocelini Chronica*, p. 40.   [2] *Jocelini Chronica*, p. 68.

there comes to him one of the Lord Bishop's men or monks, with a message from his Lordship, " That he now begged permission to cut down the requisite trees in Elmswell Wood,"—so said the monk: Elms*well*, where there are no trees but scrubs and shrubs, instead of Elm*set*, our true *nemus* and high-towering oak-wood, here on Melford Manor! Elmswell? The Lord Abbot, in surprise, inquires privily of Richard his Forester; Richard answers that my Lord of Ely has already had his *carpentarii* in Elm*set*, and marked out for his own use all the best trees in the compass of it. Abbot Samson thereupon answers the monk: " Elmswell? Yes surely, be it as my Lord Bishop wishes." The successful monk, on the morrow morning, hastens home to Ely; but, on the morrow morning, ' directly after mass,' Abbot Samson too was busy! The successful monk, arriving at Ely, is rated for a goose and an owl; is ordered back to say that Elmset was the place meant. Alas, on arriving at Elmset, he finds the Bishop's trees, they ' and a hundred more,' all felled and piled, and the stamp of St. Edmund's Monastery burnt into them,—for roofing of the great tower we are building there! Your importunate Bishop must seek wood for Glemsford edifices in some other *nemus* than this. A practical Abbot!

We said withal there was a terrible flash of anger in him; witness his address to old Herbert the Dean, who in a too thrifty manner has erected a windmill for himself on his glebe-lands at Haberdon. On the morrow, after mass, our Lord Abbot orders the Cellerarius to send off his carpenters to demolish the said structure *brevi manu*, and lay up the wood in safe keeping. Old Dean Herbert, hearing what was toward, comes tottering along hither, to plead humbly for himself and his mill. The Abbot answers: " I am obliged to thee as if thou hadst cut off both my feet! By God's face, *per os Dei*, I will not eat bread till that fabric be torn in pieces. Thou art an old man, and shouldst have known that neither the King nor his Justiciary dare change aught within the Liberties without consent of Abbot and Convent: and thou hast presumed on such a thing? I tell thee, it will

not be without damage to my mills; for the Townsfolk
will go to thy mill, and grind their corn (*bladum suum*) at
their own good pleasure; nor can I hinder them, since
they are free men. I will allow no new mills on such
principle. Away, away; before thou gettest home again,
thou shalt see what thy mill has grown to!" [1]—The very
reverend the old Dean totters home again, in all haste;
tears the mill in pieces by his own *carpentarii*, to save at
least the timber; and Abbot Samson's workmen, coming
up, find the ground already clear of it.

Easy to bully-down poor old rural Deans, and blow
their windmills away: but who is the man that dare
abide King Richard's anger; cross the Lion in his path,
and take him by the whiskers! Abbot Samson too; he
is that man, with justice on his side. The case was this.
Adam de Cokefield, one of the chief feudatories of St.
Edmund, and a principal man in the Eastern Counties,
died, leaving large possessions, and for heiress a daughter
of three months; who by clear law, as all men know,
became thus Abbot Samson's ward; whom accordingly
he proceeded to dispose of to such person as seemed
fittest. But now King Richard has another person in
view, to whom the little ward and her great possessions
were a suitable thing. He, by letter, requests that Abbot
Samson will have the goodness to give her to this person.
Abbot Samson, with deep humility, replies that she is
already given. New letters from Richard, of severer
tenor; answered with new deep humilities, with gifts and
entreaties, with no promise of obedience. King Richard's
ire is kindled; messengers arrive at St. Edmundsbury, with
emphatic message to obey or tremble! Abbot Samson,
wisely silent as to the King's threats, makes answer:
"The King can send if he will, and seize the ward: force
and power he has to do his pleasure, and abolish the
whole Abbey. But I, for my part, never can be bent to
wish this that he seeks, nor shall it by me be ever done.
For there is danger lest such things be made a precedent
of, to the prejudice of my successors. *Videat Altissimus,*

[1] *Jocelini Chronica*, p. 43.

Let the Most High look on it. Whatsoever thing shall befall I will patiently endure."

Such was Abbot Samson's deliberate decision. Why not? Cœur-de-Lion is very dreadful, but not the dreadfulest. *Videat Altissimus.* I reverence Cœur-de-Lion to the marrow of my bones, and will in all right things be *homo suus ;* but it is not, properly speaking, with terror, with any fear at all. On the whole, have I not looked on the face of ' Satan with outspread wings; ' steadily into Hell-fire these seven-and-forty years;—and was not melted into terror even at that, such the Lord's goodness to me? Cœur-de-Lion!

Richard swore tornado oaths, worse than our armies in Flanders, To be revenged on that proud Priest. But in the end he discovered that the Priest was right; and forgave him, and even loved him. ' King Richard wrote, soon after, to Abbot Samson, That he wanted one or two of the St. Edmundsbury dogs, which he heard were good.' Abbot Samson sent him dogs of the best; Richard replied by the present of a ring, which Pope Innocent the Third had given him. Thou brave Richard, thou brave Samson! Richard too, I suppose, ' loved a man,' and knew **one** when he saw him.

No one will accuse our Lord Abbot of wanting worldly wisdom, due interest in worldly things. A skilful man; full of cunning insight, lively interests; always discerning the road to his object, be it circuit, be it short-cut, and victoriously travelling forward thereon. Nay rather it might seem, from Jocelin's Narrative, as if he had his eye all but exclusively directed on terrestrial matters, and was much too secular for a devout man. But this too, if we examine it, was right. For it is *in* the world that a man, devout or other, has his life to lead, his work waiting to be done. The basis of Abbot Samson's, we shall discover, was truly religion, after all. Returning from his dusty pilgrimage, with such welcome as we saw, ' he sat down at the foot of St. Edmund's Shrine.' Not a talking theory, that; no, a silent practice: Thou, St. Edmund, with what lies in thee, thou now must help me, or none will!

This also is a significant fact: the zealous interest our

Abbot took in the Crusades. To all noble Christian
hearts of that era, what earthly enterprise so noble?
'When Henry II., having taken the cross, came to St.
Edmund's, to pay his devotions before setting out, the
Abbot secretly made for himself a cross of linen cloth:
and, holding this in one hand and a threaded needle in
the other, asked 'leave of the King to assume it.' The
King could not spare Samson out of England;—the King
himself indeed never went. But the Abbot's eye was
set on the Holy Sepulchre, as on the spot of this Earth
where the true cause of Heaven was deciding itself. 'At
the retaking of Jerusalem by the Pagans, Abbot Samson
put on a cilice and hair-shirt, and wore under-garments of
hair-cloth ever after; he abstained also from flesh and
flesh-meats (*carne et carneis*) thenceforth to the end of
his life.' Like a dark cloud eclipsing the hopes of
Christendom, those tidings cast their shadow over St.
Edmundsbury too: Shall Samson Abbas take pleasure
while Christ's Tomb is in the hands of the Infidel?
Samson, in pain of body, shall daily be reminded of it,
daily be admonished to grieve for it.

The great antique heart: how like a child's in its simplicity, like a man's in its earnest solemnity and depth!
Heaven lies over him wheresoever he goes or stands on
the Earth; making all the Earth a mystic Temple to him,
the Earth's business all a kind of worship. Glimpses of
bright creatures flash in the common sunlight; angels yet
hover doing God's messages among men: that rainbow
was set in the clouds by the hand of God! Wonder,
miracle encompass the man; he lives in an element of
miracle; Heaven's splendour over his head, Hell's darkness under his feet. A great Law of Duty, high as these
two Infinitudes, dwarfing all else, annihilating all else,—
making royal Richard as small as peasant Samson, smaller
if need be!—The 'imaginative faculties?' 'Rude poetic
ages?' The 'primeval poetic element?' Oh, for God's
sake, good reader, talk no more of all that! It was not a
Dilettantism this of Abbot Samson. It was a Reality,
and it is one. The garment only of it is dead; the essence
of it lives through all Time and all Eternity!—

And truly, as we said above, is not this comparative silence of Abbot Samson as to his religion precisely the healthiest sign of him and of it? 'The Unconscious is the alone Complete.' Abbot Samson all along a busy working man, as all men are bound to be, his religion, his worship was like his daily bread to him;—which he did not take the trouble to talk much about; which he merely ate at stated intervals, and lived and did his work upon! This is Abbot Samson's Catholicism of the Twelfth Century;—something like the *Ism* of all true men in all true centuries, I fancy! Alas, compared with any of the *Isms* current in these poor days, what a thing! Compared with the respectablest, morbid, struggling Methodism, never so earnest; with the respectablest, ghastly, dead or galvanised Dilettantism, never so spasmodic!

Methodism with its eye forever turned on its own navel; asking itself with torturing anxiety of Hope and Fear, " Am I right? am I wrong? Shall I be saved? shall I not be damned? "—what is this, at bottom, but a new phasis of *Egoism*, stretched out into the Infinite; not always the heavenlier for its infinitude! Brother, so soon as possible, endeavour to rise above all that. " Thou *art* wrong; thou art like to be damned: " consider that as the fact, reconcile thyself even to that, if thou be a man; —then first is the devouring Universe subdued under thee, and from the black murk of midnight and noise of greedy Acheron, dawn as of an everlasting morning, how far above all Hope and all Fear, springs for thee, enlightening thy steep path, awakening in thy heart celestial Memnon's music!

But of our Dilettantisms, and galvanised Dilettantisms; of Puseyism—O Heavens, what shall we say of Puseyism, in comparison to Twelfth-Century Catholicism? Little or nothing; for indeed it is a matter to strike one dumb.

> The Builder of this Universe was wise,
> He plann'd all souls, all systems, planets, particles:
> The Plan He shap'd all Worlds and Æons by,
> Was—Heavens!—Was thy small Nine-and-thirty Articles?

That certain human souls, living on this practical Earth, should think to save themselves and a ruined world by

noisy theoretic demonstrations and laudations of *the*
Church, instead of some unnoisy, unconscious, but
practical, total, heart-and-soul demonstration of *a* Church:
this, in the circle of revolving ages, this also was a thing
we were to see. A kind of penultimate thing, precursor
of very strange consummations; last thing but one? If
there is no atmosphere, what will it serve a man to
demonstrate the excellence of lungs? How much pro-
fitabler, when you can, like Abbot Samson, breathe; and
go along your way!

CHAPTER XVI

ST. EDMUND

ABBOT SAMSON built many useful, many pious edifices;
human dwellings, churches, church-steeples, barns;—all
fallen now and vanished, but useful while they stood.
He built and endowed ' the Hospital of Babwell;' built
' fit houses for the St. Edmundsbury Schools.' Many
are the roofs once ' thatched with reeds ' which he ' caused
to be covered with tiles;' or if they were churches, probably ' with lead.' For all ruinous incomplete things,
buildings or other, were an eye-sorrow to the man. We
saw his ' great tower of St. Edmund's;' or at least the
roof-timbers of it, lying cut and stamped in Elmset Wood.
To change combustible decaying reed-thatch into tile or
lead; and material, still more, moral wreck into rain-tight
order, what a comfort to Samson!

One of the things he could not in any wise but rebuild
was the great Altar, aloft on which stood the Shrine itself;
the great Altar, which had been damaged by fire, by the
careless rubbish and careless candle of two somnolent
Monks, one night,—the Shrine escaping almost as if by
miracle! Abbot Samson read his Monks a severe lecture:
" A Dream one of us had, that he saw St. Edmund naked
and in lamentable plight. Know ye the interpretation of
that Dream? St. Edmund proclaims himself naked,

because ye defraud the naked Poor of your old clothes, and give with reluctance what ye are bound to give them of meat and drink: the idleness moreover and negligence of the Sacristan and his people is too evident from the late misfortune by fire. Well might our Holy Martyr seem to lie cast out from his Shrine, and say with groans that he was stript of his garments, and wasted with hunger and thirst!"

This is Abbot Samson's interpretation of the Dream; —diametrically the reverse of that given by the Monks themselves, who scruple not to say privily, "It is *we* that are the naked and famished limbs of the Martyr; we whom the Abbot curtails of all our privileges, setting his own official to control our very Cellarer!" Abbot Samson adds, that this judgment by fire has fallen upon them for murmuring about their meat and drink.

Clearly enough, meanwhile, the Altar, whatever the burning of it mean or foreshadow, must needs be reëdified. Abbot Samson reëdifies it, all of polished marble; with the highest stretch of art and sumptuosity, reëmbellishes the Shrine for which it is to serve as pediment. Nay farther, as had ever been among his prayers, he enjoys, he sinner, a glimpse of the glorious Martyr's very Body in the process; having solemnly opened the *Loculus*, Chest or sacred Coffin, for that purpose. It is the culminating moment of Abbot Samson's life. Bozzy Jocelin himself rises into a kind of Psalmist solemnity on this occasion; the laziest monk ' weeps ' warm tears, as *Te Deum* is sung.

Very strange;—how far vanished from us in these unworshipping ages of ours! The Patriot Hampden, best beatified man we have, had lain in like manner some two centuries in his narrow home, when certain dignitaries of us, ' and twelve grave-diggers with pulleys,' raised him also up, under cloud of night, cut off his arm with pen-knives, pulled the scalp off his head,—and otherwise worshipped our Hero Saint in the most amazing manner! [1] Let the modern eye look earnestly on that old midnight hour in St. Edmundsbury Church, shining yet on us,

---

[1] *Annual Register* (year 1828, Chronicle, p. 93), *Gentleman's Magazine*, etc., etc.

ruddy-bright, through the depths of seven hundred years; and consider mournfully what our Hero-worship once was, and what it now is! We translate with all the fidelity we can:

'The Festival of St. Edmund now approaching, the marble blocks are polished, and all things are in readiness for lifting of the Shrine to its new place. A fast of three days was held by all the people, the cause and meaning thereof being publicly set forth to them. The Abbot announces to the Convent that all must prepare themselves for transferring of the Shrine, and appoints time and way for the work. Coming therefore that night to matins, we found the great Shrine (*feretrum magnum*) raised upon the Altar, but empty; covered all over with white doeskin leather, fixed to the wood with silver nails; but one pannel of the Shrine was left down below, and resting thereon, beside its old column of the Church, the Loculus with the Sacred Body yet lay where it was wont. Praises being sung, we all proceeded to commence our disciplines (*ad disciplinas suscipiendas*). These finished, the Abbot and certain with him are clothed in their albs; and, approaching reverently, set about uncovering the Loculus. There was an outer cloth of linen, enwrapping the Loculus and all; this we found tied on the upper side with strings of its own: within this was a cloth of silk, and then another linen cloth, and then a third; and so at last the Loculus was uncovered, and seen resting on a little tray of wood, that the bottom of it might not be injured by the stone. Over the breast of the Martyr, there lay, fixed to the surface of the Loculus, a Golden Angel about the length of a human foot; holding in one hand a golden sword, and in the other a banner: under this there was a hole in the lid of the Loculus, on which the ancient servants of the Martyr had been wont to lay their hands for touching the Sacred Body. And over the figure of the Angel was this verse inscribed:

'*Martiris ecce zoma servat Michaelis agalma.*[1]

At the head and foot of the Loculus were iron rings whereby it could be lifted.

[1] 'This is the Martyr's Garment, which Michael's Image guards.'

' Lifting the Loculus and Body, therefore, they carried it to the Altar; and I put-to my sinful hand to help in carrying, though the Abbot had commanded that none should approach except called. And the Loculus was placed in the Shrine; and the pannel it had stood on was put in its place, and the Shrine for the present closed. We all thought that the Abbot would show the Loculus to the people; and bring out the Sacred Body again, at a certain period of the Festival. But in this we were wofully mistaken, as the sequel shows.

' For in the fourth holiday of the Festival, while the Convent were all singing *Completorium*, our Lord Abbot spoke privily with the Sacristan and Walter the Medicus; and order was taken that twelve of the Brethren should be appointed against midnight, who were strong for carrying the pannel-planks of the Shrine, and skilful in unfixing them, and putting them together again. The Abbot then said that it was among his prayers to look once upon the Body of his Patron; and that he wished the Sacristan and Walter the Medicus to be with him. The Twelve appointed Brethren were these: The Abbot's two Chaplains, the two Keepers of the Shrine, the two Masters of the Vestry; and six more, namely, the Sacristan Hugo, Walter the Medicus, Augustin, William of Dice, Robert and Richard. I, alas, was not of the number.

' The Convent therefore being all asleep, these Twelve, clothed in their albs, with the Abbot, assembled at the Altar; and opening a pannel of the Shrine, they took out the Loculus; laid it on a table, near where the Shrine used to be; and made ready for unfastening the lid, which was joined and fixed to the Loculus with sixteen very long nails. Which when, with difficulty, they had done, all except the two fore-named associates are ordered to draw back. The Abbot and they two were alone privileged to look in. The Loculus was so filled with the Sacred Body that you could scarcely put a needle between the head and the wood, or between the feet and the wood: the head lay united to the body, a little raised with a small pillow. But the Abbot, looking close, found

now a silk cloth veiling the whole Body, and then a
linen cloth of wondrous whiteness; and upon the head
was spread a small linen cloth, and then another small
and most fine silk cloth, as if it were the veil of a nun.
These coverings being lifted off, they found now the
Sacred Body all wrapt in linen; and so at length the
lineaments of the same appeared. But here the Abbot
stopped; saying he durst not proceed farther, or look
at the sacred flesh naked. Taking the head between his
hands, he thus spake, groaning: "Glorious Martyr, holy
Edmund, blessed be the hour when thou wert born.
Glorious Martyr, turn it not to my perdition that I have
so dared to touch thee, I miserable and sinful; thou
knowest my devout love, and the intention of my mind."
And proceeding, he touched the eyes; and the nose,
which was very massive and prominent (*valde grossum et
valde eminentem*); and then he touched the breast and
arms; and raising the left arm he touched the fingers,
and placed his own fingers between the sacred fingers.
And proceeding he found the feet standing stiff up, like
the feet of a man dead yesterday; and he touched the
toes and counted them (*tangendo numeravit*).

' And now it was agreed that the other Brethren should
be called forward to see the miracles; and accordingly
those ten now advanced, and along with them six others
who had stolen in without the Abbot's assent, namely,
Walter of St. Alban's, Hugh the Infirmirarius, Gilbert
brother of the Prior, Richard of Henham, Jocellus our
Cellarer, and Turstan the Little; and all these saw the
Sacred Body, but Turstan alone of them put forth his
hand, and touched the Saint's knees and feet. And that
there might be abundance of witnesses, one of our
Brethren, John of Dice, sitting on the roof of the Church,
with the servants of the Vestry, and looking through,
clearly saw all these things.'

What a scene; shining luminous effulgent, as the lamps
of St. Edmund do, through the dark Night; John of
Dice, with vestrymen, clambering on the roof to look
through; the Convent all asleep, and the Earth all asleep,

—and since then, Seven Centuries of Time mostly gone to sleep! Yes, there, sure enough, is the martyred Body of Edmund, landlord of the Eastern Counties, who, nobly doing what he liked with his own, was slain three hundred years ago: and a noble awe surrounds the memory of him, symbol and promoter of many other right noble things.

But have not we now advanced to strange new stages of Hero-worship, now in the little Church of Hampden, with our penknives out, and twelve grave-diggers with pulleys? The manner of men's Hero-worship, verily it is the innermost fact of their existence, and determines all the rest,—at public hustings, in private drawing-rooms, in church, in market, and wherever else. Have true reverence, and what indeed is inseparable therefrom, reverence the right man, all is well; have sham-reverence, and what also follows, greet with it the wrong man, then all is ill, and there is nothing well. Alas, if Hero-worship become Dilettantism, and all except Mammonism be a vain grimace, how much, in this most earnest Earth, has gone and is evermore going to fatal destruction, and lies wasting in quiet lazy ruin, no man regarding it! Till at length no heavenly *Ism* any longer coming down upon us, *Isms* from the other quarter have to mount up. For the Earth, I say, is an earnest place; Life is no grimace, but a most serious fact. And so, under universal Dilettantism much having been stript bare, not the souls of men only, but their very bodies and bread-cupboards having been stript bare, and life now no longer possible,—all is reduced to desperation, to the iron law of Necessity and very Fact again; and to temper Dilettantism, and astonish it, and burn it up with infernal fire, arises Chartism, *Bare-back-ism*, Sansculottism so-called! May the gods, and what of unworshipped heroes still remain among us, avert the omen!—

But however this may be, St. Edmund's Loculus, we find, has the veils of silk and linen reverently replaced, the lid fastened down again with its sixteen ancient nails; is wrapt in a new costly covering of silk, the gift of Hubert

Archbishop of Canterbury: and through the sky-window
John of Dice sees it lifted to its place in the Shrine, the
pannels of this latter duly refixed, fit parchment docu-
ments being introduced withal;—and now John and his
vestry-men can slide down from the roof, for all is over,
and the Convent wholly awakens to matins. 'When we
assembled to sing matins,' says Jocelin, 'and understood
what had been done, grief took hold of all that had not
seen these things, each saying to himself, "Alas, I was
deceived." Matins over, the Abbot called the Convent
to the great Altar; and briefly recounting the matter,
alleged that it had not been in his power, nor was it permissible or fit, to invite us all to the sight of such things.
At hearing of which, we all wept, and with tears sang
Te deum laudamus; and hastened to toll the bells in the
Choir.'

Stupid blockheads, to reverence their St. Edmund's
dead Body in this manner? Yes, brother;—and yet, on
the whole, who knows how to reverence the Body of a
Man? It is the most reverend phenomenon under this
Sun. For the Highest God dwells visible in that mystic
unfathomable Visibility, which calls itself "I" on the
Earth. 'Bending before men,' says Novalis, 'is a reverence done to this Revelation in the Flesh. We touch
Heaven when we lay our hand on a human Body.' And
the Body of one Dead;—a temple where the Hero-soul
once was and now is not: Oh, all mystery, all pity, all
mute *awe* and wonder; *Super*naturalism brought home
to the very dullest; Eternity laid open, and the nether
Darkness and the upper Light-Kingdoms, do conjoin there,
or exist nowhere! Sauerteig used to say to me, in his
peculiar way: "A Chancery Lawsuit; justice, nay justice
in mere money, denied a man, for all his pleading, till
twenty, till forty years of his Life are gone seeking it: and
a Cockney Funeral, Death reverenced by hatchments,
horse-hair, brass-lacquer, and unconcerned bipeds carrying long poles and bags of black silk:—are not these two
reverences, this reverence for Death and that reverence
for Life, a notable pair of reverences among you English?"

Abbot Samson, at this culminating point of his existence,

may, and indeed must, be left to vanish with his Life-scenery from the eyes of modern men. He had to run into France, to settle with King Richard for the military service there of his St. Edmundsbury Knights; and with great labour got it done. He had to decide on the dilapidated Coventry Monks; and with great labour, and much pleading and journeying, got them reinstated; dined with them all, and with the ' Masters of the Schools of Oxneford,'—the veritable Oxford *Caput* sitting there at dinner, in a dim but undeniable manner, in the City of Peeping Tom! He had, not without labour, to controvert the intrusive Bishop of Ely, the intrusive Abbot of Cluny. Magnanimous Samson, his life is but a labour and a journey; a bustling and a justling, till the still Night come. He is sent for again, over sea, to advise King Richard touching certain Peers of England, who had taken the Cross, but never followed it to Palestine; whom the Pope is inquiring after. The magnanimous Abbot makes preparation for departure; departs, and——And Jocelin's Boswellean Narrative, suddenly shorn-through by the scissors of Destiny, *ends*. There are no words more; but a black line, and leaves of blank paper. Irremediable: the miraculous hand, that held all this theatric-machinery, suddenly quits hold; impenetrable Time-Curtains rush down; in the mind's eye all is again dark, void; with loud dinning in the mind's ear, our real-phantasmagory of St. Edmundsbury plunges into the bosom of the Twelfth Century again, and all is over. Monks, Abbot, Hero-worship, Government, Obedience, Cœur-de-Lion and St. Edmund's Shrine, vanish like Mirza's Vision; and there is nothing left but a mutilated black Ruin amid green botanic expanses, and oxen, sheep and dilettanti pasturing in their places.

CHAPTER XVII

THE BEGINNINGS

WHAT a singular shape of a Man, shape of a Time, have we in this Abbot Samson and his history; how strangely do modes, creeds, formularies, and the date and place of a man's birth, modify the figure of the man!

Formulas too, as we call them, have a *reality* in Human Life. They are real as the very *skin* and *muscular tissue* of a Man's Life; and a most blessed indispensable thing, so long as they have *vitality* withal, and are a *living* skin and tissue to him! No man, or man's life, can go abroad and do business in the world without skin and tissues. No; first of all, these have to fashion themselves,—as indeed they spontaneously and inevitably do. Foam itself, and this is worth thinking of, can harden into oyster-shell; all living objects do by necessity form to themselves a skin.

And yet, again, when a man's Formulas become *dead* ; as all Formulas, in the progress of living growth, are very sure to do! When the poor man's integuments, no longer nourished from within, become dead skin, mere adscititious leather and callosity, wearing thicker and thicker, uglier and uglier; till no *heart* any longer can be felt beating through them, so thick, callous, calcified are they; and all over it has now grown mere calcified oyster-shell, or were it polished mother-of-pearl, inwards almost to the very heart of the poor man:—yes then, you may say, his usefulness once more is quite obstructed; once more, he cannot go abroad and do business in the world; it is time that *he* take to bed, and prepare for departure, which cannot now be distant!

Ubi homines sunt modi sunt. Habit is the deepest law of human nature. It is our supreme strength; if also, in certain circumstances, our miserablest weakness.— From Stoke to Stowe is as yet a field, all pathless, untrodden; from Stoke where I live, to Stowe where I have to make my merchandises, perform my businesses, consult

supplemental

my heavenly oracles, there is as yet no path or human
footprint; and I, impelled by such necessities, must
nevertheless undertake the journey. Let me go once,
scanning my way with any earnestness of outlook, and
successfully arriving, my footprints are an invitation to
me a second time to go by the same way. It is easier
than any other way: the industry of 'scanning' lies
already invested in it for me; I can go this time with
less of scanning, or without scanning at all. Nay the
very sight of my footprints, what a comfort for me; and
in a degree, for all my brethren of mankind! The footprints are trodden and retrodden; the path wears ever
broader, smoother, into a broad highway, where even
wheels can run; and many travel it;—till—till the Town
of Stowe disappear from that locality (as towns have been
known to do), or no merchandising, heavenly oracle, or
real business any longer exist for one there: then why
should anybody travel the way?—Habit is our primal,
fundamental law; Habit and Imitation, there is nothing
more perennial in us than these two. They are the source
of all Working and all Apprenticeship, of all Practice and
all Learning, in this world.

Yes, the wise man too speaks, and acts, in Formulas; all
men do so. And in general, the more completely cased
with Formulas a man may be, the safer, happier is it for
him. Thou who, in an All of rotten Formulas, seemest to
stand nigh bare, having indignantly shaken off the superannuated rags and unsound callosities of Formulas,—
consider how thou too art still clothed! This English
Nationality, whatsoever from uncounted ages is genuine
and a fact among thy native People, in their words and
ways: all this, has it not made for thee a skin or second-
skin, adhesive actually as thy natural skin? This thou
hast not stript off, this thou wilt never strip off: the
humour that thy mother gave thee has to show itself
through this. A common, or it may be an uncommon
Englishman thou art: but, good Heavens, what sort of
Arab, Chinaman, Jew-Clothesman, Turk, Hindoo, African
Mandingo, wouldst thou have been, *thou* with those
mother-qualities of thine!

It strikes me dumb to look over the long series of faces, such as any full Church, Courthouse, London-Tavern Meeting, or miscellany of men will show them. Some score or two of years ago, all these were little red-coloured pulpy infants; each of them capable of being kneaded, baked into any social form you chose: yet see now how they are fixed and hardened,—into artisans, artists, clergy, gentry, learned serjeants, unlearned dandies, and can and shall now be nothing else henceforth!

Mark on that nose the colour left by too copious port and viands; to which the profuse cravat with exorbitant breastpin, and the fixed, forward, and as it were menacing glance of the eyes correspond. That is a ' Man of Business;' prosperous manufacurer, house-contractor, engineer, law-manager; his eye, nose, cravat have, in such work and fortune, got such a character: deny him not thy praise, thy pity. Pity him too, the Hard-handed, with bony brow, rudely-combed hair, eyes looking out as in labour, in difficulty and uncertainty; rude mouth, the lips coarse, loose, as in hard toil and lifelong fatigue they have got the habit of hanging:—hast thou seen aught more touching than the rude intelligence, so cramped, yet energetic, unsubduable, true, which looks out of that marred visage? Alas, and his poor wife, with her own hands, washed that cotton neckcloth for him, buttoned that coarse shirt, sent him forth creditably trimmed as she could. In such imprisonment lives he, for his part; man cannot now deliver him: the red pulpy infant has been baked and fashioned *so*.

Or what kind of baking was it that this other brother mortal got, which has baked him into the genus Dandy? Elegant Vacuum; serenely looking down upon all Plenums and Entities as low and poor to his serene Chimaership and *Non*entity laboriously attained! Heroic Vacuum; inexpugnable, while purse and present condition of society hold out; curable by no hellebore. The doom of Fate was, Be thou a Dandy! Have thy eye-glasses, opera-glasses, thy Long-Acre cabs with white-breeched tiger, thy yawning impassivities, pococurantisms; *fix* thyself in Dandyhood, undeliverable; it is thy doom.

*caring little
indifference
nonchalance.*

And all these, we say, were red-coloured infants; of the same pulp and stuff, few years ago; now irretrievably shaped and kneaded as we see! Formulas? There is no mortal extant, out of the depths of Bedlam, but lives all skinned, thatched, covered over with Formulas; and is, as it were, held in from delirium and the Inane by his Formulas! They are withal the most beneficent, indispensable of human equipments: blessed he who has a skin and tissues, so it be a living one, and the heart-pulse everywhere discernible through it. Monachism, Feudalism, with a real King Plantagenet, with real Abbots Samson, and their other living realities, how blessed!—

Not without a mournful interest have we surveyed that authentic image of a Time now wholly swallowed. Mournful reflections crowd on us;—and yet consolatory. How many brave men have lived before Agamemnon! Here is a brave governor Samson, a man fearing God, and fearing nothing else; of whom as First Lord of the Treasury, as King, Chief Editor, High Priest, we could be so glad and proud; of whom nevertheless Fame has altogether forgotten to make mention! The faint image of him, revived in this hour, is found in the gossip of one poor Monk, and in Nature nowhere else. Oblivion had so nigh swallowed him altogether, even to the echo of his ever having existed. What regiments and hosts and generations of such has Oblivion already swallowed! Their crumbled dust makes up the soil our life-fruit grows on. Said I not, as my old Norse Fathers taught me, The Life-tree Igdrasil, which waves round thee in this hour, whereof thou in this hour art portion, has its roots down deep in the oldest Death-Kingdoms; and grows; the Three Nornas, or *Times*, Past, Present, Future, watering it from the Sacred Well!

For example, who taught thee to *speak ?* From the day when two hairy-naked or fig-leaved Human Figures began, as uncomfortable dummies, anxious no longer to be dumb, but to impart themselves to one another; and endeavoured, with gaspings, gesturings, with unsyllabled cries, with painful pantomime and interjections, in a very

unsuccessful manner,—up to the writing of this present
copyright Book, which also is not very successful! Between
that day and this, I say, there has been a pretty space of
time; a pretty spell of work, which *somebody* has done!
Thinkest thou there were no poets till Dan Chaucer?
No heart burning with a thought, which it could not hold,
and had no word for; and needed to shape and coin a
word for,—what thou callest a metaphor, trope, or the
like? For every word we have, there was such a man
and poet. The coldest word was once a glowing new
metaphor, and bold questionable originality. ' Thy very
ATTENTION, does it not mean an *attentio*, a STRETCHING-
TO?' Fancy that act of the mind, which all were conscious
of, which none had yet named,—when this new ' poet '
first felt bound and driven to name it! His questionable
originality, and new glowing metaphor, was found adoptable, intelligible; and remains our name for it to this day.

Literature:—and look at Paul's Cathedral, and the
Masonries and Worships and Quasi-Worships that are
there; not to speak of Westminster Hall and its wigs!
Men had not a hammer to begin with, not a syllabled
articulation: they had it all to make;—and they have
made it. What thousand thousand articulate, semi-
articulate, earnest-stammering *Prayers* ascending up to
Heaven, from hut and cell, in many lands, in many
centuries, from the fervent kindled souls of innumerable
men, each struggling to pour itself forth incompletely, as
it might, before the incompletest *Liturgy* could be com-
piled! The Liturgy, or adoptable and generally adopted
Set of Prayers and Prayer-Method, was what we can call
the Select Adoptabilities, ' Select Beauties ' well edited
(by Œcumenic Councils and other Useful-Knowledge
Societies) from that wide waste imbroglio of Prayers
already extant and accumulated, good and bad. The
good were found adoptable by men; were gradually got
together, well-edited, accredited: the bad, found in-
appropriate, unadoptable, were gradually forgotten, dis-
used and burnt. It is the way with human things. The
first man who, looking with opened soul on this august
Heaven and Earth, this Beautiful and Awful, which we

name Nature, Universe and suchlike, the essence of which remains for ever UNNAMEABLE; he who first, gazing into this, fell on his knees awestruck, in silence as is likeliest, —he, driven by inner necessity, the 'audacious original' that he was, had done a thing, too, which all thoughtful hearts saw straightway to be an expressive, altogether adoptable thing! To bow the knee was ever since the attitude of supplication. Earlier than any spoken Prayers, *Litanias,* or *Leitourgias ;* the beginning of all Worship,— which needed but a beginning, so rational was it. What a poet he! Yes, this bold original was a successful one withal. The wellhead this one, hidden in the primeval dusks and distances, from whom as from a Nile-source all *Forms of Worship* flow:—such a Nile-river (somewhat muddy and malarious now!) of Forms of Worship sprang there, and flowed, and flows, down to Puseyism, Rotatory Calabash, Archbishop Laud at St. Catherine Creed's, and perhaps lower!

Things rise, I say, in that way. The *Iliad* Poem, and indeed most other poetic, especially epic things, have risen as the Liturgy did. The great *Iliad* in Greece, and the small *Robin Hood's Garland* in England, are each, as I understand, the well-edited 'Select Beauties' of an immeasurable waste imbroglio of Heroic Ballads in their respective centuries and countries. Think what strumming of the seven-stringed heroic lyre, torturing of the less heroic fiddle-catgut, in Hellenic Kings' Courts, and English wayside Public Houses; and beating of the studious Poetic brain, and gasping here too in the semi-articulate windpipe of Poetic men, before the Wrath of a Divine Achilles, the Prowess of a Will Scarlet or Wakefield Pindar, could be adequately sung! Honour to you, ye nameless great and greatest ones, ye long-forgotten brave!

Nor was the Statute *De Tallagio non concedendo,* nor any Statute, Law-method, Lawyer's-wig, much less were the Statute-Book and Four Courts, with Coke upon Lyttelton and Three Estates of Parliament in the rear of them, got together without human labour,—mostly forgotten now! From the time of Cain's slaying Abel by swift head-breakage, to this time of killing your man in

Chancery by inches, and slow heart-break for forty years, —there too is an interval! Venerable Justice herself began by Wild-Justice; all Law is as a tamed furrow-field, slowly worked out, and rendered arable, from the waste jungle of Club-Law. Valiant Wisdom tilling and draining; escorted by owl-eyed Pedantry, by owlish and vulturish and many other forms of Folly;—the valiant husbandman assiduously tilling; the blind greedy enemy *too* assiduously sowing tares! It is because there is yet in venerable wigged Justice some wisdom, amid such mountains of wiggeries and folly, that men have not cast her into the River; that she still sits there, like Dryden's Head in the *Battle of the Books*,—a huge helmet, a huge mountain of greased parchment, of unclean horse-hair, first striking the eye; and then in the innermost corner, visible at last, in size as a hazelnut, a real fraction of God's Justice, perhaps not yet unattainable to some, surely still indispensable to all;—and men know not what to do with her! Lawyers were not all pedants, voluminous voracious persons; Lawyers too were poets, were heroes, —or their Law had been past the Nore long before this time. Their Owlisms, Vulturisms, to an incredible extent, will disappear by and by, their Heroisms only remaining, and the helmet be reduced to something like the size of the head, we hope!—

It is all work and forgotten work, this peopled, clothed, articulate-speaking, high-towered, wide-acred World. The hands of forgotten brave men have made it a World for us;—they,—honour to them; they, in *spite* of the idle and the dastard. This English Land, here and now, is the summary of what was found of wise, and noble, and accordant with God's Truth, in all the generations of English Men. Our English Speech is speakable because there were Hero-Poets of our blood and lineage; speakable in proportion to the number of these. This Land of England has its conquerors, possessors, which change from epoch to epoch, from day to day; but its real conquerors, creators, and eternal proprietors are these following, and their representatives if you can find them: All the Heroic Souls that ever were in England, each in their degree; all the men that ever cut a thistle, drained a puddle out of England, contrived a wise scheme in England, did or said a true and valiant thing in England. I tell thee, they had not a hammer to begin with; and yet Wren built St. Paul's: not an articulated syllable; and yet there have come English Literatures, Elizabethan Literatures, Satanic-School, Cockney-School, and other Literatures;—once more, as in the old time of the *Leitourgia*, a most waste imbroglio, and world-wide jungle and jumble; waiting terribly to be 'well-edited' and 'well burnt'! Arachne started with forefinger and thumb, and had not even a distaff; yet thou seest Manchester, and Cotton Cloth, which will shelter naked backs, at twopence an ell.

Work? The quantity of done and forgotten work that lies silent under my feet in this world, and escorts and attends me, and supports and keeps me alive, wheresoever I walk or stand, whatsoever I think or do, gives rise to reflections! Is it not enough, at any rate, to strike the thing called 'Fame' into total silence for a wise man? For fools and unreflective persons, she is and will be very noisy, this 'Fame,' and talks of her 'immortals' and so forth: but if you will consider it, what is she? Abbot Samson was not nothing because nobody *said* anything of him. Or thinkest thou, the Right Honourable Sir Jabez Windbag can be made something by Paliamentary Majorities and Leading Articles? Her 'immortals'! Scarcely two hundred years back can Fame recollect articulately at all; and there she but maunders and mumbles. She manages to recollect a Shakspeare or so; and prates, considerably like a goose, about him;—and in the rear of that, onwards to the birth of Theuth, to Hengst's Invasion, and the bosom of Eternity, it was all blank; and the respectable Teutonic Languages, Teutonic Practices, Existences, all came of their own accord, as the grass springs, as the trees grow; no Poet, no work from the inspired heart of a Man needed there; and Fame has not an articulate word to say about it! Or ask her, What, with all conceivable appliances and mnemonics, including apotheosis and human sacrifices among the number, she

608

carries in her head with regard to a Wodan, even a Moses, or other such? She begins to be uncertain as to what they were, whether spirits of men or mould,—gods, charlatans; begins sometimes to have a misgiving that they were mere symbols, ideas of the mind; perhaps nonentities and Letters of the Alphabet! She is the noisiest, inarticulately babbling, hissing, screaming, foolishest, unmusicalest of fowls that fly; and needs no 'trumpet,' I think, but her own enormous goose-throat, —measuring several degrees of celestial latitude, so to speak. Her 'wings,' in these days, have grown far swifter than ever; but her goose-throat hitherto seems only larger, louder and foolisher than ever. _She_ is transitory, futile, a goose-goddess:—if she were not transitory, what would become of us! It is a chief comfort that she forgets us all; all, even to the very Wodans; and grows to consider us, at last, as probably nonentities and Letters of the Alphabet.

Yes, a noble Abbot Samson resigns himself to Oblivion too; feels _it_ no hardship, but a comfort; counts it as a still resting-place, from much sick fret and fever and stupidity, which in the night-watches often made his strong heart sigh. Your most sweet voices, making one enormous goose-voice, O Bobus and Company, how can they be a guidance for any Son of Adam? In _silence_ of you and the like of you, the 'small still voices' will speak to him better; in which does lie guidance.

My friend, all speech and rumour is short-lived, foolish, untrue. Genuine WORK alone, what thou workest faithfully, that is eternal, as the Almighty Founder and World-Builder himself. Stand thou by that; and let 'Fame' and the rest of it go prating.

> 'Heard are the Voices,
> Heard are the Sages,
> The Worlds and the Ages:
> "Choose well; your choice is
> Brief and yet endless.
>
> Here eyes do regard you,
> In Eternity's stillness;
> Here is all fulness,
> Ye brave, to reward you;
> Work, and despair not." '—_Goethe._

BOOK III.—THE MODERN WORKER

CHAPTER I

PHENOMENA

But, it is said, our religion is gone: we no longer believe in St. Edmund, no longer see the figure of him 'on the rim of the sky,' minatory or confirmatory! God's absolute Laws, sanctioned by an eternal Heaven and an eternal Hell, have become Moral Philosophies, sanctioned by able computations of Profit and Loss, by weak considerations of Pleasures of Virtue and the Moral Sublime.

It is even so. To speak in the ancient dialect, we ' have forgotten God;'—in the most modern dialect and very truth of the matter, we have taken up the Fact of this Universe as it *is not*. We have quietly closed our eyes to the eternal Substance of things, and opened them only to the Shows and Shams of things. We quietly believe this Universe to be intrinsically a great unintelligible PERHAPS; extrinsically, clear enough, it is a great, most extensive Cattlefold and Workhouse, with most extensive Kitchen-ranges, Dining-tables,—whereat he is wise who can find a place! All the Truth of this Universe is uncertain; only the profit and loss of it, the pudding and praise of it, are and remain very visible to the practical man.

There is no longer any God for us! God's Laws are become a Greatest-Happiness Principle, a Parliamentary Expediency: the Heavens over-arch us only as an Astronomical Time-keeper; a butt for Herschel-telescopes to shoot science at, to shoot sentimentalities at:—in our and old Jonson's dialect, man has lost the *soul* out of him; and now, after the due period,—begins to find the want of it! This is verily the plague-spot; centre of the universal Social Gangrene, threatening all modern things with

frightful death.   To him that will consider it, here is the
stem, with its roots and taproot, with its world-wide upas-
boughs and accursed poison-exudations, under which the
world lies writhing in atrophy and agony.   You touch the
focal-centre of all our disease, of our frightful nosology of
diseases, when you lay your hand on this.   There is no
religion; there is no God; man has lost his soul, and vainly
seeks antiseptic salt.   Vainly: in killing Kings, in passing
Reform Bills, in French Revolutions, Manchester Insurrections, is found no remedy.   The foul elephantine
leprosy, alleviated for an hour, reappears in new force and
desperateness next hour.

For actually this is *not* the real fact of the world; the
world is not made so, but otherwise!—Truly, any Society
setting out from this No-God hypothesis will arrive at a
result or two.   The *Un*veracities, escorted, each Unveracity of them by its corresponding Misery and Penalty;
the Phantasms, and Fatuities, and ten-years Corn-Law
Debatings, that shall walk the Earth at noonday,—must
needs be numerous!   The Universe *being* intrinsically a
Perhaps, being too probably an ' infinite Humbug,' why
should any minor Humbug astonish us?   It is all according to the order of Nature; and Phantasms riding with
huge clatter along the streets, from end to end of our
existence, astonish nobody.   Enchanted St. Ives' Workhouses and Joe-Manton Aristocracies; giant Working
Mammonism near strangled in the partridge-nets of giant-
looking Idle Dilettantism,—this, in all its branches, in its
thousand-thousand modes and figures, is a sight familiar
to us.

The Popish Religion, we are told, flourishes extremely
in these years; and is the most vivacious-looking religion
to be met with at present.   " *Elle a trois cents ans dans
le ventre*," counts M. Jouffroy; " *c'est pourquoi je la
respecte!*"—The old Pope of Rome, finding it laborious
to kneel so long while they cart him through the streets
to bless the people on *Corpus-Christi* Day, complains of
rheumatism; whereupon his Cardinals consult;—construct him, after some study, a stuffed cloaked figure, of

iron and wood, with wool or baked hair; and place it in a kneeling posture. Stuffed figure, or rump of a figure; to this stuffed rump he, sitting at his ease on a lower level, joins, by the aid of cloaks and drapery, his living head and outspread hands: the rump with its cloaks kneels, the Pope looks, and holds his hands spread; and so the two in concert bless the Roman population on *Corpus-Christi* Day, as well as they can.

I have considered this amphibious Pope, with the wool-and-iron back, with the flesh head and hands; and endeavoured to calculate his horoscope. I reckon him the remarkablest Pontiff that has darkened God's daylight, or painted himself in the human retina, for these several thousand years. Nay, since Chaos first shivered, and 'sneezed,' as the Arabs say, with the first shaft of sunlight shot through it, what stranger product was there of Nature and Art working together? Here is a Supreme Priest who believes God to be—What, in the name of God, *does* he believe God to be?—and discerns that all worship of God is a scenic phantasmagory of wax-candles, organ-blasts, Gregorian chants, mass-brayings, purple monsignori, wool-and-iron rumps, artistically spread out,—to save the ignorant from worse.

O reader, I say not who are Belial's elect. This poor amphibious Pope too gives loaves to the Poor; has in him more good latent than he is himself aware of. His poor Jesuits, in the late Italian Cholera, were, with a few German Doctors, the only creatures whom dastard terror had not driven mad: they descended fearless into all gulfs and bedlams; watched over the pillow of the dying, with help, with counsel and hope; shone as luminous fixed stars, when all else had gone out in chaotic night: honour to them! This poor Pope,—who knows what good is in him? In a Time otherwise too prone to forget, he keeps up the mournfulest ghastly memorial of the Highest, Blessedest, which once was; which, in new fit forms, will again partly have to be. Is he not as a perpetual death's-head and cross-bones, with their *Resurgam*, on the grave of a Universal Heroism,—grave of a Christianity? Such Noblenesses, purchased by the world's best heart's blood, must not be lost; we cannot afford to lose them, in what confusions soever. To all of us the day will come, to a few of us it has already come, when no mortal, with his heart yearning for a ' Divine Humility,' or other ' Highest form of Valour,' will need to look for it in death's-heads, but will see it round him in here and there a beautiful living head.

Besides, there is in this poor Pope, and his practice of the Scenic Theory of Worship, a frankness which I rather honour. Not half and half, but with undivided heart does *he* set about worshipping by stage-machinery; as if there were now, and could again be, in Nature no other. He will ask you, What other? Under this my Gregorian Chant, and beautiful wax-light Phantasmagory, kindly hidden from you is an Abyss, of Black Doubt, Scepticism, nay Sansculottic Jacobinism; an Orcus that has no bottom. Think of that. ' Groby Pool *is* thatched with pancakes,'—as Jeannie Deans's Innkeeper defied it to be! The Bottomless of Scepticism, Atheism, Jacobinism, behold, it is thatched over, hidden from your despair, by stage-properties judiciously arranged. This stuffed rump of mine saves not me only from rheumatism, but you also from what other *isms !* In this your Life-pilgrimage Nowhither, a fine Squallacci marching-music, and Gregorian Chant, accompanies you, and the hollow Night of Orcus is well hid!

Yes truly, few men that worship by the rotatory Calabash of the Calmucks do it in half so great, frank or effectual a way. Drury-Lane, it is said, and that is saying much, might learn from him in the dressing of parts, in the arrangement of lights and shadows. He is the greatest Play-actor that at present draws salary in this world. Poor Pope; and I am told he is fast growing bankrupt too; and will, in a measurable term of years (a great way *within* the ' three hundred '), not have a penny to make his pot boil! His old rheumatic back will then get to rest; and himself and his stage-properties sleep well in Chaos forevermore.

Or, alas, why go to Rome for Phantasms walking the streets? Phantasms, ghosts, in this midnight hour, hold

jubilee, and screech and jabber; and the question rather
were, What high Reality anywhere is yet awake? Aristocracy has become Phantasm-Aristocracy, no longer able
to *do* its work, not in the least conscious that it has any
work longer to do. Unable, totally careless to *do* its
work; careful only to clamour for the *wages* of doing its
work,—nay for higher, and *palpably* undue wages, and
Corn-Laws and *increase* of rents; the old rate of wages not
being adequate now! In hydra-wrestle, giant ' *Millo-
cracy* ' so-called, a real giant, though as yet a blind one
and but half-awake, wrestles and wrings in choking
nightmare, ' like to be strangled in the partridge-nets of
Phantasm-Aristocracy,' as we said, which fancies itself
still to be a giant. Wrestles, as under nightmare, till it
do awaken; and gasps and struggles thousandfold, we
may say, in a truly painful manner, through all fibres of
our English Existence, in these hours and years! Is our
poor English Existence wholly becoming a Nightmare;
full of mere Phantasms?—

The Champion of England, cased in iron or tin, rides
into Westminster Hall, ' being lifted into his saddle with
little assistance,' and there asks, If in the four quarters of
the world, under the cope of Heaven, is any man or
demon that dare question the right of this King? Under
the cope of Heaven no man makes intelligible answer,—
as several men ought already to have done. Does not
this Champion too know the world; that it is a huge
Imposture, and bottomless Inanity, thatched over with
bright cloth and other ingenious tissues? Him let us
leave there, questioning all men and demons.

Him we have left to his destiny; but whom else have
we found? From this the highest apex of things, downwards through all strata and breadths, how many fully
awakened Realities have we fallen in with:—alas, on the
contrary, what troops and populations of Phantasms, not
God-Veracities but Devil-Falsities, down to the very
lowest stratum,—which now, by such superincumbent
weight of Unveracities, lies enchanted in St. Ives' Workhouses, broad enough, helpless enough! You will walk
in no public thoroughfare or remotest byway of English

Existence but you will meet a man, an interest of men, that has given up hope in the Everlasting, True, and placed its hope in the Temporary, half or wholly False. The Honourable Member complains unmusically that there is ' devil's-dust ' in Yorkshire cloth. Yorkshire cloth,—why, the very Paper I now write on is made, it seems, partly of plaster-lime well smoothed, and obstructs my writing! You are lucky if you can find now any good Paper,—any work really *done ;* search where you will, from highest Phantasm apex to lowest Enchanted basis.

Consider, for example, that great Hat seven-feet high, which now perambulates London Streets; which my Friend Sauerteig regarded justly as one of our English notabilities; " the topmost point as yet," said he, " would it were your culminating and returning point, to which English Puffery has been observed to reach!"—The Hatter in the Strand of London, instead of making better felt-hats than another, mounts a huge lath-and-plaster Hat, seven feet high, upon wheels; sends a man to drive it through the streets; hoping to be saved *thereby !* He has not attempted to *make* better hats, as he was appointed by the Universe to do, and as with this ingenuity of his he could very probably have done; but his whole industry is turned to *persuade* us that he has made such! He too knows that the Quack has become God. Laugh not at him, O reader; or do not laugh only. He has ceased to be comic; he is fast becoming tragic. To me this all-deafening blast of Puffery, of poor Falsehood grown necessitous, of poor Heart-Atheism fallen now into Enchanted Workhouses, sounds too surely like a Doom's-blast! I have to say to myself in old dialect: " God's blessing is not written on all this; His curse is written on all this!" Unless perhaps the Universe *be* a chimera; —some old totally deranged eightday clock, dead as brass; which the Maker, if there ever was any Maker, has long ceased to meddle with?—To my Friend Sauerteig this poor seven-feet Hat-manufacturer, as the top-stone of English Puffery, was very notable.

Alas, that we natives note him little, that we view him

as a thing of course, is the very burden of the misery. We take it for granted, the most rigorous of us, that all men who have made anything are expected and entitled to make the loudest possible proclamation of it, and call on a discerning public to reward them for it. Every man his own trumpeter! that is, to a really alarming extent, the accepted rule. Make loudest possible proclamation of your Hat: true proclamation if that will do; if that will not do, then false proclamation,—to such extent of falsity as will serve your purpose; as will not seem too false to be credible!—I answer, once for all, that the fact is not so. Nature requires no man to make proclamation of his doings and hat-makings; Nature forbids all men to make such. There is not a man or hat-maker born into the world but feels, or has felt, that he is degrading himself if he speak of his excellencies and prowesses, and supremacy in his crafts: his inmost heart says to him, "Leave thy friends to speak of these; if possible, thy enemies to speak of these; but at all events, thy friends!" He feels that he is already a poor braggart; fast hastening to be a falsity and speaker of the Untruth.

Nature's Laws, I must repeat, are eternal: her small still voice, speaking from the inmost heart of us, shall not, under terrible penalties, be disregarded. No one man can depart from the truth without damage to himself; no one million of men; no Twenty-seven Millions of men. Show me a Nation fallen everywhere into this course, so that each expects it, permits it to others and himself, I will show you a Nation travelling with one assent on the broad way. The broad way, however many Banks of England, Cotton-Mills and Duke's Palaces it may have. Not at happy Elysian fields, and everlasting crowns of victory, earned by silent Valour, will this Nation arrive; but at precipices, devouring gulfs, if it pause not. Nature has appointed happy fields, victorious laurel-crowns; but only to the brave and true: *Un*nature, what we call Chaos, holds nothing in it but vacuities, devouring gulfs. What are Twenty-seven Millions, and their unanimity? Believe them not; the Worlds and the Ages, God and Nature and All Men say otherwise.

'Rhetoric all this?' No, my brother, very singular to say, it is Fact all this. Cocker's Arithmetic is not truer. Forgotten in these days, it is old as the foundations of the Universe, and will endure till the Universe cease. It is forgotten now; and the first mention of it puckers thy sweet countenance into a sneer: but it will be brought to mind again,—unless indeed the Law of Gravitation chance to cease, and men find that they *can* walk on vacancy. Unanimity of the Twenty-seven Millions will do nothing; walk not thou with them; fly from them as for thy life. Twenty-seven Millions travelling on such courses, with gold jingling in every pocket, with vivats heaven-high, are incessantly advancing, let me again remind thee, towards the *firm-land's end*,— towards the end and extinction of what Faithfulness, Veracity, real Worth, was in their way of life. Their noble ancestors have fashioned for them a 'life-road;' —in how many thousand senses, this! There is not an old wise Proverb on their tongue, an honest Principle articulated in their hearts into utterance, a wise true method of doing and despatching any work or commerce of men, but helps yet to carry them forward. Life is still possible to them, because all is not yet Puffery, Falsity, Mammon-worship and Unnature; because somewhat is yet Faithfulness, Veracity and Valour. With a certain very considerable finite quantity of Unveracity and Phantasm, social life is still possible; not with an infinite quantity! Exceed your certain quantity, the seven-feet Hat, and all things upwards to the very Champion cased in tin, begin to reel and flounder,—in Manchester Insurrections, Chartisms, Sliding-scales; the Law of Gravitation not forgetting to act. You advance incessantly towards the land's end; you are, literally enough, 'consuming the way.' Step after step, Twenty-seven Million unconscious men;—till you are *at* the land's end; till there is not Faithfulness enough among you any more: and the next step now is lifted *not* over land, but into air, over ocean-deeps and roaring abysses:—unless perhaps the Law of Gravitation have forgotten to act?

Oh, it is frightful when a whole Nation, as our Fathers

used to say, has ' forgotten God; ' has remembered only
Mammon, and what Mammon leads to! When your self-
trumpeting Hatmaker is the emblem of almost all makers,
and workers, and men, that make anything,—from soul-
overseerships, body-overseerships, epic poems, acts of
parliament, to hats and shoe-blacking! Not one false
man but does uncountable mischief: how much, in a
generation or two, will Twenty-seven Millions, mostly
false, manage to accumulate? The sum of it, visible
in every street, market-place, senate-house, circulating-
library, cathedral, cotton-mill, and union-workhouse, fills
one *not* with a comic feeling!

pursuit only of wealth

CHAPTER II

GOSPEL OF MAMMONISM

READER, even Christian Reader as thy title goes, hast
thou any notion of Heaven and Hell? I rather appre-
hend, not. Often as the words are on our tongue, they
have got a fabulous or semi-fabulous character for most
of us, and pass on like a kind of transient similitude, like
a sound signifying little.

Yet it is well worth while for us to know, once and
always, that they are not a similitude, nor a fable nor
semi-fable; that they are an everlasting highest fact!
" No Lake of Sicilian or other sulphur burns now anywhere in these ages," sayest thou? Well, and if there
did not! Believe that there does not; believe it if thou
wilt, nay hold by it as a real increase, a rise to higher
stages, to wider horizons and empires. All this has
vanished, or has not vanished; believe as thou wilt as
to all this. But that an Infinite of Practical Importance,
speaking with strict arithmetical exactness, an *Infinite*,
has vanished or can vanish from the Life of any Man:
this thou shalt not believe! O brother, the Infinite of
Terror, of Hope, of Pity, did it not at any moment disclose itself to thee, indubitable, unnameable? Came it
never, like the gleam of *preter*natural eternal Oceans, like

the voice of old Eternities, far-sounding through thy heart
of hearts? Never? Alas, it was not thy Liberalism,
then; it was thy Animalism! The Infinite is more sure
than any other fact. But only men can discern it; mere
building beavers, spinning arachnes, much more the
predatory vulturous and vulpine species, do not discern
it well!—

'The word Hell,' says Sauerteig, 'is still frequently in
use among the English people: but I could not without
difficulty ascertain what they meant by it. Hell generally
signifies the Infinite Terror, the thing a man *is* infinitely
afraid of, and shudders and shrinks from, struggling with
his whole soul to escape from it. There is a Hell therefore, if you will consider, which accompanies man, in all
stages of his history, and religious or other development:
but the Hells of men and Peoples differ notably. With
Christians it is the infinite terror of being found guilty
before the Just Judge. With old Romans, I conjecture,
it was the terror not of Pluto, for whom probably they
cared little, but of doing unworthily, doing unvirtuously,
which was their word for un*man*fully. And now what
is it, if you pierce through his Cants, his oft-repeated
Hearsays, what he calls his Worships and so forth,—what
is it that the modern English soul does, in very truth,
dread infinitely, and contemplate with entire despair?
What *is* his Hell, after all these reputable, oft-repeated
Hearsays, what is it? With hesitation, with astonishment, I pronounce it to be: The terror of " Not succeed-
ing; " of not making money, fame, or some other figure
in the world,—chiefly of not making money! Is not
that a somewhat singular Hell?'

Yes, O Sauerteig, it is very singular. If we do not
'succeed,' where is the use of us? We had better never
have been born. " Tremble intensely," as our friend the
Emperor of China says: *there* is the black Bottomless of
Terror; what Sauerteig calls the 'Hell of the English' !
—But indeed this Hell belongs naturally to the Gospel of
Mammonism, which also has its corresponding Heaven.
For there *is* one Reality among so many Phantasms;
about one thing we are entirely in earnest: The making

of money. Working Mammonism does divide the world with idle game-preserving Dilettantism:—thank Heaven that there is even a Mammonism, *any*thing we are in earnest about! Idleness is worst, Idleness alone is without hope: work earnestly at anything, you will by degrees learn to work at almost all things. There is endless hope in work, were it even work at making money.

True, it must be owned, we for the present, with our Mammon-Gospel, have come to strange conclusions. We call it a Society; and go about professing openly the totalest separation, isolation. Our life is not a mutual helpfulness; but rather, cloaked under due laws-of-war, named 'fair competition' and so forth, it is a mutual hostility. We have profoundly forgotten everywhere that *Cash-payment* is not the sole relation of human beings; we think, nothing doubting, that *it* absolves and liquidates all engagements of man. "My starving workers?" answers the rich mill-owner: "Did not I hire them fairly in the market? Did I not pay them, to the last sixpence, the sum covenanted for? What have I to do with them more?"—Verily Mammon-worship is a melancholy creed. When Cain, for his own behoof, had killed Abel, and was questioned, "Where is thy brother?" he too made answer, "Am I my brother's keeper?" Did I not pay my brother *his* wages, the thing he had merited from me?

O sumptuous Merchant-Prince, illustrious game-preserving Duke, is there no way of 'killing' thy brother but Cain's rude way! 'A good man by the very look of him, by his very presence with us as a fellow wayfarer in this Life-pilgrimage, *promises* so much:' woe to him if he forget all such promises, if he never know that they were given! To a deadened soul, seared with the brute Idolatry of Sense, to whom going to Hell is equivalent to not making money, all 'promises,' and moral duties, that cannot be pleaded for in Courts of Requests, address themselves in vain. Money he can be ordered to pay, but nothing more. I have not heard in all Past History, and expect not to hear in all Future History, of any Society anywhere under God's Heaven supporting itself on such Philosophy. The Universe is not made so; it is made otherwise than so. The man or nation of men that thinks it is made so, marches forward nothing doubting, step after step; but marches—whither we know! In these last two centuries of Atheistic Government (near two centuries now, since the blessed restoration of his Sacred Majesty, and Defender of the Faith, Charles Second), I reckon that we have pretty well exhausted what of 'firm earth' there was for us to march on;—and are now, very ominously, shuddering, reeling, and let us hope trying to recoil, on the cliff's edge!—

For out of this that we call Atheism come so many other *isms* and falsities, each falsity with its misery at its heels!—A soul is not like wind (*spiritus*, or breath) contained within a capsule; the ALMIGHTY MAKER is not like a Clockmaker that once, in old immemorial ages, having *made* his Horologe of a Universe, sits ever since and sees it go! Not at all. Hence comes Atheism; come, as we say, many other *isms ;* and as the sum of all, comes Valetism, the *reverse* of Heroism; sad root of all woes whatsoever. For indeed, as no man ever saw the above-said wind-element enclosed within its capsule, and finds it at bottom more deniable than conceivable; so too he finds, in spite of Bridgwater Bequests, your Clockmaker Almighty an entirely questionable affair, a deniable affair;—and accordingly denies it, and along with it so much else. Alas, one knows not what and how much else! For the faith in an Invisible, Unnameable, Godlike, present everywhere in all that we see and work and suffer, is the essence of all faith whatsoever; and that once denied, or still worse, asserted with lips only, and out of bound prayerbooks only, what other thing remains believable? That Cant well-ordered is marketable Cant; that Heroism means gas-lighted Histrionism; that seen with 'clear eyes' (as they call Valet-eyes), no man is a Hero, or ever was a Hero, but all men are Valets and Varlets. The accursed practical quintessence of all sorts of Unbelief! For if there be now no Hero, and the Histrio himself begin to be seen into, what hope is there for the seed of Adam here below? We are the doomed everlasting prey of the Quack; who, now in this guise, now in that, is to filch us, to pluck and eat us, by such modes as are convenient for him. For the modes and guises I care little. The Quack once inevitable, let him come swiftly, let him pluck and eat me;—swiftly, that I may at least have done with him; for in his Quack-world I can have no wish to linger. Though he slay me, yet will I *not* trust in him. Though he conquer nations, and have all the Flunkies of the Universe shouting at his heels, yet will I know well that *he* is an Inanity; that for him and his there is no continuance appointed, save only in Gehenna and the Pool. Alas, the Atheist world, from its utmost summits of Heaven and Westminster-Hall, downwards through poor seven-feet Hats and ' Unveracities fallen hungry,' down to the lowest cellars and neglected hunger-dens of it, is very wretched.

One of Dr. Alison's Scotch facts struck us much.[1]   A poor Irish Widow, her husband having died in one of the Lanes of Edinburgh, went forth with her three children, bare of all resource, to solicit help from the Charitable Establishments of that City. At this Charitable Establishment and then at that she was refused; referred from one to the other, helped by none;—till she had exhausted them all; till her strength and heart failed her: she sank down in typhus-fever; died, and infected her Lane with fever, so that ' seventeen other persons ' died of fever there in consequence. The humane Physician asks thereupon, as with a heart too full for speaking, Would it not have been *economy* to help this poor Widow? She took typhus-fever, and killed seventeen of you!—Very curious. The forlorn Irish Widow applies to her fellow-creatures, as if saying, " Behold I am sinking, bare of help: ye must help me! I am your sister, bone of your bone; one God made us: ye must help me! " They answer, " No, impossible; thou art no sister of ours." But she proves her sisterhood; her typhus-fever kills *them* : they actually were her brothers, though denying it! Had human creature ever to go lower for a proof?

[1] *Observations on the Management of the Poor in Scotland :* by William Pulteney Alison, M.D. (Edinburgh, 1840.)

For, as indeed was very natural in such case, all
government of the Poor by the Rich has long ago been
given over to Supply-and-demand, Laissez-faire and suchlike, and universally declared to be 'impossible.' " You
are no sister of ours; what shadow of proof is there?
Here are our parchments, our padlocks, proving indisputably our money-safes to be *ours*, and you to have no
business with them. Depart! It is impossible!"—Nay,
what wouldst thou thyself have us do? cry indignant
readers. Nothing, my friends,—till you have got a
soul for yourselves again. Till then all things are
'impossible.' Till then I cannot even bid you buy, as
the old Spartans would have done, twopence worth of
powder and lead, and compendiously shoot to death this
poor Irish Widow: even that is 'impossible' for you.
Nothing is left but that she prove her sisterhood by
dying, and infecting you with typhus. Seventeen of you
lying dead will not deny such proof that she *was* flesh
of your flesh; and perhaps some of the living may lay
it to heart.

'Impossible:' of a certain two-legged animal with
feathers it is said, if you draw a distinct chalk-circle round
him, he sits imprisoned, as if girt with an iron ring of Fate;
and will die there, though within sight of victuals,—or
sit in sick misery there, and be fatted to death. The name
of this poor two-legged animal is—Goose; and they make
of him, when well fattened, *Pâté de foie gras*, much prized
by some!

CHAPTER III

GOSPEL OF DILETTANTISM

But after all, the Gospel of Dilettantism, producing a
Governing Class who do not govern, nor understand in
the least that they are bound or expected to govern, is
still mournfuler than that of Mammonism. Mammonism,
as we said, at least works; this goes idle. Mammonism

has seized some portion of the message of Nature to man; and seizing that, and following it, will seize and appropriate more and more of Nature's message: but Dilettantism has missed it wholly. 'Make money:' that will mean withal, 'Do work in order to make money.' But, 'Go gracefully idle in Mayfair,' what does or can that mean? An idle, game-preserving, and even corn-lawing Aristocracy, in such an England as ours: has the world, if we take thought of it, ever seen such a phenomenon till very lately? Can it long continue to see such?

Accordingly the impotent, insolent Donothingism in Practice and Saynothingism in Speech, which we have to witness on that side of our affairs, is altogether amazing. A Corn-Law demonstrating itself openly, for ten years or more, with 'arguments' to make the angels, and some other classes of creatures, weep! For men are not ashamed to rise in Parliament and elsewhere, and speak the things they do *not* think. 'Expediency,' 'Necessities of Party,' etc. etc.! It is not known that the Tongue of Man is a sacred organ; that Man himself is definable in Philosophy as an 'Incarnate *Word*;' the Word not there, you have no Man there either, but a Phantasm instead! In this way it is that Absurdities may live long enough,—still walking, and talking for themselves, years and decades after the brains are quite out! How are 'the knaves and dastards' ever to be got 'arrested' at that rate?—

"No man in this fashionable London of yours," friend Sauerteig would say, "speaks a plain word to me. Every man feels bound to be something more than plain; to be pungent withal, witty, ornamental. His poor fraction of sense has to be perked into some epigrammatic shape, that it may prick into me;—perhaps (this is the commonest) to be topsyturvied, left standing on its head, that I may remember it the better! Such grinning inanity is very sad to the soul of man. Human faces should not grin on one like masks; they should look on one like faces! I love honest laughter, as I do sunlight; but not dishonest: most kinds of dancing too; but the St.-Vitus kind not at all! A fashionable wit, *ach Himmel!* if you ask, Which,

K 608

he or a Death's-head, will be the cheerier company for
me? pray send *not* him!"

Insincere Speech, truly, is the prime material of insincere Action. Action hangs, as it were, *dissolved* in
Speech, in Thought whereof Speech is the Shadow; and
precipitates itself therefrom. The kind of Speech in a
man betokens the kind of Action you will get from him.
Our Speech, in these modern days, has become amazing.
Johnson complained, "Nobody speaks in earnest, Sir;
there is no serious conversation." To us all serious speech
of men, as that of Seventeenth-Century Puritans, Twelfth-
Century Catholics, German Poets of this Century, has
become jargon, more or less insane. Cromwell was mad
and a quack; Anselm, Becket, Goethe, *ditto ditto.*

Perhaps few narratives in History or Mythology are
more significant than that Moslem one, of Moses and the
Dwellers by the Dead Sea. A tribe of men dwelt on the
shores of that same Asphaltic Lake; and having forgotten,
as we are all too prone to do, the inner facts of Nature,
and taken up with the falsities and outer semblances of
it, were fallen into sad conditions, — verging indeed
towards a certain far deeper Lake. Whereupon it pleased
kind Heaven to send them the Prophet Moses, with an
instructive word of warning, out of which might have
sprung 'remedial measures' not a few. But no: the men
of the Dead Sea discovered, as the valet-species always
does in heroes or prophets, no comeliness in Moses;
listened with real tedium to Moses, with light grinning, or
with splenetic sniffs and sneers, affecting even to yawn;
and signified, in short, that they found him a humbug,
and even a bore. Such was the candid theory these men
of the Asphalt Lake formed to themselves of Moses, That
probably he was a humbug, that certainly he was a bore.

Moses withdrew; but Nature and her rigorous veracities
did not withdraw. The men of the Dead Sea, when we
next went to visit them, were all 'changed into Apes;'[1]
sitting on the trees there, grinning now in the most *un-*
affected manner; gibbering and chattering very genuine
nonsense; finding the whole Universe now a most indis-

[1] Sale's *Koran* (Introduction).

putable Humbug! The Universe has *become* a Humbug to these Apes who thought it one. There they sit and chatter, to this hour: only, I believe, every Sabbath there returns to them a bewildered half-consciousness, half-reminiscence; and they sit, with their wizened smoke-dried visages, and such an air of supreme tragicality as Apes may; looking out through those blinking smoke-bleared eyes of theirs, into the wonderfulest universal smoky Twilight and undecipherable disordered Dusk of Things; wholly an Uncertainty, Unintelligibility, they and it; and for commentary thereon, here and there an unmusical chatter or mew:—truest, tragicalest Humbug conceivable by the mind of man or ape! They made no use of their souls; and so have lost them. Their worship on the Sabbath now is to roost there, with unmusical screeches, and half-remember that they had souls.

Didst thou never, O Traveller, fall-in with parties of this tribe? Meseems they are grown somewhat numerous in our day.

CHAPTER IV

HAPPY

ALL work, even cotton-spinning, is noble; work is alone noble: be that here said and asserted once more. And in like manner too, all dignity is painful; a life of ease is not for any man, nor for any god. The life of all gods figures itself to us as a Sublime Sadness,—earnestness of Infinite Battle against Infinite Labour. Our highest religion is named the 'Worship of Sorrow.' For the son of man there is no noble crown, well worn or even ill worn, but is a crown of thorns!—These things, in spoken words, or still better, in felt instincts alive in every heart, were once well known.

Does not the whole wretchedness, the whole *Atheism* as I call it, of man's ways, in these generations, shadow itself for us in that unspeakable Life-philosophy of his: The pretension to be what he calls ' happy '? Every pitifulest

whipster that walks within a skin has his head filled with
the notion that he is, shall be, or by all human and divine
laws ought to be 'happy.' His wishes, the pitifulest
whipster's, are to be fulfilled for him; his days, the
pitifulest whipster's, are to flow on in ever-gentle current
of enjoyment, impossible even for the gods. The prophets
preach to us, Thou shalt be happy; thou shalt love
pleasant things, and find them. The people clamour,
Why have we not found pleasant things?

We construct our theory of Human Duties, not on
any Greatest-Nobleness Principle, never so mistaken;
no, but on a Greatest-Happiness Principle. 'The word
Soul with us, as in some Slavonic dialects, seems to be
synonymous with *Stomach*.' We plead and speak, in our
Parliaments and elsewhere, not as from the Soul, but
from the Stomach;—wherefore indeed our pleadings are
so slow to profit. We plead not for God's Justice; we
are not ashamed to stand clamouring and pleading for
our own 'interests,' our own rents and trade-profits; we
say, They are the 'interests' of so many; there is such
an intense desire in us for them! We demand Free-Trade,
with much just vociferation and benevolence, That the
poorer classes, who are terribly ill-off at present, may
have cheaper New-Orleans bacon. Men ask on Free-
trade platforms, How can the indomitable spirit of
Englishmen be kept up without plenty of bacon? We
shall become a ruined Nation!—Surely, my friends, plenty
of bacon is good and indispensable: but, I doubt, you
will never get even bacon by aiming only at that. You
are men, not animals of prey, well-used or ill-used! Your
Greatest-Happiness Principle seems to me fast becoming
a rather unhappy one.—What if we should cease babbling
about 'happiness,' and leave *it* resting on its own basis,
as it used to do!

A gifted Byron rises in his wrath; and feeling too
surely that he for his part is not 'happy,' declares the
same in very violent language, as a piece of news that
may be interesting. It evidently has surprised him
much. One dislikes to see a man and poet reduced to
proclaim on the streets such tidings: but on the whole,

as matters go, that is not the most dislikable. Byron
speaks the *truth* in this matter. Byron's large audience
indicates how true it is felt to be.

' Happy,' my brother? First of all, what difference
is it whether thou art happy or not! Today becomes
Yesterday so fast, all Tomorrows become Yesterdays;
and then there is no question whatever of the 'happiness,'
but quite another question. Nay, thou hast such a
sacred pity left at least for thyself, thy very pains, once
gone over into Yesterday, become joys to thee. Besides,
thou knowest not what heavenly blessedness and indispensable sanative virtue was in them; thou shalt only
know it after many days, when thou art wiser!—A
benevolent old Surgeon sat once in our company, with a
Patient fallen sick by gourmandising, whom he had just,
too briefly in the Patient's judgment, been examining.
The foolish Patient still at intervals continued to break
in on our discourse, which rather promised to take a
philosophic turn: " But I have lost my appetite," said
he, objurgatively, with a tone of irritated pathos; " I
have no appetite; I can't eat! "—" My dear fellow,"
answered the Doctor in mildest tone, " it isn't of the
slightest consequence; "—and continued his philosophical
discoursings with us!

Or does the reader not know the history of that
Scottish iron Misanthrope? The inmates of some town-
mansion, in those Northern parts, were thrown into the
fearfulest alarm by indubitable symptoms of a ghost
inhabiting the next house, or perhaps even the partition-
wall! Ever at a certain hour, with preternatural gnarring, growling, and screeching, which attended as running
bass, there began, in a horrid, semi-articulate, unearthly
voice, this song: " Once I was hap-hap-happy, but now
I'm *mees*erable! Clack-clack-clack, gnarr-r-r, whuz-z:
Once I was hap-hap-happy, but now I'm *mees*erable! "—
Rest, rest, perturbed spirit;—or indeed, as the good old
Doctor said: My dear fellow, it isn't of the slightest consequence! But no; the perturbed spirit could not rest;
and to the neighbours, fretted, affrighted, or at least
insufferably bored by him, it *was* of such consequence

that they had to go and examine in his haunted chamber. In his haunted chamber, they find that the perturbed spirit is an unfortunate—Imitator of Byron? No, is an unfortunate rusty Meat-jack, gnarring and creaking with rust and work; and this, in Scottish dialect, is *its* Byronian musical Life-philosophy, sung according to ability!

Truly, I think the man who goes about pothering and uproaring for his ' happiness,'—pothering, and were it ballot-boxing, poem-making, or in what way soever fussing and exerting himself,—he is not the man that will help us to ' get our knaves and dastards arrested ' ! No; he rather is on the way to increase the number,— by at least one unit and his tail! Observe, too, that this is all a modern affair; belongs not to the old heroic times, but to these dastard new times. ' Happiness our being's end and aim,' all that very paltry speculation is at bottom, if we will count well, not yet two centuries old in the world.

The only happiness a brave man ever troubled himself with asking much about was, happiness enough to get his work done. Not " I can't eat! " but " I can't work! " that was the burden of all wise complaining among men. It is, after all, the one unhappiness of a man, That he cannot work; that he cannot get his destiny as a man fulfilled. Behold, the day is passing swiftly over, our life is passing swiftly over; and the night cometh, wherein no man can work. The night once come, our happiness, our unhappiness,—it is all abolished; vanished, clean gone; a thing that has been: ' not of the slightest con- sequence ' whether we were happy as eupeptic Curtis, as the fattest pig of Epicurus, or unhappy as Job with potsherds, as musical Byron with Giaours and sensibilities of the heart; as the unmusical Meat-jack with hard labour and rust! But our work,—behold that is not abolished, that has not vanished: our work, behold, it remains, or the want of it remains;—for endless Times and Eternities, remains; and that is now the sole question with us forevermore! Brief brawling Day, with its noisy phantasms, its poor paper-crowns tinsel-gilt, is gone; and

divine everlasting Night, with her star-diadems, with her
silences and her veracities, is come! What hast thou
done, and how? Happiness, unhappiness: all that was
but the *wages* thou hadst; thou hast spent all that, in
sustaining thyself hitherward; not a coin of it remains
with thee, it is all spent, eaten: and now thy work,
where is thy work? Swift, out with it; let us see thy
work!

Of a truth, if man were not a poor hungry dastard,
and even much of a blockhead withal, he would cease
criticising his victuals to such extent; and criticise himself rather, what he does with his victuals!

happiness transitory — work remains.

CHAPTER V

THE ENGLISH

AND yet, with all thy theoretic platitudes, what a depth
of practical sense in thee, great England! A depth of
sense, of justice, and courage; in which, under all
emergencies and world-bewilderments, and under this
most complex of emergencies we now live in, there is still
hope, there is still assurance!

The English are a dumb people. They can do great
acts, but not describe them. Like the old Romans, and
some few others, *their* Epic Poem is written on the Earth's
surface: England her Mark! It is complained that they
have no artists: one Shakspeare indeed; but for Raphael
only a Reynolds; for Mozart nothing but a Mr. Bishop:
not a picture, not a song. And yet they did produce one
Shakspeare: consider how the element of Shakspearean
melody does lie imprisoned in their nature; reduced to
unfold itself in mere Cotton-mills, Constitutional Governments, and suchlike;—all the more interesting when it
does become visible, as even in such unexpected shapes
it succeeds in doing! Goethe spoke of the Horse, how
impressive, almost affecting it was that an animal of

such qualities should stand obstructed so; its speech nothing but an inarticulate neighing, its handiness mere *hoof*iness, the fingers all constricted, tied together, the finger-nails coagulated into a mere hoof, shod with iron. The more significant, thinks he, are those eye-flashings of the generous noble quadruped; those prancings, curvings of the neck clothed with thunder.

A Dog of Knowledge has free utterance; but the War-horse is almost mute, very far from free! It is even so. Truly, your freest utterances are not by any means always the best: they are the worst rather; the feeblest, trivialest; their meaning prompt, but small, ephemeral. Commend me to the silent English, to the silent Romans. Nay the silent Russians, too, I believe to be worth something: are they not even now drilling, under much obloquy, an immense semi-barbarous half-world from Finland to Kamtschatka, into rule, subordination, civilisation,— really in an old Roman fashion; speaking no word about it; quietly hearing all manner of vituperative Able Editors speak! While your ever-talking, ever-gesticulating French, for example, what are they at this moment drilling?—Nay of all animals, the freest of utterance, I should judge, is the genus *Simia :* go into the Indian woods, say all Travellers, and look what a brisk, adroit, unresting Ape-population it is!

The spoken Word, the written Poem, is said to be an epitome of the man; how much more the done work. Whatsoever of morality and of intelligence; what of patience, perseverance, faithfulness, of method, insight, ingenuity, energy; in a word, whatsoever of Strength the man had in him will lie written in the Work he does. To work: why, it is to try himself against Nature, and her everlasting unerring Laws; these will tell a true verdict as to the man. So much of virtue and of faculty did *we* find in him; so much and no more! He had such capacity of harmonising himself with *me* and my un-alterable ever-veracious Laws; of co-operating and work-ing as *I* bade him;—and has prospered, and has not prospered, as you see!—Working as great Nature bade him: does not that mean virtue of a kind; nay of all kinds? Cotton can be spun and sold, Lancashire operatives can be got to spin it, and at length one has the woven webs and sells them, by following Nature's regulations in that matter: by not following Nature's regulations, you have them not. You have them not;—there is no Cotton-web to sell: Nature finds a bill against you; your 'Strength' is not Strength, but Futility! Let faculty be honoured, so far as it is faculty. A man that can succeed in working is to me always a man.

How one loves to see the burly figure of him, this thick-skinned, seemingly opaque, perhaps sulky, almost stupid Man of Practice, pitted against some light adroit Man of Theory, all equipt with clear logic, and able anywhere to give you Why for Wherefore! The adroit Man of Theory, so light of movement, clear of utterance, with his bow full-bent and quiver full of arrow-arguments,— surely he will strike down the game, transfix everywhere the heart of the matter; triumph everywhere, as he proves that he shall and must do? To your astonishment, it turns out oftenest No. The cloudy-browed, thick-soled, opaque Practicality, with no logic utterance, in silence mainly, with here and there a low grunt or growl, has in him what transcends all logic-utterance: a Congruity with the Unuttered. The Speakable, which lies atop, as a superficial film, or outer skin, is his or is not his: but the Doable, which reaches down to the World's centre, you find him there!

The rugged Brindley has little to say for himself; the rugged Brindley, when difficulties accumulate on him, retires silent, ' generally to his bed; ' retires ' sometimes for three days together to his bed, that he may be in perfect privacy there,' and ascertain in his rough head how the difficulties can be overcome. The ineloquent Brindley, behold he *has* chained seas together; his ships do visibly float over valleys, invisibly through the hearts of mountains; the Mersey and the Thames, the Humber and the Severn have shaken hands: Nature most audibly answers, Yea! The Man of Theory twangs his full-bent bow: Nature's Fact ought to fall stricken, but does not:

his logic-arrow glances from it as from a scaly dragon, and the obstinate Fact keeps walking its way. How singular! At bottom, you will have to grapple closer with the dragon; take it home to you, by real faculty, not by seeming faculty; try whether you are stronger, or it is stronger. Close with it, wrestle it: sheer obstinate toughness of muscle; but much more, what we call tough- ness of heart, which will mean persistence hopeful and even desperate, unsubduable patience, composed candid openness, clearness of mind: all this shall be 'strength' in wrestling your dragon; the whole man's real strength is in this work, we shall get the measure of him here.

Of all the Nations in the world at present the English are the stupidest in speech, the wisest in action. As good as a 'dumb' Nation, I say, who cannot speak, and have never yet spoken,—spite of the Shakspeares and Miltons who show us what possibilities there are!—O Mr. Bull, I look in that surly face of thine with a mixture of pity and laughter, yet also with wonder and veneration. Thou complainest not, my illustrious friend; and yet I believe the heart of thee is full of sorrow, of unspoken sadness, seriousness,—profound melancholy (as some have said) the basis of thy being. Unconsciously, for thou speakest of nothing, this great Universe is great to thee. Not by levity of floating, but by stubborn force of swimming, shalt thou make thy way. The Fates sing of thee that thou shalt many times be thought an ass and a dull ox, and shalt with a godlike indifference believe it. My friend,—and it is all untrue, nothing ever falser in point of fact! Thou art of those great ones whose greatness the small passer-by does not discern. Thy very stupidity is wiser than their wisdom. A grand *vis inertiæ* is in thee; how many grand qualities unknown to small men! Nature alone knows thee, acknowledges the bulk and strength of thee: thy Epic, unsung in words, is written in huge characters on the face of this Planet,—sea-moles, cotton- trades, railways, fleets and cities, Indian Empires, Americas, New Hollands; legible throughout the Solar System!

But the dumb Russians too, as I said, they, drilling

all wild Asia and wild Europe into military rank and file, a terrible yet hitherto a prospering enterprise, are still dumber. The old Romans also could not *speak*, for many centuries:—not till the world was theirs; and so many speaking Greekdoms, their logic-arrows all spent, had been absorbed and abolished. The logic-arrows, how they glanced futile from obdurate thick-skinned Facts; Facts to be wrestled down only by the real vigour of Roman thews!—As for me, I honour, in these loud-babbling days, all the Silent rather. A grand Silence that of Romans; —nay the grandest of all, is it not that of the gods! Even Triviality, Imbecility, that can sit silent, how respectable is it in comparison! The 'talent of silence' is our fundamental one. Great honour to him whose Epic is a melodious hexameter Iliad; not a jingling Sham Iliad, nothing true in it but the hexameters and forms merely. But still greater honour, if his Epic be a mighty Empire slowly built together, a mighty Series of Heroic Deeds,—a mighty Conquest over Chaos; *which* Epic the 'Eternal Melodies' have, and must have, informed and dwelt in, as *it* sung itself! There is no mistaking that latter Epic. Deeds are greater than Words. Deeds have such a life, mute but undeniable, and grow as living trees and fruit-trees do; they people the vacuity of Time, and make it green and worthy. Why should the oak prove logically that it ought to grow, and will grow? Plant it, try it; what gifts of diligent judicious assimilation and secretion it has, of progress and resistance, of *force* to grow, will then declare themselves. My much-honoured, illustrious, extremely inarticulate Mr. Bull!—

Ask Bull his spoken opinion of any matter,—oftentimes the force of dulness can no farther go. You stand silent, incredulous, as over a platitude that borders on the Infinite. The man's Churchisms, Dissenterisms, Puseyisms, Benthamisms, College Philosophies, Fashionable Literatures, are unexampled in this world. Fate's prophecy is fulfilled; you call the man an ox and an ass. But set him once to work,— respectable man! His spoken sense is next to nothing, nine-tenths of it palpable *non*sense: but his unspoken sense, his inner silent feeling of what is true, what does agree with fact, what is doable and what is not doable,—this seeks its fellow in the world. A terrible worker; irresistible against marshes, mountains, impediments, disorder, incivilisation; everywhere vanquishing disorder, leaving it behind him as method and order. He 'retires to his bed three days,' and considers!

Nay withal, stupid as he is, our dear John,—ever, after infinite tumblings, and spoken platitudes innumerable from barrel-heads and parliament-benches, he does settle down somewhere about the just conclusion; you are certain that his jumblings and tumblings will end, after years or centuries, in the stable equilibrium. Stable equilibrium, I say; centre-of-gravity lowest;—not the unstable, with centre-of-gravity highest, as I have known it done by quicker people! For indeed, do but jumble and tumble sufficiently, you avoid that worst fault, of settling with your centre-of-gravity highest; your centre-of-gravity is certain to come lowest, and to stay there. If slowness, what we in our impatience call 'stupidity' be the price of stable equilibrium over unstable, shall we grudge a little slowness? Not the least admirable quality of Bull is, after all, that of remaining insensible to logic; holding out for considerable periods, ten years or more, as in this of the Corn-Laws, after all arguments and shadow of arguments have faded away from him, till the very urchins on the street titter at the arguments he brings. Logic,—Λογική, the 'Art of Speech,'—does indeed speak so and so; clear enough: nevertheless Bull still shakes his head; will see whether nothing else *illogical*, not yet 'spoken,' not yet able to be 'spoken,' do not lie in the business, as there so often does!—My firm belief is, that, finding himself now enchanted, hand-shackled, foot-shackled, in Poor-Law Bastilles and elsewhere, he will retire three days to his bed, and *arrive* at a conclusion or two! His three-years 'total stagnation of trade,' alas, is not that a painful enough 'lying in bed to consider himself?' Poor Bull!

Bull is a born Conservative; for this too I inexpressibly honour him. All great Peoples are conservative;

slow to believe in novelties; patient of much error in actualities; deeply and forever certain of the greatness that is in LAW, in Custom once solemnly established, and now long recognised as just and final.—True, O Radical Reformer, there is no Custom that can, properly speaking, be final; none. And yet thou seest *Customs* which, in all civilised countries, are accounted final; nay, under the Old-Roman name of *Mores*, are accounted *Morality*, Virtue, Laws of God Himself. Such, I assure thee, not a few of them are; such almost all of them once were. And greatly do I respect the solid character,—a blockhead, thou wilt say; yes, but a well-conditioned blockhead, and the best-conditioned,—who esteems all ' Customs once solemnly acknowledged' to be ultimate, divine, and the rule for a man to walk by, nothing doubting, not inquiring farther. What a time of it had we, were all men's life and trade still, in all parts of it, a problem, a hypothetic seeking, to be settled by painful Logics and Baconian Inductions! The Clerk in Eastcheap cannot spend the day in verifying his Ready-Reckoner; he must take it as verified, true and indisputable; or his Book-keeping by Double Entry will stand still. " Where is your Posted Ledger? " asks the Master at night.—" Sir," answers the other, " I was verifying my Ready-Reckoner, and find some errors. The Ledger is—! "—Fancy such a thing!

True, all turns on your Ready-Reckoner being moderately correct, being *not* insupportably incorrect! A Ready-Reckoner which has led to distinct entries in your Ledger such as these: *Creditor* an English People by fifteen hundred years of good Labour; and *Debtor* to lodging in enchanted Poor-Law Bastilles: *Creditor* by con-quering the largest Empire the Sun ever saw; and *Debtor* to Donothingism and " Impossible " written on all departments of the government thereof: *Creditor* by mountains of gold ingots earned; and *Debtor* to No Bread purchasable by them: '—*such* Ready-Reckoner, methinks, is beginning to be suspect; nay is ceasing, and has ceased, to be suspect! Such Ready-Reckoner is a Solecism in Eastcheap; and must, whatever be the press of business,

and will and shall be rectified a little.   Business can go on
no longer with it.   The most Conservative English People,
thickest-skinned, most patient of Peoples, is driven alike
by its Logic and its Unlogic, by things 'spoken,' and by
things not yet spoken or very speakable, but only felt and
very unendurable, to be wholly a Reforming People.
Their Life, as it is, has ceased to be longer possible for
them.

Urge not this noble silent People; rouse not the
Berserkir rage that lies in them! Do you know their
Cromwells, Hampdens, their Pyms and Bradshaws?
Men very peaceable, but men that can be made very
terrible! Men who, like their old Teutsch Fathers in
Agrippa's days, 'have a soul that despises death;' to
whom 'death,' compared with falsehoods and injustices,
is light;—' in whom there is a rage unconquerable by the
immortal gods!'   Before this, the English People have
taken very preternatural-looking Spectres by the beard;
saying virtually: "And if thou *wert* 'preternatural'?
Thou with thy 'divine-rights' grown diabolic-wrongs?
Thou,—not even 'natural;' decapitable; totally extin-
guishable!"——Yes, just so godlike as this People's
patience was, even so godlike will and must its impatience
be. Away, ye scandalous Practical Solecisms, children
actually of the Prince of Darkness; ye have near broken
our hearts; we can and will endure you no longer.
Begone, we say; depart, while the play is good! By the
Most High God, whose sons and born missionaries true
men are, ye shall not continue here! You and we have
become incompatible; can inhabit one house no longer.
Either you must go, or we. Are ye ambitious to try *which*
it shall be?

O my Conservative friends, who still specially name
and struggle to approve yourselves 'Conservative,' would
to Heaven I could persuade you of this world-old fact,
than which Fate is not surer, That Truth and Justice alone
are *capable* of being 'conserved' and preserved! The
thing which is unjust, which is *not* according to God's Law,
will you, in a God's Universe, try to conserve that? It is so
old, say you? Yes, and the hotter haste ought *you*, of all

others, to be in, to let it grow no older! If but the faintest whisper in your hearts intimate to you that it is not fair,—hasten, for the sake of Conservatism itself, to probe it rigorously, to cast it forth at once and forever if guilty. How will or can you preserve *it*, the thing that is not fair? ' Impossibility ' a thousandfold is marked on that. And ye call yourselves Conservatives, Aristocracies:—ought not honour and nobleness of mind, if they had departed from all the Earth elsewhere, to find their last refuge with you? Ye unfortunate!

The bough that is dead shall be cut away, for the sake of the tree itself. Old? Yes, it is too old. Many a weary winter has it swung and creaked there, and gnawed and fretted, with its dead wood, the organic substance and still living fibre of this good tree; many a long summer has its ugly naked brown defaced the fair green umbrage; every day it has done mischief, and that only: off with it, for the tree's sake, if for nothing more; let the Conservatism that would preserve cut *it* away. Did no wood-forester apprise you that a dead bough with its dead root left sticking there is extraneous, poisonous; is as a dead iron spike, some horrid rusty ploughshare driven into the living substance;—nay is far worse; for in every wind-storm (' commercial crisis ' or the like), it frets and creaks, jolts itself to and fro, and cannot lie quiet as your dead iron spike would.

If I were the Conservative Party of England (which is another bold figure of speech), I would not for a hundred thousand pounds an hour allow those Corn-Laws to continue! Potosi and Golconda put together would not purchase my assent to them. Do you count what treasuries of bitter indignation they are laying up for you in every just English heart? Do you know what questions, not as to Corn-prices and Sliding-scales alone, they are *forcing* every reflective Englishman to ask himself? Questions insoluble, or hitherto unsolved; deeper than any of our Logic-plummets hitherto will sound: questions deep enough,—which it were better that we did not name even in thought! You are forcing us to think of them, to begin uttering them. The utterance of them is begun;

and where will it be ended, think you? When two
millions of one's brother-men sit in Workhouses, and five
millions, as is insolently said, ' rejoice in potatoes,' there
are various things that must be begun, let them end where
they can.

CHAPTER VI

TWO CENTURIES

THE Settlement effected by our ' Healing Parliament '
in the Year of Grace 1660, though accomplished under
universal acclamations from the four corners of the
British Dominions, turns out to have been one of the
mournfulest that ever took place in this land of ours. It
called and thought itself a Settlement of brightest hope and
fulfilment, bright as the blaze of universal tar-barrels and
bonfires could make it: and we find it now, on looking
back on it with the insight which trial has yielded, a
Settlement as of despair. Considered well, it was a
Settlement to govern henceforth without God, with only
some decent Pretence of God.

Governing by the Christian Law of God had been found
a thing of battle, convulsion, confusion, an infinitely difficult thing: wherefore let us now abandon it, and govern
only by so much of God's Christian Law as—as may prove
quiet and convenient for us. What is the end of Government? To guide men in the way wherein they should go;
towards their true good in this life, the portal of infinite
good in a life to come? To guide men in such way, and
ourselves in such way, as the Maker of men, whose eye is
upon us, will sanction at the Great Day?—Or alas, perhaps
at bottom *is* there no Great Day, no sure outlook of any
life to come; but only this poor life, and what of taxes,
felicities, Nell-Gwyns and entertainments we can manage
to muster here? In that case, the end of Government
will be, To suppress all noise and disturbance, whether of
Puritan preaching, Cameronian psalm-singing, thieves'-
riot, murder, arson, or what noise soever, and—be careful

that supplies do not fail! A very notable conclusion, if we will think of it, and not without an abundance of fruits for us. Oliver Cromwell's body hung on the Tyburn gallows, as the type of Puritanism found futile, inexecutable, execrable,—yes, that gallows-tree has been a finger-post into very strange country indeed. Let earnest Puritanism die; let decent Formalism, whatsoever cant it be or grow to, live! We have had a pleasant journey in that direction; and are—arriving at our inn?

To support the Four Pleas of the Crown, and keep Taxes coming in: in very sad seriousness, has not this been, ever since, even in the best times, almost the one admitted end and aim of Government? Religion, Christian Church, Moral Duty; the fact that man had a soul at all; that in man's life there was any eternal truth or justice at all,—has been as good as left quietly out of sight. Church indeed,—alas, the endless talk and struggle we have had of High-Church, Low-Church, Church-Extension, Church-in-Danger: we invite the Christian reader to think whether it has not been a too miserable screech-owl phantasm of talk and struggle, as for a 'Church,'—which one had rather not define at present!

But now in these godless two centuries, looking at England and her efforts and doings, if we ask, What of England's doings the Law of Nature had accepted, Nature's King had actually furthered and pronounced to have truth in them,—where is our answer? Neither the 'Church' of Hurd and Warburton, nor the Anti-Church of Hume and Paine; not in any shape the Spiritualism of England: all this is already seen, or beginning to be seen, for what it is; a thing that Nature does *not* own. On the one side is dreary Cant, with a *reminiscence* of things noble and divine; on the other is but acrid Candour, with a *prophecy* of things brutal, infernal. Hurd and Warburton are sunk into the sere and yellow leaf; no considerable body of true-seeing men looks thitherward for healing: the Paine-and-Hume Atheistic theory, of 'things well let alone,' with Liberty, Equality and the like, is

also in these days declaring itself nought, unable to keep
the world from taking fire.

The theories and speculations of both these parties,
and, we may say, of all intermediate parties and persons,
prove to be things which the Eternal Veracity did not
accept; things superficial, ephemeral, which already a
near Posterity, finding them already dead and brown-
leafed, is about to suppress and forget. The Spiritualism
of England, for those godless years, is, as it were, all
forgettable. Much has been written: but the perennial
Scriptures of Mankind have small accession: from all
English Books, in rhyme or prose, in leather binding or
in paper wrappage, how many verses have been added to
these? Our most melodious Singers have sung as from
the throat outwards: from the inner Heart of Man, from
the great Heart of Nature, through no Pope or Philips,
has there come any tone. The Oracles have been dumb.
In brief, the Spoken Word of England has not been true.
The Spoken Word of England turns out to have been
trivial; of short endurance; not valuable, not available
as a Word, except for the passing day. It has been
accordant with transitory Semblance; discordant with
eternal Fact. It has been unfortunately not a Word, but
a Cant; a helpless involuntary Cant, nay too often a
cunning voluntary one: either way, a very mournful
Cant; the Voice not of Nature and Fact, but of something
other than these.

With all its miserable shortcomings, with its wars, controversies, with its trades-unions, famine-insurrections,—
it is her Practical Material Work alone that England has
to show for herself! This, and hitherto almost nothing
more; yet actually this. The grim inarticulate veracity
of the English People, unable to speak its meaning in
words, has turned itself silently on things; and the dark
powers of Material Nature have answered, "Yes, this at
least is true, this is not false!" So answers Nature.
"Waste desert-shrubs of the Tropical swamps have
become Cotton-trees; and here, under my furtherance, are
verily woven shirts,—hanging unsold, undistributed, but
capable to be distributed, capable to cover the bare backs

of my children of men. Mountains, old as the Creation,
I have permitted to be bored through; bituminous fuel-
stores, the wreck of forests that were green a million years
ago,—I have opened them from my secret rock-chambers,
and they are yours, ye English. Your huge fleets, steam-
ships, do sail the sea; huge Indias do obey you; from
huge *New* Englands and Antipodal Australias comes
profit and traffic to this Old England of mine!" So
answers Nature. The Practical Labour of England is
not a chimerical Triviality: it is a Fact, acknowledged by
all the Worlds; which no man and no demon will con-
tradict. It is, very audibly, though very inarticulately
as yet, the one God's Voice we have heard in these two
atheistic centuries.

And now to observe with what bewildering obscurations and impediments all this as yet stands entangled,
and is yet intelligible to no man! How, with our gross
Atheism, we hear it not to be the Voice of God to us, but
regard it merely as a Voice of earthly Profit-and-Loss.
And have a Hell in England,—the Hell of not making
money. And coldly see the all-conquering valiant Sons
of Toil sit enchanted, by the million, in their Poor-Law
Bastille, as if this were Nature's Law;—mumbling to
ourselves some vague janglement of Laissez-faire, Supply-
and-demand, Cash-payment the one nexus of man to
man: Free-trade, Competition, and Devil take the hindmost, our latest Gospel yet preached!

As if, in truth, there were no God of Labour; as if godlike
Labour and brutal Mammonism were convertible terms.
A serious, most earnest Mammonism grown Midas-eared;
an unserious Dilettantism, earnest about nothing, grinning
with inarticulate incredulous incredible jargon about all
things, as the *enchanted* Dilettanti do by the Dead Sea!
It is mournful enough, for the present hour; were there
not an endless hope in it withal. Giant LABOUR, truest
emblem there is of God the World-Worker, Demiurgus,
and Eternal Maker; noble LABOUR, which is yet to be
the King of this Earth, and sit on the highest throne,—
staggering hitherto like a blind irrational giant, hardly

allowed to have his common place on the street-pavements; idle Dilettantism, Dead-Sea Apism crying out, " Down with him; he is dangerous ! "

Labour must become a seeing rational giant, with a *soul* in the body of him, and take his place on the throne of things,—leaving his Mammonism, and several other adjuncts, on the lower steps of said throne.

CHAPTER VII

OVER-PRODUCTION

BUT what will reflective readers say of a Governing Class, such as ours, addressing its Workers with an indictment of ' Over-production ' ! Over-production: runs it not so? " Ye miscellaneous, ignoble manufacturing individuals, ye have produced too much! We accuse you of making above two-hundred thousand shirts for the bare backs of mankind. Your trousers too, which you have made, of fustian, of cassimere, of Scotch-plaid, of jane, nankeen and woollen broadcloth, are they not manifold? Of hats for the human head, of shoes for the human foot, of stools to sit on, spoons to eat with— Nay, what say we hats or shoes? You produce gold-watches, jewelries, silver-forks, and epergnes, commodes, chiffoniers, stuffed sofas — Heavens, the Commercial Bazaar and multitudinous Howel-and-Jameses cannot contain you. You have produced, produced;—he that seeks your indictment, let him look around. Millions of shirts, and empty pairs of breeches, hang there in judgment against you. We accuse you of over-producing: you are criminally guilty of producing shirts, breeches, hats, shoes and commodities, in a frightful over-abundance. And now there is a glut, and your operatives cannot be fed ! "

Never surely, against an earnest Working Mammonism was there brought, by Game-preserving aristocratic Dilettantism, a stranger accusation, since this world began. My lords and gentlemen,—why, it was *you* that were appointed, by the fact and by the theory of your position on the Earth, to ' make and administer Laws,'— that is to say, in a world such as ours, to guard against ' gluts '; against honest operatives, who had done their work, remaining unfed! I say, *you* were appointed to preside over the Distribution and Apportionment of the Wages of Work done; and to see well that there went no labourer without his hire, were it of money-coins, were it of hemp gallows-ropes: that function was yours, and from immemorial time has been; yours, and as yet no other's. These poor shirt-spinners have forgotten much, which by the virtual unwritten law of their position they should have remembered: but by any written recognised law of their position, what have they forgotten? They were set to make shirts. The Community with all its voices commanded them, saying, " Make shirts; "—and there the shirts are! Too many shirts? Well, that is a novelty, in this intemperate Earth, with its nine-hundred millions of bare backs! But the Community commanded you, saying, " See that the shirts are well apportioned, that our Human Laws be emblem of God's Laws; "—and where is the apportionment? Two million shirtless or ill-shirted workers sit enchanted in Workhouse Bastilles, five million more (according to some) in Ugolino Hunger-cellars; and for remedy, you say,—what say you?— " Raise *our* rents! " I have not in my time heard any stranger speech, not even on the Shores of the Dead Sea. You continue addressing those poor shirt-spinners and over-producers in really a *too* triumphant manner!

" Will you bandy accusations, will you accuse *us* of over-production? We take the Heavens and the Earth to witness that we have produced nothing at all. Not from us proceeds this frightful overplus of shirts. In the wide domains of created Nature circulates no shirt or thing of our producing. Certain fox-brushes nailed upon our stable-door, the fruit of fair audacity at Melton Mowbray; these we have produced, and they are openly nailed up there. He that accuses us of producing, let him show himself, let him name what and when. We

are innocent of producing;—ye ungrateful, what mountains of things have we not, on the contrary, had to
' consume ' and make away with! Mountains of those
your heaped manufactures, wheresoever edible or wearable,
have they not disappeared before us, as if we had the
talent of ostriches, of cormorants, and a kind of divine
faculty to eat? Ye ungrateful!—and did you not grow
under the shadow of our wings? Are not your filthy mills
built on these fields of ours; on this soil of England,
which belongs to—whom think you? And we shall not
offer you our own wheat at the price that pleases us,
but that partly pleases you? A precious notion! What
would become of you, if we chose, at any time, to decide
on growing no wheat more? "

Yes, truly, *here* is the ultimate rock-basis of all Corn-
Laws; whereon, at the bottom of much arguing, they
rest, as securely as they can: What would become of you,
if we decided, some day, on growing no more wheat at
all? If we chose to grow only partridges henceforth, and
a modicum of wheat for our own uses? Cannot we do
what we like with our own?—Yes, indeed! For my share,
if I could melt Gneiss Rock, and create Law of Gravitation;
if I could stride out to the Dogger-bank, some morning,
and striking down my trident there into the mud-waves,
say, " Be land, be fields, meadows, mountains and fresh-
rolling streams! " by Heaven, I should incline to have
the letting of *that* land in perpetuity, and sell the wheat
of it, or burn the wheat of it, according to my own good
judgment! My Corn-Lawing friends, you affright me.

To the ' Millo-cracy ' so-called, to the Working Aristocracy, steeped too deep in mere ignoble Mammonism, and
as yet all unconscious of its noble destinies, as yet but
an irrational or semi-rational giant, struggling to awake
some soul in itself,—the world will have much to say,
reproachfully, reprovingly, admonishingly. But to the
Idle Aristocracy, what will the world have to say? Things
painful, and not pleasant!

To the man who *works*, who attempts, in never so un-
gracious barbarous a way, to get forward with some work,
you will hasten out with furtherances, with encourage-

ments, corrections; you will say to him: " Welcome;
thou art ours; our care shall be of thee." To the Idler,
again, never so gracefully going idle, coming forward with
never so many parchments, you will not hasten out; you
will sit still, and be disinclined to rise. You will say to
him: " Not welcome, O complex Anomaly; would thou
hadst stayed out of doors: for who of mortals knows
what to do with thee? Thy parchments: yes, they are
old, of venerable yellowness; and we too honour parchment, old-established settlements, and venerable use-and-
wont. Old parchments in very truth:—yet on the whole,
if thou wilt remark, they are young to the Granite Rocks,
to the Ground-plan of God's Universe! We advise thee
to put up thy parchments; to go home to thy place, and
make no needless noise whatever. Our heart's wish is to
save thee: yet there as thou art, hapless Anomaly, with
nothing but thy yellow parchments, noisy futilities, and
shotbelts and fox-brushes, who of gods or men can avert
dark Fate? Be counselled, ascertain if no work exist
for thee on God's Earth; if thou find no commanded-duty
there but that of going gracefully idle? Ask, inquire
earnestly, with a half-frantic earnestness; for the answer
means Existence or Annihilation to thee. We apprise
thee of the world-old fact, becoming sternly disclosed
again in these days, That he who cannot work in this
Universe cannot get existed in it: had he parchments
to thatch the face of the world, these, combustible fallible
sheepskin, cannot avail him. Home, thou unfortunate;
and let us have at least no noise from thee!"

Suppose the unfortunate Idle Aristocracy, as the unfortunate Working one has done, were to ' retire three
days to *its* bed,' and consider itself there, what o'clock
it had become?—

How have we to regret not only that men have ' no
religion,' but that they have next to no reflection; and
go about with heads full of mere extraneous noises, with
eyes wide-open but visionless,—for most part in the
somnambulist state!

CHAPTER VIII

UNWORKING ARISTOCRACY

IT is well said, ' Land is the right basis of an Aristocracy; ' whoever possesses the Land, he, more emphatically than any other, is the Governor, Viceking of the people on the Land. It is in these days as it was in those of Henry Plantagenet and Abbot Samson; as it will in all days be. The Land is *Mother* of us all; nourishes, shelters, gladdens, lovingly enriches us all; in how many ways, from our first wakening to our last sleep on her blessed mother-bosom, does she, as with blessed mother-arms, enfold us all!

The Hill I first saw the Sun rise over, when the Sun and I and all things were yet in their auroral hour, who can divorce me from it? Mystic, deep as the world's centre, are the roots I have struck into my Native Soil; no *tree* that grows is rooted so. From noblest Patriotism to humblest industrial Mechanism; from highest dying for your country, to lowest quarrying and coal-boring for it, a Nation's Life depends upon its Land. Again and again we have to say, there can be no true Aristocracy but must possess the Land.

Men talk of ' selling ' Land. Land, it is true, like Epic Poems and even higher things, in such a trading world, has to be presented in the market for what it will bring, and as we say be ' sold: ' but the notion of ' selling,' for certain bits of metal, the *Iliad* of Homer, how much more the *Land* of the World-Creator, is a ridiculous impossibility! We buy what is saleable of it; nothing more was ever buyable. Who can or could sell it to us? Properly speaking, the Land belongs to these two: To the Almighty God; and to all His Children of Men that have ever worked well on it, or that shall ever work well on it. No generation of men can or could, with never such solemnity and effort, sell Land on any other principle: it is not the property of any generation, we say, but that of all the past generations that have worked on it, and of all the future ones that shall work on it.

Again, we hear it said, The soil of England, or of any country, is properly worth nothing, except ' the labour bestowed on it.' This, speaking even in the language of Eastcheap, is not correct. The rudest space of country equal in extent to England, could a whole English Nation, with all their habitudes, arrangements, skills, with whatsoever they do carry within the skins of them and cannot be stript of, suddenly take wing and alight on it,—would be worth a very considerable thing! Swiftly, within year and day, this English Nation, with its multiplex talents of ploughing, spinning, hammering, mining, road-making and trafficking, would bring a handsome value out of such a space of country. On the other hand, fancy what an English Nation, once ' on the wing,' could have done with itself, had there been simply no soil, not even an inarable one, to alight on? Vain all its talents for ploughing, hammering, and whatever else; there is no Earth-room for this Nation with its talents: this Nation will have to *keep* hovering on the wing, dolefully shrieking to and fro; and perish piecemeal; burying itself, down to the last soul of it, in the waste unfirmamented seas. Ah yes, soil, with or without ploughing, is the gift of God. The soil of all countries belongs evermore, in a very considerable degree, to the Almighty Maker! The last stroke of labour bestowed on it is not the making of its value, but only the increasing thereof.

It is very strange, the degree to which these truisms are forgotten in our days; how, in the ever-whirling chaos of Formulas, we have quietly lost sight of Fact,—which it is so perilous not to keep forever in sight. Fact, if we do not see it, will make us *feel* it by and by!—From much loud controversy, and Corn-Law debating there rises, loud though inarticulate, once more in these years, this very question among others, Who made the Land of England? Who made it, this respectable English Land, wheat-growing, metalliferous, carboniferous, which will let readily hand over head for seventy millions or upwards, as it here lies: who did make it?—" We! " answer the much-*consuming* Aristocracy; " We! " as they ride in, moist with the sweat of Melton Mowbray: " It is we that made it; or are the heirs, assigns and representatives of those who did!"—My brothers, You? Everlasting honour to you, then; and Corn-Laws as many as you will, till your own deep stomachs cry Enough, or some voice of Human pity for our famine bids you Hold! Ye are as gods, that can create soil. Soil-creating gods there is no withstanding. They have the might to sell wheat at what price they list; and the right, to all lengths, and famine-lengths,—if they be pitiless infernal gods! Celestial gods, I think, would stop short of the famine-price; but no infernal nor any kind of god can be bidden stop!—— Infatuated mortals, into what questions are you driving every thinking man in England?

I say, you did *not* make the Land of England; and, by the possession of it, you *are* bound to furnish guidance and governance to England! That is the law of your position on this God's-Earth; an everlasting act of Heaven's Parliament, not repealable in St. Stephen's or elsewhere! True government and guidance; not no-government and Laissez-faire; how much less, *mis*-government and Corn-Law! There is not an imprisoned Worker looking out from these Bastilles but appeals, very audibly in Heaven's High Courts, against you, and me, and every one who is not imprisoned, " Why am I here? " His appeal is audible in Heaven; and will become audible enough on Earth too, if it remain unheeded here. His appeal is against you, foremost of all; you stand in the front-rank of the accused; you, by the very place you hold, have first of all to answer him and Heaven!

What looks maddest, miserablest in these mad and miserable Corn-Laws is independent altogether of their ' effect on wages,' their effect on ' increase of trade,' or any other such effect: it is the continual maddening proof they protrude into the faces of all men, that our Governing Class, called by God and Nature and the inflexible law of Fact, either to do something towards governing, or to die and be abolished,—have not yet learned even to sit still and do no mischief! For no Anti-Corn-Law League yet asks more of them than this;—Nature and Fact, very imperatively, asking so much more of them. Anti-Corn-Law League asks not, Do something; but, Cease your destructive misdoing, Do ye nothing!

Nature's message will have itself obeyed: messages of mere Free-Trade, Anti-Corn-Law League and Laissez-faire, will then need small obeying!—Ye fools, in name of Heaven, work, work, at the Ark of Deliverance for yourselves and us, while hours are still granted you! No: instead of working at the Ark, they say, "We cannot get our hands kept rightly warm;" and *sit obstinately burning the planks*. No madder spectacle at present exhibits itself under this Sun.

The Working Aristocracy; Mill-owners, Manufacturers, Commanders of Working Men: alas, against them also much shall be brought in accusation; much,—and the freest Trade in Corn, total abolition of Tariffs, and uttermost 'Increase of Manufactures' and 'Prosperity of Commerce,' will permanently mend no jot of it. The Working Aristocracy must strike into a new path; must understand that money alone is *not* the representative either of man's success in the world, or of man's duties to man; and reform their own selves from top to bottom, if they wish England reformed. England will not be habitable long, unreformed.

The Working Aristocracy—Yes, but on the threshold of all this, it is again and again to be asked, What of the Idle Aristocracy? Again and again, What shall we say of the Idle Aristocracy, the Owners of the Soil of England; whose recognised function is that of handsomely consuming the rents of England, shooting the partridges of England, and as an agreeable amusement (if the purchase-money and other conveniences serve), dilettante-ing in Parliament and Quarter-Sessions for England? We will say mournfully, in the presence of Heaven and Earth,—that we stand speechless, stupent, and know not what to say! That a class of men entitled to live sumptuously on the marrow of the earth; permitted simply, nay entreated, and as yet entreated in vain, to do nothing at all in return, was never heretofore seen on the face of this Planet. That such a class is transitory, exceptional, and,

unless Nature's Laws fall dead, cannot continue. That
it has continued now a moderate while; has, for the
last fifty years, been rapidly attaining its state of perfection. That it will have to find its duties and do
them; or else that it must and will cease to be seen on
the face of this Planet, which is a Working one, not an
Idle one.

Alas, alas, the Working Aristocracy, admonished by
Trades-unions, Chartist conflagrations, above all by their
own shrewd sense kept in perpetual communion with the
fact of things, will assuredly reform themselves, and a
working world will still be possible:—but the fate of the
Idle Aristocracy, as one reads its horoscope hitherto in
Corn-Laws and suchlike, is an abyss that fills one with
despair. Yes, my rosy fox-hunting brothers, a terrible
Hippocratic look reveals itself (God knows, not to
my joy) through those fresh buxom countenances of
yours. Through your Corn-Law Majorities, Sliding-Scales,
Protecting - Duties, Bribery - Elections, and triumphant
Kentish-fire, a thinking eye discerns ghastly images of
ruin, too ghastly for words; a handwriting as of MENE,
MENE. Men and brothers, on your Sliding-scale you
seem sliding, and to have slid,—you little know whither!
Good God! did not a French Donothing Aristocracy,
hardly above half a century ago, declare in like manner,
and in its featherhead believe in like manner, " We cannot
exist, and continue to dress and parade ourselves, on the
just rent of the soil of France; but we must have farther
payment than rent of the soil, we must be exempted from
taxes too,"—we must have a Corn-Law to extend our rent?
This was in 1789: in four years more—Did you look into
the Tanneries of Meudon, and the long-naked making for
themselves breeches of human skins! May the merciful
Heavens avert the omen; may we be wiser, that so we be
less wretched.

A High Class without duties to do is like a tree planted
on precipices; from the roots of which all the earth has
been crumbling. Nature owns no man who is not a
Martyr withal. Is there a man who pretends to live

luxuriously housed up; screened from all work, from want, danger, hardship, the victory over which is what we name work;—he himself to sit serene, amid down-bolsters and appliances, and have all his work and battling done by other men? And such man calls himself a *noble*-man? His fathers worked for him, he says; or successfully gambled for him: here *he* sits; professes, not in sorrow but in pride, that he and his have done no work, time out of mind. It is the law of the land, and is thought to be the law of the Universe, that he, alone of recorded men, shall have no task laid on him, except that of eating his cooked victuals, and not flinging himself out of window. Once more I will say, there was no stranger spectacle ever shown under this Sun. A veritable fact in our England of the Nineteenth Century. His victuals he does eat: but as for keeping in the inside of the window,—have not his friends, like me, enough to do? Truly, looking at his Corn-Laws, Game-Laws, Chandos-Clauses, Bribery-Elections and much else, you do shudder over the tumbling and plunging he makes, held back by the lapels and coat-skirts; only a thin fence of window-glass before him,—and in the street mere horrid iron spikes! My sick brother, as in hospital-maladies men do, thou dreamest of Paradises and Eldorados, which are far from thee. 'Cannot I do what I like with my own?' Gracious Heaven, my brother, this that thou seest with those sick eyes is no firm Eldorado, and Corn-Law Paradise of Donothings, but a dream of thy own fevered brain. It is a glass-window, I tell thee, so many stories from the street; where are iron spikes and the law of gravitation!

What is the meaning of nobleness, if this be 'noble?' In a valiant suffering for others, not in a slothful making others suffer for us, did nobleness ever lie. The chief of men is he who stands in the van of men; fronting the peril which frightens back all others; which, if it be not vanquished, will devour the others. Every noble crown is, and on Earth will forever be, a crown of thorns. The Pagan Hercules, why was he accounted a hero? Because he had slain Nemean Lions, cleansed Augean Stables, undergone Twelve Labours only not too heavy for a god.

In modern, as in ancient and all societies, the Aristocracy, they that assume the functions of an Aristocracy, doing them or not, have taken the post of honour; which is the post of difficulty, the post of danger,—of death, if the difficulty be not overcome. *Il faut payer de sa vie.* Why was our life given us, if not that we should manfully give it? Descend, O Donothing Pomp; quit thy down-cushions; expose thyself to learn what wretches feel, and how to cure it! The Czar of Russia became a dusty toiling shipwright; worked with his axe in the Docks of Saardam; and his aim was small to thine. Descend thou: under-take this horrid 'living chaos of Ignorance and Hunger' weltering round thy feet; say, " I will heal it, or behold I will die foremost in it." Such is verily the law. Every-where and everywhen a man has to ' *pay* with his life;' to do his work, as a soldier does, at the expense of life. In no Piepowder earthly Court can you sue an Aristocracy to do its work, at this moment: but in the Higher Court, which even *it* calls ' Court of Honour,' and which is the Court of Necessity withal, and the eternal Court of the Universe, in which all Fact comes to plead, and every Human Soul is an apparitor,—the Aristocracy is answer-able, and even now answering, *there.*

Parchments? Parchments are venerable: but they ought at all times to represent, as near as they by possi-bility can, the writing of the Adamant Tablets; otherwise they are not so venerable! Benedict the Jew in vain pleaded parchments; his usuries were too many. The King said, " Go to, for all thy parchments, thou shalt pay just debt; down with thy dust, or observe this tooth-forceps!" Nature, a far juster Sovereign, has far terribler forceps. Aristocracies, actual and imaginary, reach a time when parchment pleading does not avail them. " Go to, for all thy parchments, thou shalt pay due debt! " shouts the Universe to them, in an emphatic manner. They refuse to pay, confidently pleading parch-ment: their best grinder-tooth, with horrible agony, goes out of their jaw. Wilt thou pay now? A second grinder, again in horrible agony, goes: a second, and a third, and if need be, all the teeth and grinders, and the life itself with them;—and *then* there is free payment, and an anatomist-subject into the bargain!

Reform Bills, Corn-Law Abrogation Bills, and then Land-Tax Bill, Property-Tax Bill, and still dimmer list of etceteras; grinder after grinder:—my lords and gentlemen, it were better for you to arise and begin doing your work, than sit there and plead parchments!

We write no Chapter on the Corn-Laws, in this place; the Corn-Laws are too mad to have a Chapter. There is a certain immorality, when there is not a necessity, in speaking about things finished; in chopping into small pieces the already slashed and slain. When the brains are out, why does not a Solecism die? It is at its own peril if it refuse to die; it ought to make all conceivable haste to die, and get itself buried! The trade of Anti-Corn-Law Lecturer in these days, still an indispensable, is a highly tragic one.

The Corn-Laws will go, and even soon go: would we were all as sure of the Millennium as they are of going! They go swiftly in these present months; with an increase of velocity, an ever-deepening, ever-widening sweep of momentum, truly notable. It is at the Aristocracy's own damage and peril, still more than at any other's whatsoever, that the Aristocracy maintains them;—at a damage, say only, as above computed, of a 'hundred thousand pounds an hour'! The Corn-Laws keep all the air hot: fostered by their fever-warmth, much that is evil, but much also, how much that is good and indispensable, is rapidly coming to life among us!

CHAPTER IX

WORKING ARISTOCRACY

A POOR Working Mammonism getting itself 'strangled in the partridge-nets of an Unworking Dilettantism,' and bellowing dreadfully, and already black in the face, is surely a disastrous spectacle! But of a Midas-eared Mammonism, which indeed at bottom all pure Mammonisms are, what better can you expect? No better;— if not this, then something other equally disastrous, if not still more disastrous. Mammonisms, grown asinine, have to become human again, and rational; they have, on the whole, to cease to be Mammonisms, were it even on compulsion, and pressure of the hemp round their neck!—My friends of the Working Aristocracy, there are now a great many things which you also, in your extreme need, will have to consider.

The Continental people, it would seem, are 'exporting our machinery, beginning to spin cotton and manufacture for themselves, to cut us out of this market and then out of that!' Sad news indeed; but irremediable;—by no means the saddest news. The saddest news is, that we should find our National Existence, as I sometimes hear it said, depend on selling manufactured cotton at a farthing an ell cheaper than any other People. A most narrow stand for a great Nation to base itself on! A stand which, with all the Corn-Law Abrogations conceivable, I do not think will be capable of enduring.

My friends, suppose we quitted that stand; suppose we came honestly down from it, and said: " This is our minimum of cotton-prices. We care not, for the present, to make cotton any cheaper. Do you, if it seem so blessed to you, make cotton cheaper. Fill your lungs with cotton-fuzz, your hearts with copperas-fumes, with rage and mutiny; become ye the general gnomes of Europe, slaves of the lamp! "—I admire a Nation which fancies it will die if it do not undersell all other Nations, to the end of the world. Brothers, we will cease to *under*sell them: we will be content to *equal*-sell them; to be happy selling equally with them! I do not see the use of underselling them. Cotton-cloth is already two-pence a yard or lower; and yet bare backs were never more numerous among us. Let inventive men cease to spend their existence incessantly contriving how cotton can be made cheaper; and try to invent, a little, how cotton at its present cheapness could be somewhat justlier divided among us. Let inventive men consider, Whether the Secret of this Universe, and of Men's Life there, does, after all, as we rashly fancy it, consist in making money? There is One God, just, supreme, almighty: but is Mammon the name of him?—With a Hell which means 'Failing to make money,' I do not think there is any Heaven possible that would suit one well; nor so much as an Earth that can be habitable long! In brief, all this Mammon-Gospel, of Supply-and-demand, Competition, Laissez-faire, and Devil take the hindmost, begins to be one of the shabbiest Gospels ever preached; or altogether the shabbiest. Even with Dilettante partridge-nets, and at a horrible expenditure of pain, who shall regret to see the entirely transient, and at best somewhat despicable life strangled out of *it*? At the best, as we say, a somewhat despicable, unvenerable thing, this same ' Laissez-faire; ' and now, at the *worst*, fast growing an altogether detestable one!

"But what is to be done with our manufacturing population, with our agricultural, with our ever-increasing population? " cry many.—Ay, what? Many things can be done with them, a hundred things, and a thousand things,—had we once got a soul, and begun to try. This one thing, of doing for them by ' underselling all people,' and filling our own bursten pockets and appetites by the road; and turning over all care for any ' population,' or human or divine consideration except cash only, to the winds, with a " Laissez-faire " and the rest of it: this is evidently not the thing. Farthing cheaper per yard? No great Nation can stand on the apex of such a pyramid; screwing itself higher and higher; balancing itself on its great-toe! Can England not subsist without being *above*

all people in working? England never deliberately pur-
posed such a thing. If England work better than all
people, it shall be well. England, like an honest worker,
will work as well as she can; and hope the gods may allow
her to live on that basis. Laissez-faire and much else
being once well dead, how many 'impossibles' will become
possible! They are impossible, as cotton-cloth at two-
pence an ell was—till men set about making it. The
inventive genius of great England will not forever sit
patient with mere wheels and pinions, bobbins, straps and
billy-rollers whirring in the head of it. The inventive
genius of England is not a Beaver's, or a Spinner's or
Spider's genius: it is a *Man's* genius, I hope, with a God
over him!

Laissez-faire, Supply-and-demand,—one begins to be
weary of all that. Leave all to egoism, to ravenous greed
of money, of pleasure, of applause:—it is the Gospel of
Despair! Man *is* a Patent-Digester, then: only give
him Free Trade, Free digesting-room; and each of us
digest what he can come at, leaving the rest to Fate!
My unhappy brethren of the Working Mammonism, my
unhappier brethren of the Idle Dilettantism, no world
was ever held together in that way for long. A world
of mere Patent-Digesters will soon have nothing to digest:
such world ends, and by Law of Nature must end, in
'over-population;' in howling universal famine, 'impossibility,' and suicidal madness, as of endless dog-
kennels run rabid. Supply-and-demand shall do its full
part, and Free Trade shall be free as air;—thou of the
shotbelts, see thou forbid it not, with those paltry, *worse*
than Mammonish swindleries and Sliding-scales of thine,
which are seen to be swindleries for all thy canting, which
in times like ours are very scandalous to see! And Trade
never so well freed, and all Tariffs settled or abolished,
and Supply-and-demand in full operation,—let us all
know that we have yet done nothing; that we have merely
cleared the ground for doing.

Yes, were the Corn-Laws ended to-morrow, there is
nothing yet ended; there is only room made for all
manner of things beginning. The Corn-Laws gone, and

Trade made free, it is as good as certain this paralysis of industry will pass away. We shall have another period of commercial enterprise, of victory and prosperity; during which, it is likely, much money will again be made, and all the people may, by the extant methods, still for a space of years, be kept alive and physically fed. The strangling band of Famine will be loosened from our necks; we shall have room again to breathe; time to bethink ourselves, to repent and consider! A precious and thrice-precious space of years; wherein to struggle as for life in reforming our foul ways; in alleviating, instructing, regulating our people; seeking, as for life, that something like spiritual food be imparted them, some real governance and guidance be provided them! It will be a priceless time. For our new period or paroxysm of commercial prosperity will and can, on the old methods of ' Competition and Devil take the hindmost,' prove but a paroxysm: a new paroxysm,—likely enough, if we do not use it better, to be our *last*. In this, of itself, is no salvation. If our Trade in twenty years, ' flourishing ' as never Trade flourished, could double itself; yet then also, by the old Laissez-faire method, our Population is doubled: we shall then be as we are, only twice as many of us, twice and ten times as unmanageable!

All this dire misery, therefore; all this of our poor Workhouse Workmen, of our Chartisms, Trades-strikes, Corn-Laws, Toryisms, and the general downbreak of Laissez-faire in these days,—may we not regard it as a voice from the dumb bosom of Nature, saying to us: " Behold! supply-and-demand is not the one Law of Nature; Cash-payment is not the sole nexus of man with man,—how far from it! Deep, far deeper than Supply-and-demand, are Laws, Obligations sacred as Man's Life itself: these also, if you will continue to do work, you shall now learn and obey. He that will learn them, behold Nature is on his side, he shall yet work and prosper with noble rewards. He that will not learn them, Nature is against him, he shall not be able to do work in Nature's empire,—not in hers. Perpetual mutiny, contention, hatred, isolation, execration shall wait on his footsteps, till all men discern that the thing which he attains, however golden it look or be, is not success, but the want of success."

Supply-and-demand,—alas! For what noble work was there ever yet any audible ' demand ' in that poor sense? The man of Macedonia, speaking in vision to an Apostle Paul, " Come over and help us," did not specify what rate of wages he would give! Or was the Christian Religion itself accomplished by Prize-Essays, Bridgwater Bequests, and a ' minimum of Four thousand five hundred a year ' ? No demand that I heard of was made then, audible in any Labour-market, Manchester Chamber of Commerce, or other the like emporium and hiring establishment; silent were all these from any whisper of such demand;— powerless were all these to ' supply ' it, had the demand been in thunder and earthquake, with gold Eldorados and Mahometan Paradises for the reward. Ah me, into what waste latitudes, in this Time-Voyage, have we wandered; like adventurous Sindbads;—where the men go about as if by galvanism, with meaningless glaring eyes, and have no soul, but only a beaver-faculty and stomach! The haggard despair of Cotton-factory, Coal-mine operatives, Chandos Farm-labourers, in these days, is painful to behold; but not so painful, hideous to the inner sense, as that brutish godforgetting Profit-and-Loss Philosophy and Life-theory, which we hear jangled on all hands of us, in senate-houses, spouting-clubs, leading-articles, pulpits and platforms, everywhere as the Ultimate Gospel and candid Plain-English of Man's Life, from the throats and pens and thoughts of all-but all men!—

Enlightened Philosophies, like Molière Doctors, will tell you: " Enthusiasms, Self-sacrifice, Heaven, Hell and suchlike: yes, all that was true enough for old stupid times; all that used to be true: but we have changed all that, *nous avons changé tout cela !* " Well; if the heart be got round now into the right side, and the liver to the left; if man have no heroism in him deeper than the wish to eat, and in his soul there dwell now no Infinite of Hope and Awe, and no divine Silence can become

imperative because it is not Sinai Thunder, and no tie
will bind if it be not that of Tyburn gallows-ropes,—
then verily you have changed all that; and for it, and
for you, and for me, behold the Abyss and nameless
Annihilation is ready. So scandalous a beggarly Universe
deserves indeed nothing else; I cannot say I would save
it from Annihilation. Vacuum, and the serene Blue, will
be much handsomer; easier too for all of us. I, for one,
decline living as a Patent-Digester. Patent-Digester,
Spinning-Mule, Mayfair Clothes-Horse: many thanks,
but your Chaosships will have the goodness to excuse me!

CHAPTER X

PLUGSON OF UNDERSHOT

ONE thing I do know: Never, on this Earth, was the
relation of man to man long carried on by Cash-payment
alone. If, at any time, a philosophy of Laissez-faire,
Competition and Supply-and-demand, start up as the
exponent of human relations, expect that it will soon end.
Such philosophies will arise: for man's philosophies
are usually the 'supplement of his practice;' some
ornamental Logic-varnish, some outer skin of Articulate
Intelligence, with which he strives to render his dumb
Instinctive Doings presentable when they are done. Such
philosophies will arise; be preached as Mammon-Gospels,
the ultimate Evangel of the World; be believed, with
what is called belief, with much superficial bluster, and
a kind of shallow satisfaction real in its way:—but they
are ominous gospels! They are the sure, and even swift,
forerunner of great changes. Expect that the old System
of Society is done, is dying and fallen into dotage, when
it begins to rave in that fashion. Most Systems that I
have watched the death of, for the last three thousand
years, have gone just so. The Ideal, the True and Noble
that was in them having faded out, and nothing now
remaining but naked Egoism, vulturous Greediness, they

cannot live; they are bound and inexorably ordained by the oldest Destinies, Mothers of the Universe, to die. Curious enough: they thereupon, as I have pretty generally noticed, devise some light comfortable kind of ' wine-and-walnuts philosophy ' for themselves, this of Supply-and-demand or another; and keep saying, during hours of mastication and rumination, which they call hours of meditation: " Soul, take thy ease; it is all *well* that thou art a vulture-soul; "—and pangs of dissolution come upon them, oftenest before they are aware!

Cash-payment never was, or could except for a few years be, the union-bond of man to man. Cash never yet paid one man fully his deserts to another; nor could it, nor can it, now or henceforth to the end of the world. I invite his Grace of Castle-Rackrent to reflect on this;— does he think that a Land Aristocracy when it becomes a Land Auctioneership can have long to live? Or that Sliding-scales will increase the vital stamina of it? The indomitable Plugson too, of the respected Firm of Plugson, Hunks and Company, in St. Dolly Undershot, is invited to reflect on this; for to him also it will be new, perhaps even newer. Book-keeping by double entry is admirable, and records several things in an exact manner. But the Mother-Destinies also keep their Tablets; in Heaven's Chancery also there goes on a recording; and things, as my Moslem friends say, are ' written on the iron leaf.'

Your Grace and Plugson, it is like, go to Church occasionally: did you never in vacant moments, with perhaps a dull parson droning to you, glance into your New Testament, and the cash-account stated four times over, by a kind of quadruple entry,—in the Four Gospels there? I consider that a cash-account, and balance-statement of work done and wages paid, worth attending to. Precisely *such*, though on a smaller scale, go on at all moments under this Sun; and the statement and balance of them in the Plugson Ledgers and on the Tablets of Heaven's Chancery are discrepant exceedingly;—which ought really to teach, and to have long since taught, an indomitable common-sense Plugson of Undershot, much more an unattackable *un*common-sense Grace of Rackrent, a thing or two!—In brief, we shall have to dismiss the Cash-Gospel rigorously into its own place: we shall have to know, on the threshold, that either there is some infinitely deeper Gospel, subsidiary, explanatory and daily and hourly corrective, to the Cash one; or else that the Cash one itself and all others are fast travelling!

For all human things do require to have an Ideal in them; to have some Soul in them, as we said, were it only to keep the Body unputrefied. And wonderful it is to see how the Ideal or Soul, place it in what ugliest Body you may, will irradiate said Body with its own nobleness; will gradually, incessantly, mould, modify, new-form or reform said ugliest Body, and make it at last beautiful, and to a certain degree divine!—Oh, if you could dethrone that Brute-god Mammon, and put a Spirit-god in his place! One way or other, he must and will have to be dethroned.

Fighting, for example, as I often say to myself, Fighting with steel murder-tools is surely a much uglier operation than Working, take it how you will. Yet even of Fighting, in religious Abbot Samson's days, see what a Feudalism there had grown,—a 'glorious Chivalry,' much besung down to the present day. Was not that one of the 'impossiblest' things? Under the sky is no uglier spectacle than two men with clenched teeth, and hell-fire eyes, hacking one another's flesh; converting precious living bodies, and priceless living souls, into nameless masses of putrescence, useful only for turnip-manure. How did a Chivalry ever come out of that; how anything that was not hideous, scandalous, infernal? It will be a question worth considering by and by.

I remark, for the present, only two things: first, that the Fighting itself was not, as we rashly suppose it, a Fighting without cause, but more or less with cause. Man is created to fight; he is perhaps best of all definable as a born soldier; his life 'a battle and a march,' under the right General. It is forever indispensable for a man to fight: now with Necessity, with Barrenness, Scarcity, with Puddles, Bogs, tangled Forests, unkempt Cotton;—

now also with the hallucinations of his poor fellow **Men.** Hallucinatory visions rise in the head of my poor fellow man; make him claim over me rights which are not his. All fighting, as we noticed long ago, is the dusty conflict of strengths, each thinking itself the strongest, or, in other words, the justest;—of Mights which do in the long-run, and forever will in this just Universe in the long-run, mean Rights. In conflict the perishable part of them, beaten sufficiently, flies off into dust: this process ended, appears the imperishable, the true and exact.

And now let us remark a second thing: how, in these baleful operations, a noble devout-hearted Chevalier will comport himself, and an ignoble godless Bucanier and Chactaw Indian. Victory is the aim of each. But deep in the heart of the noble man it lies forever legible, that as an Invisible Just God made him, so will and must God's Justice and this only, were it never so invisible, ultimately prosper in all controversies and enterprises and battles whatsoever. What an Influence; ever-present,—like a Soul in the rudest Caliban of a body; like a ray of Heaven, and illuminative creative *Fiat-Lux*, in the wastest terrestrial Chaos! Blessed divine Influence, traceable even in the horror of Battlefields and garments rolled in blood: how it ennobles even the Battlefield; and, in place of a Chactaw Massacre, makes it a Field of Honour! A Battlefield too is great. Considered well, it is a kind of Quintessence of Labour; Labour distilled into its utmost concentration; the significance of years of it compressed into an hour. Here too thou shalt be strong, and not in muscle only, if thou wouldst prevail. Here too thou shalt be strong of heart, noble of soul; thou shalt dread no pain or death, thou shalt not love ease or life; in rage, thou shalt remember mercy, justice; —thou shalt be a Knight and not a Chactaw, if thou wouldst prevail! It is the rule of all battles, against hallucinating fellow Men, against unkempt Cotton, or whatsoever battles they may be, which a man in this world has to fight.

Howel Davies dyes the West-Indian Seas with blood, piles his decks with plunder; approves himself the expertest Seaman, the daringest Seafighter: but he gains no lasting victory, lasting victory is not possible for him. Not, had he fleets larger than the combined British Navy all united with him in bucaniering. He, once for all, cannot prosper in his duel. He strikes down his man: yes; but his man, or his man's representative, has no notion to lie struck down; neither, though slain ten times, will he keep so lying;—nor has the Universe any notion to keep him so lying! On the contrary, the Universe and he have, at all moments, all manner of motives to start up again, and desperately fight again. Your Napoleon is flung out, at last, to St. Helena; the latter end of him sternly compensating the beginning. The Bucanier strikes down a man, a hundred or a million men: but what profits it? He has one enemy never to be struck down; nay two enemies: Mankind and the Maker of Men. On the great scale or on the small, in fighting of men or fighting of difficulties, I will not embark my venture with Howel Davies: it is not the Bucanier, it is the Hero only that can gain victory, that can do more than *seem* to succeed. These things will deserve meditating; for they apply to all battle and soldiership, all struggle and effort whatsoever in this Fight of Life. It is a poor Gospel, Cash-Gospel or whatever name it have, that does not, with clear tone, uncontradictable, carrying conviction to all hearts, forever keep men in mind of these things.

Unhappily, my indomitable friend Plugson of Undershot has, in a great degree, forgotten them;—as, alas, all the world has; as, alas, our very Dukes and Soul-Overseers have, whose special trade it was to remember them! Hence these tears.—Plugson, who has indomitably spun Cotton merely to gain thousands of pounds, I have to call as yet a Bucanier and Chactaw; till there come something better, still more indomitable from him. His hundred Thousand-pound Notes, if there be nothing other, are to me but as the hundred Scalps in a Chactaw wigwam. The blind Plugson: he was a Captain of Industry, born member of the Ultimate genuine Aristocracy of this Universe, could he have known it! These thousand men that span and toiled round him, they were a regiment whom he had enlisted, man by man; to make war on a very genuine enemy: Bareness of back, and disobedient Cotton-fibre, which will not, unless forced to it, consent to cover bare backs. Here is a most genuine enemy; over whom all creatures will wish him victory. He enlisted his thousand men: said to them, "Come, brothers, let us have a dash at Cotton!" They follow with cheerful shout; they gain such a victory over Cotton as the Earth has to admire and clap hands at: but, alas, it is yet only of the Bucanier or Chactaw sort,—as good as no victory! Foolish Plugson of St. Dolly Undershot: does he hope to become illustrious by hanging up the scalps in his wigwam, the hundred thousands at his banker's, and saying, Behold my scalps? Why, Plugson, even thy own host is all in mutiny: Cotton is conquered; but the ' bare backs'—are worse covered than ever! Indomitable Plugson, thou must cease to be a Chactaw; thou and others; thou thyself, if no other!

Did William the Norman Bastard, or any of his Taillefers, *Ironcutters*, manage so? Ironcutter, at the end of the campaign, did not turn-off his thousand fighters, but said to them: "Noble fighters, this is the land we have gained; be I Lord in it,—what we will call *Law-ward*, maintainer and *keeper* of Heaven's *Laws* : be I *Law-ward*, or in brief orthoepy *Lord* in it, and be ye Loyal Men around me in it; and we will stand by one another, as soldiers round a captain, for again we shall have need of one another!" Plugson, bucanier-like, says to them: "Noble spinners, this is the Hundred Thousand we have gained, wherein I mean to dwell and plant vineyards; the hundred thousand is mine, the three and sixpence daily was yours: adieu, noble spinners; drink my health with this groat each, which I give you over and above!" The entirely unjust Captain of Industry, say I; not Chevalier, but Bucanier! 'Commercial Law' does indeed acquit him; asks, with wide eyes, What else? So too Howel Davies asks, Was it not according to the strictest Bucanier Custom? Did I depart in any jot or tittle from the Laws of the Bucaniers?

After all, money, as they say, is miraculous. Plugson wanted victory; as Chevaliers and Bucaniers, and all men alike do. He found money recognised, by the whole world with one assent, as the true symbol, exact equivalent and synonym of victory;—and here we have him, a grim-browed, indomitable Bucanier, coming home to us with a ' victory,' which the whole world is *ceasing* to clap hands at! The whole world, taught somewhat impressively, is beginning to recognise that such victory is but half a victory; and that now, if it please the Powers, we must—have the other half!

Money is miraculous. What miraculous facilities has it yielded, will it yield us; but also what never-imagined confusions, obscurations has it brought in; down almost to total extinction of the moral-sense in large masses of mankind! ' Protection of property,' of what is ' *mine*,' means with most men protection of money,—the thing which, had I a thousand padlocks over it, is least of all *mine ;* is, in a manner, scarcely worth calling mine! The symbol shall be held sacred, defended everywhere with tipstaves, ropes and gibbets; the thing signified shall be composedly cast to the dogs. A human being who has worked with human beings clears all scores with them, cuts himself with triumphant completeness forever loose from them, by paying down certain shillings and pounds. Was it not the wages I promised you? There they are, to the last sixpence,—according to the Laws of the Bucaniers! —Yes, indeed;—and, at such times, it becomes impera-tively necessary to ask all persons, bucaniers and others, Whether these same respectable Laws of the Bucaniers are written on God's eternal Heavens at all, on the inner Heart of Man at all; or on the respectable Bucanier Log-book merely, for the convenience of bucaniering merely? What a question;—whereat Westminster Hall shudders to its driest parchment; and on the dead wigs each particular horsehair stands on end!

The Laws of Laissez-faire, O Westminster, the laws of industrial Captain and industrial Soldier, how much more of idle Captain and industrial Soldier, will need to be remodelled, and modified, and rectified in a hundred and a hundred ways,—and *not* in the Sliding-scale direction, but in the totally opposite one! With two million industrial Soldiers already sitting in Bastilles, and five million pining on potatoes, methinks Westminster cannot begin too soon!—A man has other obligations laid on him, in God's Universe, than the payment of cash: these also Westminster, if it will continue to exist and have board-wages, must contrive to take some charge of:—by Westminster or by another, they must and will be taken charge of; be, with whatever difficulty, got articulated, got enforced, and to a certain approximate extent put in practice. And, as I say, it cannot be too soon! For Mammonism, left to itself, has become Midas-eared; and with all its gold mountains, sits starving for want of bread: and Dilettantism with its partridge-nets, in this extremely earnest Universe of ours, is playing somewhat too high a game. 'A man by the very look of him promises so much:' yes; and by the rent-roll of him does he promise nothing?—

Alas, what a business will this be, which our Continental friends, groping this long while somewhat absurdly about it and about it, call 'Organisation of Labour;'—which must be taken out of the hands of absurd windy persons, and put into the hands of wise, laborious, modest and valiant men, to begin with it straightway; to proceed with it, and succeed in it more and more, if Europe, at any rate if England, is to continue habitable much longer. Looking at the kind of most noble Corn-Law Dukes or Practical *Duces* we have, and also of right reverend Soul-Overseers, Christian Spiritual *Duces* 'on a minimum of four thousand five hundred,' one's hopes are a little chilled. Courage, nevertheless; there are many brave men in England! My indomitable Plugson,—nay is there not even in thee some hope? Thou art hitherto a Bucanier, as it was written and prescribed for thee by an evil world: but in that grim brow, in that indomitable heart which *can* conquer Cotton, do there not perhaps lie other ten-times nobler conquests?

CHAPTER XI

LABOUR

FOR there is a perennial nobleness, and even sacredness, in Work. Were he never so benighted, forgetful of his high calling, there is always hope in a man that actually and earnestly works: in Idleness alone is there perpetual despair. Work, never so Mammonish, mean, *is* in communication with Nature; the real desire to get Work done will itself lead one more and more to truth, to Nature's appointments and regulations, which are truth. The latest Gospel in this world is, Know thy work and do it. ' Know thyself: ' long enough has that poor ' self ' of thine tormented thee; thou wilt never get to ' know ' it, I believe! Think it not thy business, this of knowing thyself; thou art an unknowable individual: know what thou canst work at; and work at it, like a Hercules! That will be thy better plan.

It has been written, ' an endless significance lies in Work; ' a man perfects himself by working. Foul jungles are cleared away, fair seedfields rise instead, and stately cities; and withal the man himself first ceases to be a jungle and foul unwholesome desert thereby. Consider how, even in the meanest sorts of Labour, the whole soul of a man is composed into a kind of real harmony, the instant he sets himself to work! Doubt, Desire, Sorrow, Remorse, Indignation, Despair itself, all these like hell-dogs lie beleaguering the soul of the poor day-worker, as of every man: but he bends himself with free valour against his task, and all these are stilled, all these shrink murmuring far off into their caves. The man is now a man. The blessed glow of Labour in him, is it not as purifying fire, wherein all poison is burnt up, and of sour smoke itself there is made bright blessed flame!

Destiny, on the whole, has no other way of cultivating us. A formless Chaos, once set it *revolving*, grows round and ever rounder; ranges itself, by mere force of gravity, into strata, spherical courses; is no longer a Chaos, but a

round-compacted World.   What would become of the
Earth, did she cease to revolve?   In the poor old Earth,
so long as she revolves, all inequalities, irregularities
disperse themselves; all irregularities are incessantly
becoming regular.   Hast thou looked on the Potter's
wheel,—one of the venerablest objects; old as the Prophet
Ezechiel and far older?   Rude lumps of clay, how they
spin themselves up, by mere quick whirling, into beautiful
circular dishes.   And fancy the most assiduous Potter,
but without his wheel; reduced to make dishes, or rather
amorphous botches, by mere kneading and baking!
Even such a Potter were Destiny, with a human soul that
would rest and lie at ease, that would not work and spin!
Of an idle unrevolving man the kindest Destiny, like the
most assiduous Potter without wheel, can bake and
knead nothing other than a botch; let her spend on him
what expensive colouring, what gilding and enamelling
she will, he is but a botch.   Not a dish; no, a bulging,
kneaded, crooked, shambling, squint-cornered, amorphous
botch,—a mere enamelled vessel of dishonour!   Let the
idle think of this.

Blessed is he who has found his work; let him ask no
other blessedness.   He has a work, a life-purpose; he
has found it, and will follow it!   How, as a free-flowing
channel, dug and torn by noble force through the sour
mud-swamp of one's existence, like an ever-deepening
river there, it runs and flows;—draining-off the sour
festering water, gradually from the root of the remotest
grass-blade; making, instead of pestilential swamp, a
green fruitful meadow with its clear-flowing stream.   How
blessed for the meadow itself, let the stream and *its* value
be great or small!   Labour is Life: from the inmost heart
of the Worker rises his god-given Force, the sacred celestial
Life-essence breathed into him by Almighty God; from
his inmost heart awakens him to all nobleness,—to all
knowledge, ' self-knowledge ' and much else, so soon as
Work fitly begins.   Knowledge?   The knowledge that
will hold good in working, cleave thou to that; for Nature
herself accredits that, says Yea to that.   Properly thou
hast no other knowledge but what thou hast got by

working: the rest is yet all a hypothesis of knowledge; a thing to be argued of in schools, a thing floating in the clouds, in endless logic-vortices, till we try it and fix it. 'Doubt, of whatever kind, can be ended by Action alone.'

And again, hast thou valued Patience, Courage, Perseverance, Openness to light; readiness to own thyself mistaken, to do better next time? All these, all virtues, in wrestling with the dim brute Powers of Fact, in ordering of thy fellows in such wrestle, there and elsewhere not at all, thou wilt continually learn. Set down a brave Sir Christopher in the middle of black ruined Stone-heaps, of foolish unarchitectural Bishops, redtape Officials, idle Nell-Gwyn Defenders of the Faith; and see whether he will ever raise a Paul's Cathedral out of all that, yea or no! Rough, rude, contradictory are all things and persons, from the mutinous masons and Irish hodmen, up to the idle Nell-Gwyn Defenders, to blustering redtape Officials, foolish unarchitectural Bishops. All these things and persons are there not for Christopher's sake and his Cathedral's; they are there for their own sake mainly! Christopher will have to conquer and constrain all these, —if he be able. All these are against him. Equitable Nature herself, who carries her mathematics and architectonics not on the face of her, but deep in the hidden heart of her,—Nature herself is but partially for him; will be wholly against him, if he constrain her not! His very money, where is it to come from? The pious munificence of England lies far-scattered, distant, unable to speak, and say, " I am here; "—must be spoken to before it can speak. Pious munificence, and all help, is so silent, invisible like the gods; impediment, contradictions manifold are so loud and near! O brave Sir Christopher, trust thou in those notwithstanding, and front all these; understand all these; by valiant patience, noble effort, insight, by man's-strength, vanquish and compel all these,—and, on the whole, strike down victoriously the last topstone of that Paul's Edifice; thy monument for certain centuries, the stamp 'Great Man' impressed very legibly on Portland-stone there!—

Yes, all manner of help, and pious response from Men or Nature, is always what we call silent; cannot speak or come to light, till it be seen, till it be spoken to. Every noble work is at first 'impossible.' In very truth, for every noble work the possibilities will lie diffused through Immensity; inarticulate, undiscoverable except to faith. Like Gideon thou shalt spread out thy fleece at the door of thy tent; see whether under the wide arch of Heaven there be any bounteous moisture, or none. Thy heart and life-purpose shall be as a miraculous Gideon's fleece, spread out in silent appeal to Heaven: and from the kind Immensities, what from the poor unkind Localities and town and country Parishes there never could, blessed dew-moisture to suffice thee shall have fallen!

Work is of a religious nature:—work is of a *brave* nature; which it is the aim of all religion to be. All work of man is as the swimmer's: a waste ocean threatens to devour him; if he front it not bravely, it will keep its word. By incessant wise defiance of it, lusty rebuke and buffet of it, behold how it loyally supports him, bears him as its conqueror along. 'It is so,' says Goethe, 'with all things that man undertakes in this world.'

Brave Sea-captain, Norse Sea-king,—Columbus, my hero, royalest Sea-king of all! it is no friendly environment this of thine, in the waste deep waters; around thee mutinous discouraged souls, behind thee disgrace and ruin, before thee the unpenetrated veil of Night. Brother, these wild water-mountains, bounding from their deep bases (ten miles deep, I am told), are not entirely there on thy behalf! Meseems *they* have other work than floating thee forward:—and the huge Winds, that sweep from Ursa Major to the Tropics and Equators, dancing their giant-waltz through the kingdoms of Chaos and Immensity, they care little about filling rightly or filling wrongly the small shoulder-of-mutton sails in this cockle-skiff of thine! Thou art not among articulate-speaking friends, my brother; thou art among immeasurable dumb monsters, tumbling, howling wide as the world here. Secret, far off, invisible to all hearts but thine, there lies a help in them: see how thou wilt get at that. Patiently

thou wilt wait till the mad South-wester spend itself,
saving thyself by dexterous science of defence, the while:
valiantly, with swift decision, wilt thou strike in, when
the favouring East, the Possible, springs up. Mutiny of
men thou wilt sternly repress; weakness, despondency,
thou wilt cheerily encourage: thou wilt swallow down
complaint, unreason, weariness, weakness of others and
thyself;—how much wilt thou swallow down! There
shall be a depth of Silence in thee, deeper than this Sea,
which is but ten miles deep: a Silence unsoundable;
known to God only. Thou shalt be a Great Man. Yes,
my World-Soldier, thou of the World Marine-service,—
thou wilt have to be *greater* than this tumultuous unmeasured World here round thee is: thou, in thy strong
soul, as with wrestler's arms, shalt embrace it, harness it
down; and make it bear thee on,—to new Americas, or
whither God wills!

CHAPTER XII

REWARD

' RELIGION,' I said; for, properly speaking, all true Work
is Religion: and whatsoever Religion is not Work may
go and dwell among the Brahmins, Antinomians, Spinning
Dervishes, or where it will; with me it shall have no
harbour. Admirable was that of the old Monks, ' *Laborare
est Orare*, Work is Worship.'

Older than all preached Gospels was this unpreached,
inarticulate, but ineradicable, forever-enduring Gospel:
Work, and therein have well-being. Man, Son of Earth
and of Heaven, lies there not, in the innermost heart of
thee, a Spirit of active Method, a Force for Work;—and
burns like a painfully-smouldering fire, giving thee no
rest till thou unfold it, till thou write it down in beneficent
Facts around thee! What is immethodic, waste, thou
shalt make methodic, regulated, arable; obedient and
productive to thee. Wheresoever thou findest Disorder,
there is thy eternal enemy; attack him swiftly, subdue

him; make Order of him, the subject not of Chaos, but
of Intelligence, Divinity and Thee! The thistle that
grows in thy path, dig it out, that a blade of useful grass,
a drop of nourishing milk, may grow there instead.   The
waste cotton-shrub, gather its waste white down, spin it,
weave it; that, in place of idle litter, there may be folded
webs, and the naked skin of man be covered.

But above all, where thou findest Ignorance, Stupidity,
Brute-mindedness,—yes, there, with or without Church-
tithes and Shovel-hat, with or without Talfourd-Mahon
Copyrights, or were it with mere dungeons and gibbets
and crosses, attack it, I say; smite it wisely, unweariedly,
and rest not while thou livest and it lives; but smite,
smite, in the name of God! The Highest God, as I
understand it, does audibly so command thee; still
audibly, if thou have ears to hear. He, even He, with
his *un*spoken voice, awfuler than any Sinai thunders or
syllabled speech of Whirlwinds; for the SILENCE of deep
Eternities, of Worlds from beyond the morning-stars,
does it not speak to thee? The unborn Ages; the old
Graves, with their long-mouldering dust, the very tears
that wetted it now all dry,—do not these speak to thee,
what ear hath not heard? The deep Death-kingdoms,
the Stars in their never-resting courses, all Space and all
Time, proclaim it to thee in continual silent admonition.
Thou too, if ever man should, shalt work while it is called
Today.   For the Night cometh, wherein no man can
work.

All true Work is sacred; in all true Work, were it but
true hand-labour, there is something of divineness. Labour,
wide as the Earth, has its summit in Heaven. Sweat of
the brow; and up from that to sweat of the brain, sweat
of the heart; which includes all Kepler calculations,
Newton meditations, all Sciences, all spoken Epics, all
acted Heroisms, Martyrdoms,—up to that 'Agony of
bloody sweat,' which all men have called divine! O
brother, if this is not 'worship,' then I say, the more
pity for worship; for this is the noblest thing yet discovered under God's sky. Who art thou that complainest
of thy life of toil? Complain not.   Look up, my wearied

brother; see thy fellow Workmen there, in God's Eternity; surviving there, they alone surviving: sacred Band of the Immortals, celestial Bodyguard of the Empire of Mankind. Even in the weak Human Memory they survive so long, as saints, as heroes, as gods; they alone surviving; peopling, they alone, the unmeasured solitudes of Time! To thee Heaven, though severe, is *not* unkind; Heaven is kind,—as a noble Mother; as that Spartan Mother, saying while she gave her son his shield, "With it, my son, or upon it!" Thou too shalt return *home* in honour; to thy far-distant Home, in honour; doubt it not,—if in the battle thou keep thy shield! Thou, in the Eternities and deepest Death-kingdoms, art not an alien; thou everywhere art a denizen! Complain not; the very Spartans did not *complain*.

And who art thou that braggest of thy life of Idleness; complacently showest thy bright gilt equipages; sumptuous cushions; appliances for folding of the hands to mere sleep? Looking up, looking down, around, behind or before, discernest thou, if it be not in Mayfair alone, any *idle* hero, saint, god, or even devil? Not a vestige of one. In the Heavens, in the Earth, in the Waters under the Earth, is none like unto thee. Thou art an original figure in this Creation; a denizen in Mayfair alone, in this extraordinary Century or Half-Century alone! One monster there is in the world: the idle man. What is his 'Religion'? That Nature is a Phantasm, where cunning beggary or thievery may sometimes find good victual. That God is a lie; and that Man and his Life are a lie.—Alas, alas, who of us *is* there that can say, I have worked? The faithfulest of us are unprofitable servants; the faithfulest of us know that best. The faithfulest of us may say, with sad and true old Samuel, "Much of my life has been trifled away!" But he that has, and except 'on public occasions' professes to have, no function but that of going idle in a graceful or graceless manner; and of begetting sons to go idle; and to address Chief Spinners and Diggers, who at least *are* spinning and digging, "Ye scandalous persons who produce too much"—My Corn-Law friends, on what imaginary still richer Eldorados,

and true iron-spikes with law of gravitation, are ye
rushing!

As to the Wages of Work there might innumerable
things be said; there will and must yet innumerable things
be said and spoken, in St. Stephen's and out of St.
Stephen's; and gradually not a few things be ascertained
and written, on Law-parchment, concerning this very
matter:—' Fair day's-wages for a fair day's-work ' is the
most unrefusable demand! Money-wages ' to the extent
of keeping your worker alive that he may work more;'
these, unless you mean to dismiss him straightway out
of this world, are indispensable alike to the noblest Worker
and to the least noble!

One thing only I will say here, in special reference to
the former class, the noble and noblest; but throwing
light on all the other classes and their arrangements of
this difficult matter: The ' wages ' of every noble Work
do yet lie in Heaven or else Nowhere. Not in Bank-of-
England bills, in Owen's Labour-bank, or any the most
improved establishment of banking and money-changing,
needest thou, heroic soul, present thy account of earnings.
Human banks and labour-banks know thee not; or know
thee after generations and centuries have passed away,
and thou art clean gone from ' rewarding,'—all manner
of bank-drafts, shop-tills, and Downing-street Exchequers
lying very invisible, so far from thee! Nay, at bottom,
dost thou need any reward? Was it thy aim and life-
purpose to be filled with good things for thy heroism;
to have a life of pomp and ease, and be what men call
' happy,' in this world, or in any other world? I answer
for thee deliberately, No. The whole spiritual secret of
the new epoch lies in this, that thou canst answer for
thyself, with thy whole clearness of head and heart,
deliberately, No!

My brother, the brave man has to give his Life away.
Give it, I advise thee;—thou dost not expect to *sell* thy
Life in an adequate manner? What price, for example,
would content thee? The just price of thy LIFE to thee,
—why, God's entire Creation to thyself, the whole Universe

of Space, the whole Eternity of Time, and what they
hold: that is the price which would content thee; that,
and if thou wilt be candid, nothing short of that! It is
thy all; and for it thou wouldst have all. Thou art an
unreasonable mortal;—or rather thou art a poor *infinite*
mortal, who, in thy narrow clay-prison here, *seemest* so
unreasonable! Thou wilt never sell thy Life, or any part
of thy Life, in a satisfactory manner. Give it, like a royal
heart; let the price be Nothing: thou *hast* then, in a
certain sense, got All for it! The heroic man,—and is
not every man, God be thanked, a potential hero?—has
to do so, in all times and circumstances. In the most
heroic age, as in the most unheroic, he will have to say,
as Burns said proudly and humbly of his little Scottish
Songs, little dewdrops of Celestial Melody in an age when
so much was unmelodious: " By Heaven, they shall either
be invaluable or of no value; I do not need your guineas
for them!" It is an element which should, and must,
enter deeply into all settlements of wages here below.
They never will be ' satisfactory ' otherwise; they cannot,
O Mammon Gospel, they never can! Money for my little
piece of work ' to the extent that will allow me to keep
working;' yes, this,—unless you mean that I shall go
my ways *before* the work is all taken out of me: but as
to ' wages '—!—

On the whole, we do entirely agree with those old
Monks, *Laborare est Orare.* In a thousand senses, from
one end of it to the other, true Work *is* Worship. He
that works, whatsoever be his work, he bodies forth the
form of Things Unseen; a small Poet every Worker is.
The idea, were it but of his poor Delf Platter, how much
more of his Epic Poem, is as yet ' seen,' half-seen, only
by himself; to all others it is a thing unseen, impossible;
to Nature herself it is a thing unseen, a thing which never
hitherto was;—very ' impossible,' for it is as yet a Nothing! The Unseen Powers had need to watch over such
a man; he works in and for the Unseen. Alas, if he look
to the Seen Powers only, he may as well quit the business;
his No-thing will never rightly issue as a Thing, but as a
Deceptivity, a Sham-thing,—which it had better not do!

Thy No-thing of an Intended Poem, O Poet who hast looked merely to reviewers, copyrights, booksellers, popularities, behold it has not yet become a Thing; for the truth is not in it! Though printed, hotpressed, reviewed, celebrated, sold to the twentieth edition: what is all that? The Thing, in philosophical uncommercial language, is still a No-thing, mostly semblance and deception of the sight;—benign Oblivion incessantly gnawing at it, impatient till Chaos, to which it belongs, do reabsorb it!—

He who takes not counsel of the Unseen and Silent, from him will never come real visibility and speech. Thou must descend to the *Mothers*, to the *Manes*, and Hercules-like long suffer and labour there, wouldst thou emerge with victory into the sunlight. As in battle and the shock of war,—for is not this a battle?—thou too shalt fear no pain or death, shalt love no ease or life; the voice of festive Lubberlands, the noise of greedy Acheron shall alike lie silent under thy victorious feet. Thy work, like Dante's, shall 'make thee lean for many years.' The world and its wages, its criticisms, counsels, helps, impediments, shall be as a waste ocean-flood; the chaos through which thou art to swim and sail. Not the waste waves and their weedy gulf-streams, shalt thou take for guidance: thy star alone,—' *Se tu segui tua stella !* ' Thy star alone, now clear-beaming over Chaos, nay now by fits gone out, disastrously eclipsed: this only shalt thou strive to follow. O, it is a business, as I fancy, that of weltering your way through Chaos and the murk of Hell! Green-eyed dragons watching you, three-headed Cerberuses,—not without sympathy of *their* sort! " *Eccovi l' uom ch' è stato all' Inferno.*" For in fine, as Poet Dryden says, you do walk hand in hand with sheer Madness, all the way,—who is by no means pleasant company! You look fixedly into Madness, and *her* undiscovered, boundless, bottomless Night-empire; that you may extort new Wisdom out of it, as an Eurydice from Tartarus. The higher the Wisdom, the closer was its neighbourhood and kindred with mere Insanity; literally so;—and thou wilt, with a speechless feeling, observe how highest

Wisdom, struggling up into this world, has oftentimes carried such tinctures and adhesions of Insanity still cleaving to it hither!

All Works, each in their degree, are a making of Madness sane;—truly enough a religious operation; which cannot be carried on without religion. You have not work otherwise; you have eye-service, greedy grasping of wages, swift and ever swifter manufacture of semblances to get hold of wages. Instead of better felt-hats to cover your head, you have bigger lath-and-plaster hats set travelling the streets on wheels. Instead of heavenly and earthly Guidance for the souls of men, you have ' Black or White Surplice ' Controversies, stuffed hair-and-leather Popes;—terrestrial *Law-wards*, Lords and Law-bringers, ' organising Labour ' in these years, by passing Corn-Laws. With all which, alas, this distracted Earth is now full, nigh to bursting. Semblances most smooth to the touch and eye; most accursed, nevertheless, to body and soul. Semblances, be they of Shamwoven Cloth or of Dilettante Legislation, which are *not* real wool or substance, but Devil's-dust, accursed of God and man! No man has worked, or can work, except religiously; not even the poor day-labourer, the weaver of your coat, the sewer of your shoes. All men, if they work not as in a Great Taskmaster's eye will work wrong, work unhappily for themselves and you.

Industrial work, still under bondage to Mammon, the rational soul of it not yet awakened, is a tragic spectacle. Men in the rapidest motion and self-motion; restless, with convulsive energy, as if driven by Galvanism, as if possessed by a Devil: tearing asunder mountains,—to no purpose, for Mammonism is always Midas-eared! This is sad, on the face of it. Yet courage: the beneficent Destinies, kind in their sternness, are apprising us that this cannot continue. Labour is not a devil, even while encased in Mammonism; Labour is ever an imprisoned god, writhing unconsciously or consciously to escape out of Mammonism! Plugson of Undershot, like Taillefer of Normandy, wants victory; how much happier will even Plugson be to have a Chivalrous victory than a Chactaw one! The

unredeemed ugliness is that of a slothful People. Show
me a People energetically busy; heaving, struggling, all
shoulders at the wheel; their heart pulsing, every muscle
swelling, with man's energy and will;—I show you a
People of whom great good is already predicable; to
whom all manner of good is yet certain, if their energy
endure. By very working, they will learn; they have,
Antæus-like, their foot on Mother Fact: how can they
but learn?

The vulgarest Plugson of a Master-Worker, who can
command Workers, and get work out of them, is already a
considerable man. Blessed and thrice-blessed symptoms
I discern of Master-Workers who are not vulgar men;
who are Nobles, and begin to feel that they must act as
such: all speed to these, they are England's hope at
present! But in this Plugson himself, conscious of almost
no nobleness whatever, how much is there! Not without
man's faculty, insight, courage, hard energy, is this rugged
figure. His words none of the wisest; but his actings
cannot be altogether foolish. Think, how were it, stoodst
thou suddenly in his shoes! He has to command a thousand men. And not imaginary commanding; no, it is
real, incessantly practical. The evil passions of so many
men (with the Devil in them, as in all of us) he has to
vanquish; by manifold force of speech and of silence, to
repress or evade. What a force of silence, to say nothing
of the others, is in Plugson! For these his thousand men
he has to provide raw-material, machinery, arrangement,
houseroom; and ever at the week's end, wages by due sale.
No Civil-List, or Goulburn-Baring Budget has he to fall
back upon, for paying of his regiment; he has to pick
his supplies from the confused face of the whole Earth
and Contemporaneous History, by his dexterity alone.
There will be dry eyes if he fail to do it!—He exclaims, at
present, ' black in the face,' near strangled with Dilettante
Legislation: " Let me have elbow-room, throat-room, and
I will not fail! No, I will spin yet, and conquer like a
giant: what ' sinews of war ' lie in me, untold resources
towards the Conquest of this Planet, if instead of
hanging me, you husband them, and help me!"—My

indomitable friend, it is *true;* and thou shalt and must be helped.

This is not a man I would kill and strangle by Corn-Laws, even if I could! No, I would fling my Corn-Laws and Shotbelts to the Devil; and try to help this man. I would teach him, by noble precept and law-precept, by noble example most of all, that Mammonism was not the essence of his or of my station in God's Universe; but the adcititious excrescence of it; the gross, terrene, godless embodiment of it; which would have to become, more or less, a godlike one. By noble *real* legislation, by true *noble's*-work, by unwearied, valiant, and were it wageless effort, in my Parliament and in my Parish, I would aid, constrain, encourage him to effect more or less this blessed change. I should know that it would have to be effected; that unless it were in some measure effected, he and I and all of us, I first and soonest of all were doomed to perdition!—Effected it will be; unless it were a Demon that made this Universe; which I, for my own part, do at no moment, under no form, in the least believe.

May it please your Serene Highnesses, your Majesties, Lordships and Law-wardships, the proper Epic of this world is not now ' Arms and the Man; ' how much less, ' Shirt-frills and the Man: ' no, it is now ' Tools and the Man: ' that, henceforth to all time, is now our Epic;— and you, first of all others, I think, were wise to take note of that!

CHAPTER XIII

DEMOCRACY

If the Serene Highnesses and Majesties do not take note of that, then, as I perceive, *that* will take note of itself! The time for levity, insincerity, and idle babble and play-acting, in all kinds, is gone by; it is a serious, grave time. Old long-vexed questions, not yet solved in logical words or parliamentary laws, are fast solving themselves in facts, somewhat unblessed to behold! This largest of questions, this question of Work and Wages, which ought, had we heeded Heaven's voice, to have begun two generations ago or more, cannot be delayed longer without hearing Earth's voice. ' Labour ' will verily need to be somewhat ' organised,' as they say,—God knows with what difficulty. Man will actually need to have his debts and earnings a little better paid by man; which, let Parliaments speak of them or be silent of them, are eternally his due from man, and cannot, without penalty and at length not without death-penalty, be withheld. How much ought to cease among us straightway; how much ought to begin straightway, while the hours yet are!

Truly they are strange results to which this of leaving all to ' Cash;' of quietly shutting-up the God's Temple, and gradually opening wide-open the Mammon's Temple, with ' Laissez faire, and Every man for himself,'—have led us in these days! We have Upper, speaking Classes, who indeed do ' speak ' as never man spake before; the withered flimsiness, the godless baseness and barrenness of whose Speech might of itself indicate what kind of Doing and practical Governing went on under it! For Speech is the gaseous element out of which most kinds of Practice and Performance, especially all kinds of moral Performance, condense themselves, and take shape; as the one is, so will the other be. Descending, accordingly, into the Dumb Class in its Stockport Cellars and Poor-Law Bastilles, have we not to announce that they also are hitherto unexampled in the History of Adam's Posterity?

Life was never a May-game for men: in all times the lot of the dumb millions born to toil was defaced with manifold sufferings, injustices, heavy burdens, avoidable and unavoidable; not play at all, but hard work that made the sinews sore and the heart sore. As bond-slaves, *villani, bordarii, sochemanni,* nay indeed as dukes, earls and kings, men were oftentimes made weary of their life; and had to say, in the sweat of their brow and of their soul, Behold, it is not sport, it is grim earnest, and our back can bear no more! Who knows not what massacrings and harryings there have been; grinding, long-continuing, unbearable injustices,—till the heart had to rise in madness, and some "*Eu Sachsen, nimith euer sachses,* You Saxons, out with your gully-knives, then!" You Saxons, some 'arrestment,' partial 'arrestment of the Knaves and Dastards' has become indispensable!—The page of Dryasdust is heavy with such details.

And yet I will venture to believe that in no time, since the beginnings of Society, was the lot of those same dumb millions of toilers so entirely unbearable as it is even in the days now passing over us. It is not to die, or even to die of hunger, that makes a man wretched; many men have died; all men must die,—the last exit of us all is in a Fire-Chariot of Pain. But it is to live miserable we know not why; to work sore and yet gain nothing; to be heart-worn, weary, yet isolated, unrelated, girt-in with a cold universal Laissez-faire: it is to die slowly all our life long, imprisoned in a deaf, dead, Infinite Injustice, as in the accursed iron belly of a Phalaris' Bull! This is and remains forever intolerable to all men whom God has made. Do we wonder at French Revolutions, Chartisms, Revolts of Three Days? The times, if we will consider them, are really unexampled.

Never before did I hear of an Irish Widow reduced to 'prove her sisterhood by dying of typhus-fever and infecting seventeen persons,'—saying in such undeniable way, "You *see* I was your sister!" Sisterhood, brotherhood, was often forgotten; but not till the rise of these ultimate Mammon and Shotbelt Gospels did I ever see it so expressly denied. If no pious Lord or *Law-ward* would remember it, always some pious Lady ('*Hlaf-dig,*' Benefactress, '*Loaf-giveress,*' they say she is,—blessings on her beautiful heart!) was there, with mild mother-voice and hand, to remember it; some pious thoughtful *Elder,* what we now call 'Prester,' *Presbyter* or 'Priest,' was there to put all men in mind of it, in the name of the God who had made all.

Not even in Black Dahomey was it ever, I think, forgotten to the typhus-fever length. Mungo Park, resourceless, had sunk down to die under the Negro Village-Tree, a horrible White object in the eyes of all. But in the poor Black Woman, and her daughter who stood aghast at him, whose earthly wealth and funded capital consisted of one small calabash of rice, there lived a heart richer than *Laissez-faire :* they, with a royal munificence, boiled their rice for him; they sang all night to him, spinning assiduous on their cotton distaffs, as he lay to sleep: "Let us pity the poor white man; no mother has he to fetch him milk, no sister to grind him corn!" Thou poor black Noble One,—thou *Lady* too: did not a God make thee too; was there not in thee too something of a God!—

Gurth, born thrall of Cedric the Saxon, has been greatly pitied by Dryasdust and others. Gurth, with the brass collar round his neck, tending Cedric's pigs in the glades of the wood, is not what I call an exemplar of human felicity: but Gurth, with the sky above him, with the free air and tinted boscage and umbrage round him, and in him at least the certainty of supper and social lodging when he came home; Gurth to me seems happy, in comparison with many a Lancashire and Buckinghamshire man of these days, not born thrall of anybody! Gurth's brass collar did not gall him: Cedric *deserved* to be his master. The pigs were Cedric's, but Gurth too would get his parings of them. Gurth had the inexpressible satisfaction of feeling himself related indissolubly, though in a rude brass-collar way, to his fellow-mortals in this Earth. He had superiors, inferiors, equals.—Gurth is now 'emancipated' long since; has what we call 'Liberty.' Liberty, I am told, is a divine thing. Liberty when it becomes the 'Liberty to die by starvation' is not so divine!

Liberty? The true liberty of a man, you would say, consisted in his finding out, or being forced to find out the right path, and to walk thereon. To learn, or to be taught, what work he actually was able for; and then by permission, persuasion, and even compulsion, to set about doing of the same! That is his true blessedness, honour, 'liberty' and maximum of wellbeing: if liberty be not that, I for one have small care about liberty. You do not allow a palpable madman to leap over precipices; you violate his liberty, you that are wise; and keep him, were it in strait-waistcoats, away from the precipices! Every stupid, every cowardly and foolish man is but a less palpable madman: his true liberty were that a wiser man, that any and every wiser man, could, by brass collars, or in whatever milder or sharper way, lay hold of him when he was going wrong, and order and compel him to go a little righter. O, if thou really art my *Senior*, Seigneur, my *Elder*, Presbyter or Priest,—if thou art in very deed my *Wiser*, may a beneficent instinct lead and impel thee to ' conquer ' me, to command me! If thou do know better than I what is good and right, I conjure thee in the name of God, force me to do it; were it by never such brass collars, whips and handcuffs, leave me not to walk over precipices! That I have been called, by all the Newspapers, a ' free man ' will avail me little, if my pilgrimage have ended in death and wreck. O that the Newspapers had called me slave, coward, fool, or what it pleased their sweet voices to name me, and I had attained not death, but life! — Liberty requires new definitions.

A conscious abhorrence and intolerance of Folly, of Baseness, Stupidity, Poltroonery and all that brood of things, dwells deep in some men: still deeper in others an *un*conscious abhorrence and intolerance, clothed moreover by the beneficent Supreme Powers in what stout appetites, energies, egoisms so-called, are suitable to it;—these latter are your Conquerors, Romans, Normans, Russians, Indo-English; Founders of what we call Aristocracies. Which indeed have they not the most ' divine right ' to found;— being themselves very truly Αριστοι, BRAVEST, BEST; and conquering generally a confused rabble of WORST, or at lowest, clearly enough, of WORSE? I think their divine right, tried, with affirmatory verdict, in the greatest Law-Court known to me, was good! A class of men who are dreadfully exclaimed against by Dryasdust; of whom nevertheless beneficent Nature has oftentimes had need; and may, alas, again have need.

When, across the hundredfold poor scepticisms, trivialisms and constitutional cobwebberies of Dryasdust,

you catch any glimpse of a William the Conqueror, a
Tancred of Hauteville or suchlike,—do you not discern
veritably some rude outline of a true God-made King;
whom not the Champion of England cased in tin, but all
Nature and the Universe were calling to the throne?   It
is absolutely necessary that he get thither.   Nature does
not mean her poor Saxon children to perish, of obesity,
stupor or other malady, as yet: a stern Ruler and Line
of Rulers therefore is called in,—a stern but most beneficent *perpetual House-Surgeon* is by Nature herself called
in, and even the appropriate *fees* are provided for him!
Dryasdust talks lamentably about Hereward and the
Fen Counties; fate of Earl Waltheof; Yorkshire and the
North reduced to ashes: all which is undoubtedly lamentable.   But even Dryasdust apprises me of one fact: ' A
child, in this William's reign, might have carried a purse of
gold from end to end of England.'   My erudite friend,
it is a fact which outweighs a thousand!   Sweep away
thy constitutional, sentimental and other cobwebberies;
look eye to eye, if thou still have any eye, in the face of
this big burly William Bastard: thou wilt see a fellow of
most flashing discernment, of most strong lion-heart;—
in whom, as it were, within a frame of oak and iron, the
gods have planted the soul of ' a man of genius '!   Dost
thou call that nothing?   I call it an immense thing!—
Rage enough was in this Willelmus Conquæstor, rage
enough for his occasions;—and yet the essential element
of him, as of all such men, is not scorching *fire*, but shining
illuminative *light*.   Fire and light are strangely inter-
changeable; nay, at bottom, I have found them different
forms of the same most godlike ' elementary substance '
in our world: a thing worth stating in these days.   The
essential element of this Conquæstor is, first of all, the most
sun-eyed perception of what *is* really what on this God's
Earth;—which, thou wilt find, does mean at bottom
' Justice,' and ' Virtues ' not a few: *Conformity* to what
the Maker has seen good to make; that, I suppose, will
mean Justice and a Virtue or two?—

Dost thou think Willelmus Conquæstor would have
tolerated ten years' jargon, one hour's jargon, on the

propriety of killing Cotton-manufacturers by partridge Corn-Laws? I fancy, this was not the man to knock out of his night's-rest with nothing but a noisy bedlamism in your mouth! "Assist us still better to bush the partridges; strangle Plugson who spins the shirts?"—"*Par la Splendeur de Dieu!*"— —Dost thou think Willelmus Conquæstor, in this new time, with Steamengine Captains of Industry on one hand of him, and Joe-Manton Captains of Idleness on the other, would have doubted which *was* really the BEST; which did deserve strangling, and which not?

I have a certain indestructible regard for Willelmus Conquæstor. A resident House-Surgeon, provided by Nature for her beloved English People, and even furnished with the requisite fees, as I said; for he by no means felt himself doing Nature's work, this Willelmus, but his own work exclusively! And his own work withal it was; informed '*par la Splendeur de Dieu.*'—I say, it is necessary to get the work out of such a man, however harsh that be! When a world, not yet doomed for death, is rushing down to ever-deeper Baseness and Confusion, it is a dire necessity of Nature's to bring in her ARISTOCRACIES, her BEST, even by forcible methods. When their descendants or representatives cease entirely to *be* the Best, Nature's poor world will very soon rush down again to Baseness; and it becomes a dire necessity of Nature's to cast them out. Hence French Revolutions, Five-point Charters, Democracies, and a mournful list of *Etceteras*, in these our afflicted times.

To what extent Democracy has now reached, how it advances irresistible with ominous, ever-increasing speed, he that will open his eyes on any province of human affairs may discern. Democracy is everywhere the inexorable demand of these ages, swiftly fulfilling itself. From the thunder of Napoleon battles, to the jabbering of Open-vestry in St. Mary Axe, all things announce Democracy. A distinguished man, whom some of my readers will hear again with pleasure, thus writes to me what in these days he notes from the Wahngasse of Weissnichtwo, where our London fashions seem to be in full vogue. Let us hear the Herr Teufelsdröckh again, were it but the smallest word!

'Democracy, which means despair of finding any Heroes to govern you, and contented putting-up with the want of them,—alas, thou too, *mein Lieber*, seest well how close it is of kin to *Atheism*, and other sad *Isms*: he who discovers no God whatever, how shall he discover Heroes, the visible Temples of God?—Strange enough meanwhile it is, to observe with what thoughtlessness, here in our rigidly Conservative Country, men rush into Democracy with full cry. Beyond doubt, his Excellenz the Titular-Herr Ritter Kauderwälsch von Pferdefuss-Quacksalber, he our distinguished Conservative Premier himself, and all but the thicker-headed of his Party, discern Democracy to be inevitable as death, and are even desperate of delaying it much!

'You cannot walk the streets without beholding Democracy announce itself: the very Tailor has become, if not properly Sansculottic, which to him would be ruinous, yet a Tailor unconsciously symbolising, and prophesying with his scissors, the reign of Equality. What now is our fashionable coat? A thing of super-finest texture, of deeply meditated cut; with Malines-lace cuffs; quilted with gold; so that a man can carry, without difficulty, an estate of land on his back? *Keines-wegs*, By no manner of means! The Sumptuary Laws have fallen into such a state of desuetude as was never before seen. Our fashionable coat is an amphibium between barn-sack and drayman's doublet. The cloth of it is studiously coarse; the colour a speckled soot-black or rust-brown gray; the nearest approach to a Peasant's. And for shape,—thou shouldst see it! The last consummation of the year now passing over us is definable as Three Bags; a big bag for the body, two small bags for the arms, and by way of collar a hem! The first Antique Cheruscan who, of felt-cloth or bear's-hide, with bone or metal needle, set about making himself a coat, before Tailors had yet awakened out of Nothing, —did not he make it even so? A loose wide poke for body, with two holes to let out the arms; this was his original coat: to which holes it was soon visible that two small loose pokes, or sleeves, easily appended, would be an improvement.

'Thus has the Tailor-art, so to speak, overset itself, like most other things; changed its centre-of-gravity; whirled suddenly over from zenith to nadir. Your Stulz, with huge somerset, vaults from his high shopboard down to the depths of primal savagery,—carrying much along with him! For I will invite thee to reflect that the Tailor, as topmost ultimate froth of Human Society, is indeed swift-passing, evanescent, slippery to decipher; yet significant of much, nay of all. Topmost evanescent froth, he is churned-up from the very lees, and from all intermediate regions of the liquor. The general outcome he, visible to the eye, of what men aimed to do, and were obliged and enabled to do, in this one public department of symbolising themselves to each other by covering of their skins. A smack of all Human Life lies in the Tailor: its wild struggles towards beauty, dignity, freedom, victory; and how, hemmed-in by Sedan and Huddersfield, by Nescience, Dulness, Prurience, and other sad necessities and laws of Nature, it has attained just to this: Gray savagery of Three Sacks with a hem!

'When the very Tailor verges towards Sansculottism, is it not ominous? The last Divinity of poor mankind dethroning himself; sinking *his* taper too, flame down-most, like the Genius of Sleep or of Death; admonitory that Tailor time shall be no more!—For, little as one could advise Sumptuary Laws at the present epoch, yet nothing is clearer than that where ranks do actually exist, strict division of costumes will also be enforced; that if we ever have a new Hierarchy and Aristocracy, acknow-ledged veritably as such, for which I daily pray Heaven, the Tailor will reawaken; and be, by volunteering and appointment, consciously and unconsciously, a safeguard of that same.'—Certain farther observations, from the same invaluable pen, on our never-ending changes of mode, our 'perpetual nomadic and even ape-like appetite for change and mere change' in all the equipments of our existence, and the 'fatal revolutionary character' thereby manifested, we suppress for the present. It may be admitted that Democracy, in all meanings of the word, is in full career; irresistible by any Ritter Kauderwälsch or other Son of Adam as times go. ' Liberty ' is a thing men are determined to have.

But truly, as I had to remark in the mean while, ' the liberty of not being oppressed by your fellow man ' is an indispensable, yet one of the most insignificant fractional parts of Human Liberty. No man oppresses thee, can bid thee fetch or carry, come or go, without reason shown. True; from all men thou art emancipated: but from Thyself and from the Devil—? No man, wiser, unwiser, can make thee come or go: but thy own futilities, bewilderments, thy false appetites for Money, Windsor Georges and suchlike? No man oppresses thee, O free and independent Franchiser: but does not this stupid Porter-pot oppress thee? No Son of Adam can bid thee come or go; but this absurd Pot of Heavy-wet, this can and does! Thou art the thrall not of Cedric the Saxon, but of thy own brutal appetites and this scoured dish of liquor. And thou pratest of thy ' liberty? ' Thou entire blockhead!

Heavy-wet and gin: alas, these are not the only kinds of thraldom. Thou who walkest in a vain show, looking out with ornamental dilettante sniff and serene supremacy at all Life and all Death; and amblest jauntily; perking up thy poor talk into crotchets, thy poor conduct into fatuous somnambulisms;—and *art* as an ' enchanted Ape ' under God's sky, where thou mightest have been a man, had proper Schoolmasters and Conquerors, and Constables with cat-o'-nine tails, been vouchsafed thee; dost thou call that ' liberty ' ? Or your unreposing Mammon-worshipper again, driven, as if by Galvanisms, by Devils, and Fixed-ideas, who rises early and sits late, chasing the impossible; straining every faculty to ' fill himself with the east wind,'—how merciful were it, could you, by mild persuasion, or by the severest tyranny so-called, check him in his mad path, and turn him into a wiser one! All painful tyranny, in that case again, were but mild 'surgery;' the pain of it cheap, as health and life, instead of galvanism and fixed-idea, are cheap at any price.

Sure enough, of all paths a man could strike into, there *is*, at any given moment, a *best path* for every man; a thing which, here and now, it were of all things *wisest* for him to do;—which could he be but led or driven to do, he were then doing 'like a man,' as we phrase it; all men and gods agreeing with him, the whole Universe virtually exclaiming Well-done to him! His success, in such case, were complete; his felicity a maximum. This path, to find this path and walk in it, is the one thing needful for him. Whatsoever forwards him in that, let it come to him even in the shape of blows and spurnings, is liberty: whatsoever hinders him, were it wardmotes, open-vestries, pollbooths, tremendous cheers, rivers of heavy-wet, is slavery.

The notion that a man's liberty consists in giving his vote at election-hustings, and saying, "Behold, now I too have my twenty-thousandth part of a Talker in our National Palaver; will not all the gods be good to me?" —is one of the pleasantest! Nature nevertheless is kind at present; and puts it into the heads of many, almost of all. The liberty especially which has to purchase itself by social isolation, and each man standing separate from the other, having 'no business with him' but a cash-account: this is such a liberty as the Earth seldom saw; —as the Earth will not long put up with, recommend it how you may. This liberty turns out, before it have long continued in action, with all men flinging up their caps round it, to be, for the Working Millions a liberty to die by want of food; for the Idle Thousands and Units, alas, a still more fatal liberty to live in want of work; to have no earnest duty to do in this God's-World any more. What becomes of a man in such predicament? Earth's Laws are silent; and Heaven's speak in a voice which is not heard. No work, and the ineradicable need of work, give rise to new very wondrous life-philosophies, new very wondrous life-practices! Dilettantism, Pococur-antism, Beau-Brummelism, with perhaps an occasional, half-mad, protesting burst of Byronism, establish them-

selves: at the end of a certain period,—if you go back
to 'the Dead Sea,' there is, say our Moslem friends, a
very strange 'Sabbath-day' transacting itself there!
—Brethren, we know but imperfectly yet, after ages of
Constitutional Government, what Liberty and Slavery are.

Democracy, the chase of Liberty in that direction,
shall go its full course; unrestrainable by him of Pferdefuss-Quacksalber, or any of *his* household. The Toiling
Millions of Mankind, in most vital need and passionate
instinctive desire of Guidance, shall cast away False-
Guidance; and hope, for an hour, that No-Guidance will
suffice them: but it can be for an hour only. The smallest
item of human Slavery is the oppression of man by his
Mock-Superiors; the palpablest, but I say at bottom the
smallest. Let him shake-off such oppression, trample it
indignantly under his feet; I blame him not, I pity and
commend him. But oppression by your Mock-Superiors
well shaken off, the grand problem yet remains to solve:
That of finding government by your Real-Superiors!
Alas, how shall we ever learn the solution of that, benighted, bewildered, sniffing, sneering, godforgetting
unfortunates as we are? It is a work for centuries; to
be taught us by tribulations, confusions, insurrections,
obstructions; who knows if not by conflagration and
despair! It is a lesson inclusive of all other lessons; the
hardest of all lessons to learn.

One thing I do know: Those Apes, chattering on the
branches by the Dead Sea, never got it learned; but
chatter there to this day. To them no Moses need come
a second time; a thousand Moseses would be but so many
painted Phantasms, interesting Fellow-Apes of new strange
aspect,—whom they would 'invite to dinner,' be glad to
meet with in lion-soirées. To them the voice of Prophecy,
of heavenly monition, is quite ended. They chatter there,
all Heaven shut to them, to the end of the world. The
unfortunates! Oh, what is dying of hunger, with honest
tools in your hand, with a manful purpose in your heart,
and much real labour lying round you done, in comparison?
You honestly quit your tools; quit a most muddy confused coil of sore work, short rations, of sorrows, dispirit-

ments and contradictions, having now honestly done with
it all;—and await, not entirely in a distracted manner,
what the Supreme Powers, and the Silences and the
Eternities may have to say to you.

A second thing I know: This lesson will have to
be learned,—under penalties! England will either learn
it, or England also will cease to exist among Nations.
England will either learn to reverence its Heroes, and dis-
criminate them from its Sham-Heroes and Valets and
gaslighted Histrios; and to prize them as the audible
God's-voice, amid all inane jargons and temporary market-
cries, and say to them with heart-loyalty, " Be ye King
and Priest, and Gospel and Guidance for us: " or else
England will continue to worship new and ever-new
forms of Quackhood, — and so, with what resiliences
and reboundings matters little, go down to the Father
of Quacks! Can I dread such things of England?
Wretched, thick-eyed, gross-hearted mortals, why will
ye worship lies, and ' Stuffed Clothes-suits created by the
ninth-parts of men!' It is not your purses that suffer;
your farm-rents, your commerces, your mill-revenues,
loud as ye lament over these; no, it is not these alone,
but a far deeper than these: it is your souls that lie dead,
crushed down under despicable Nightmares, Atheisms,
Brain-fumes; and are not souls at all, but mere succedanea
for *salt* to keep your bodies and their appetites from
putrefying! Your cotton-spinning and thrice-miraculous
mechanism, what is this too, by itself, but a larger kind of
Animalism? Spiders can spin, Beavers can build and
show contrivance; the Ant lays-up accumulation of
capital, and has, for aught I know, a Bank of Antland.
If there is no soul in man higher than all that, did it reach
to sailing on the cloud-rack and spinning sea-sand; then
I say, man is but an animal, a more cunning kind of brute:
he has no soul, but only a succedaneum for salt. Whereupon, seeing himself to be truly of the beasts that perish,
he ought to admit it, I think;—and also straightway
universally to kill himself; and so, in a manlike manner
at least *end*, and wave these brute-worlds *his* dignified
farewell!—

CHAPTER XIV

SIR JABESH WINDBAG

OLIVER CROMWELL, whose body they hung on their Tyburn gallows because he had found the Christian Religion inexecutable in this country, remains to me by far the remarkablest Governor we have had here for the last five centuries or so. For the last five centuries, there has been no Governor among us with anything like similar talent; and for the last two centuries, no Governor, we may say, with the possibility of similar talent,—with an idea in the heart of him capable of inspiring similar talent, capable of co-existing therewith. When you consider that Oliver believed in a God, the difference between Oliver's position and that of any subsequent Governor of this Country becomes, the more you reflect on it, the more immeasurable!

Oliver, no volunteer in Public Life, but plainly a balloted soldier strictly ordered thither, enters upon Public Life; comports himself there like a man who carried his own life in his hand; like a man whose Great Commander's eye was always on him. Not without results. Oliver, well-advanced in years, finds now, by Destiny and his own Deservings, or as he himself better phrased it, by wondrous successive 'Births of Providence,' the Government of England put into his hands. In senate-house and battle-field, in counsel and in action, in private and in public, this man has proved himself a man: England and the voice of God, through waste awful whirlwinds and environments, speaking to his great heart, summon him to assert formally, in the way of solemn Public Fact and as a new piece of English Law, what informally and by Nature's eternal Law needed no asserting, That he, Oliver, was the Ablest Man of England, the King of England; that he, Oliver, would undertake governing England. His way of making this same 'assertion,' the one way he had of making it, has given rise to immense criticism: but the assertion itself, in what way soever ' made,' is it not somewhat of a solemn one, somewhat of a tremendous one!

And now do but contrast this Oliver with my right honourable friend Sir Jabesh Windbag, Mr. Facing-both-ways, Viscount Mealymouth, Earl of Windlestraw, or what other Cagliostro Cagliostrino, Cagliostraccio, the course of Fortune and Parliamentary Majorities has con-stitutionally guided to that dignity, any time during these last sorrowful hundred-and-fifty years! Windbag, weak in the faith of a God, which he believes only at Church on Sundays, if even then; strong only in the faith that Paragraphs and Plausibilities bring votes; that Force of Public Opinion, as he calls it, is the primal Necessity of Things, and highest God we have:—Windbag, if we will consider him, has a problem set before him which may be ranged in the impossible class. He is a Columbus minded to sail to the indistinct country of NOWHERE, to the indistinct country of WHITHERWARD, by the *friendship* of those same waste-tumbling Water-Alps and howling waltz of All the Winds; not by conquest of them and in spite of them, but by friendship of them, when once *they* have made-up their mind! He is the most original Columbus I ever saw. Nay, his problem is not an impossible one: he will infallibly *arrive* at that same country of NOWHERE; his indistinct Whitherward will be a *Thither*ward! In the Ocean Abysses and Locker of Davy Jones, there certainly enough do he and *his* ship's company, and all their cargo and navigatings, at last find lodgment.

Oliver knew that his America lay THERE, Westward Ho;—and it was not entirely by *friendship* of the Water-Alps, and yeasty insane Froth-Oceans, that he meant to get thither! He sailed accordingly; had compass-card, and Rules of Navigation,—older and greater than these Froth-Oceans, old as the Eternal God! Or again, do but think of this. Windbag in these his probable five years of office has to prosper and get Paragraphs: the Paragraphs of these five years must be his salvation, or he is a lost man; redemption nowhere in the Worlds or in the Times discoverable for him. Oliver too would like

his Paragraphs; successes, popularities in these five years
are not undesirable to him: but mark, I say, this enormous
circumstance: *after* these five years are gone and done,
comes an Eternity for Oliver! Oliver has to appear before
the Most High Judge: the utmost flow of Paragraphs,
the utmost ebb of them, is now, in strictest arithmetic,
verily no matter at all; its exact value *zero;* an account
altogether erased! Enormous:—which a man, in these
days, hardly fancies with an effort! Oliver's Paragraphs
are all done, his battles, division-lists, successes all
summed: and now in that awful unerring Court of
Review, the real question first rises, Whether he has
succeeded at all; whether he has not been defeated
miserably forevermore? Let him come with world-wide
Io-Pæans these avail him not. Let him come covered
over with the world's execrations, gashed with ignominious
death-wounds, the gallows-rope about his neck: what
avails that? The word is, Come thou brave and faithful;
the word is, Depart thou quack and accursed!

O Windbag, my right honourable friend, in very truth
I pity thee. I say, these Paragraphs, and low or loud
votings of thy poor fellow-blockheads of mankind, will
never guide thee in any enterprise at all. Govern a
country on such guidance? Thou canst not make a pair
of shoes, sell a pennyworth of tape, on such. No, thy
shoes are vamped up falsely to meet the market; behold,
the leather only *seemed* to be tanned; thy shoes melt
under me to rubbishy pulp, and are not veritable mud-
defying shoes, but plausible vendible similitudes of shoes,
—thou unfortunate, and I! O my right honourable
friend, when the Paragraphs flowed in, who was like Sir
Jabesh? On the swelling tide he mounted; higher,
higher, triumphant, heaven-high. But the Paragraphs
again ebbed out, as unwise Paragraphs needs must:
Sir Jabesh lies stranded, sunk and forever sinking in
ignominious ooze; the Mud-nymphs, and ever-deepening bottomless Oblivion, his portion to eternal time.
' Posterity ' ? Thou appealest to Posterity, thou? My
right honourable friend, what will Posterity do for thee!
The voting of Posterity, were it continued through

centuries in thy favour, will be quite inaudible, extra-
forensic, without any effect whatever. Posterity can do
simply nothing for a man; nor even seem to do much
if the man be not brainsick. Besides, to tell the truth,
the bets are a thousand to one, Posterity will not hear
of thee, my right honourable friend! Posterity, I have
found, has generally his own windbags sufficiently
trumpeted in all market-places, and no leisure to attend
to ours. Posterity, which has made of Norse Odin a
similitude, and of Norman William a brute monster, what
will or can it make of English Jabesh? O Heavens,
' Posterity!'—

"These poor persecuted Scotch Covenanters," said I
to my inquiring Frenchman, in such stinted French as
stood at command, "*ils s'en appelaient à*"—"*A la
Postérité*," interrupted he, helping me out.—"*Ah,
Monsieur, non, mille fois non!* They appealed to the
Eternal God; not to Posterity at all! *C'était différent.*"

CHAPTER XV

MORRISON AGAIN

NEVERTHELESS, O Advanced-Liberal, one cannot promise
thee any 'New Religion,' for some time; to say truth,
I do not think we have the smallest chance of any! Will
the candid reader, by way of closing this Book Third,
listen to a few transient remarks on that subject?

Candid readers have not lately met with any man who
had less notion to interfere with their Thirty-Nine or
other Church-Articles; wherewith, very helplessly as is
like, they may have struggled to form for themselves
some not inconceivable hypothesis about this Universe,
and their own Existence there. Superstition, my friend,
is far from me; Fanaticism, for any *Fanum* likely to arise
soon on this Earth, is far. A man's Church-Articles are
surely articles of price to him; and in these times one
has to be tolerant of many strange 'Articles,' and of

many still stranger ' No-articles,' which go about placarding themselves in a very distracted manner,—the numerous long placard-poles, and questionable infirm paste-pots, interfering with one's peaceable thoroughfare sometimes!

Fancy a man, moreover, recommending his fellow men to believe in God, that so Chartism might abate, and the Manchester Operatives be got to spin peaceably! The idea is more distracted than any placard-pole seen hitherto in a public thoroughfare of men! My friend, if thou ever do come to believe in God, thou wilt find all Chartism, Manchester riot, Parliamentary incompetence, Ministries of Windbag, and the wildest Social Dissolutions, and the burning-up of this entire Planet, a most small matter in comparison. Brother, this Planet, I find, is but an inconsiderable sand-grain in the continents of Being: this Planet's poor temporary interests, thy interests and my interests there, when I look fixedly into that eternal Light-Sea and Flame-Sea with *its* eternal interests, dwindle literally into Nothing; my speech of it is—silence for the while. I will as soon think of making Galaxies and Star-Systems to guide little herring-vessels by, as of preaching Religion that the Constable may continue possible. O my Advanced-Liberal friend, this new second progress, of proceeding ' to invent God,' is a very strange one! Jacobinism unfolded into Saint-Simonism bodes innumerable blessed things; but the thing itself might draw tears from a Stoic!—As for me, some twelve or thirteen New Religions, heavy Packets, most of them unfranked, having arrived here from various parts of the world, in a space of six calendar months, I have instructed my invaluable friend the Stamped Postman to introduce no more of them, if the charge exceed one penny.

Henry of Essex, dwelling in that Thames Island, ' near to Reading Abbey,' had a religion. But was it in virtue of his seeing armed Phantasms of St. Edmund ' on the rim of the horizon,' looking minatory on him? Had that, intrinsically, anything to do with his religion at all? Henry of Essex's religion was the Inner Light or Moral Conscience of his own soul; such as is vouchsafed still to all souls of men;—which Inner Light shone here ' through such intellectual and other media ' as there were; producing ' Phantasms,' Kircherean Visual-Spectra, according to circumstances! It is so with all men. The clearer my Inner Light may shine, through the *less* turbid media, the *fewer* Phantasms it may produce,—the gladder surely shall I be, and not the sorrier! Hast thou reflected, O serious reader, Advanced-Liberal or other, that the one end, essence, use of all religion past, present and to come, was this only: To keep that same Moral Conscience or Inner Light of ours alive and shining;—which certainly the ' Phantasms ' and the ' turbid media ' were not essential for! All religion was here to remind us, better or worse, of what we already know better or worse, of the quite *infinite* difference there is between a Good man and a Bad; to bid us love infinitely the one, abhor and avoid infinitely the other,—strive infinitely to *be* the one, and not to be the other. ' All religion issues in due Practical Hero-worship.' He that has a soul unasphyxied will never want a religion; he that has a soul asphyxied, reduced to a succedaneum for salt, will never find any religion, though you rose from the dead to preach him one.

But indeed, when men and reformers ask for ' a religion,' it is analogous to their asking, ' What would you have us to do? ' and suchlike. They fancy that their religion too shall be a kind of Morrison's Pill, which they have only to swallow once, and all will be well. Resolutely once gulp-down your Religion, your Morrison's Pill, you have it all plain sailing now: you can follow your affairs, your no-affairs, go along money-hunting, pleasure-hunting, dilettanteing, dangling, and miming and chattering like a Dead-Sea Ape: your Morrison will do your business for you. Men's notions are very strange!—Brother, I say there is not, was not, nor will ever be, in the wide circle of Nature, any Pill or Religion of that character. Man cannot afford thee such; for the very gods it is impossible. I advise thee to renounce Morrison; once for all, quit hope of the Universal Pill. For body, for soul, for individual or society, there has not any such article been made. *Non extat.* In Created Nature it is not, was not, will not be. In the void imbroglios of Chaos only, and realms of Bedlam, does some shadow of it hover, to bewilder and bemock the poor inhabitants *there.*

Rituals, Liturgies, Creeds, Hierarchies; all this is not religion; all this, were it dead as Odinism, as Fetishism, does not kill religion at all! It is Stupidity alone, with never so many rituals, that kills religion. Is not this still a World? Spinning Cotton under Arkwright and Adam Smith; founding Cities by the Fountain of Juturna, on the Janiculum Mount; tilling Canaan under Prophet Samuel and Psalmist David, man is ever man; the missionary of Unseen Powers; and great and victorious, while he continues true to his mission; mean, miserable, foiled, and at last annihilated and trodden out of sight and memory, when he proves untrue. Brother, thou art a Man, I think; thou art not a mere building Beaver, or two-legged Cotton-Spider; thou hast verily a Soul in thee, asphyxied or otherwise! Sooty Manchester,—it too is built on the infinite Abysses; overspanned by the skyey Firmaments; and there is birth in it, and death in it;— and it is every whit as wonderful, as fearful, unimaginable, as the oldest Salem or Prophetic City. Go or stand, in what time, in what place we will, are there not Immensities, Eternities over us, around us, in us:

> ' Solemn before us,
>   Veiled, the dark Portal,
>   Goal of all mortal:—
>   Stars silent rest o'er us,
>   Graves under us silent! '

Between *these* two great Silences, the hum of all our spinning cylinders, Trades - Unions, Anti - Corn - Law Leagues and Carlton Clubs goes on. Stupidity itself ought to pause a little and consider that. I tell thee, through all thy Ledgers, Supply-and-demand Philosophies, and daily most modern melancholy Business and Cant, there does shine the presence of a Primeval Unspeakable; and thou wert wise to recognise, not with lips only, that same!

The Maker's Laws, whether they are promulgated in Sinai Thunder, to the ear or imagination, or quite otherwise promulgated, are the Laws of God; transcendent, everlasting, imperatively demanding obedience from all men. This, without any thunder, or with never so much thunder, thou, if there be any soul left in thee, canst know of a truth. The Universe, I say, is made by Law; the great Soul of the World is just and not unjust. Look thou, if thou have eyes or soul left, into this great shoreless Incomprehensible: in the heart of its tumultuous Appearances, Embroilments, and mad Time-vortexes, is there not, silent, eternal, an All-just, an All-beautiful; sole Reality and ultimate controlling Power of the whole? This is not a figure of speech; this is a fact. The fact of Gravitation known to all animals, is not surer than this inner Fact, which may be known to all men. He who knows this, it will sink, silent, awful, unspeakable, into his heart. He will say with Faust: "Who *dare* name HIM?" Most rituals or 'namings' he will fall in with at present, are like to be 'namings'—which shall be nameless! In silence, in the Eternal Temple, let him worship, if there be no fit word. Such knowledge, the crown of his whole spiritual being, the life of his life, let him keep and sacredly walk by. He has a religion. Hourly and daily, for himself and for the whole world, a faithful, unspoken, but not ineffectual prayer rises, "Thy will be done." His whole work on Earth is an emblematic spoken or acted prayer, Be the will of God done on earth,—not the Devil's will, or any of the Devil's servants' wills! He has a religion, this man; an everlasting Load-star that beams the brighter in the Heavens, the darker here on Earth grows the night around him. Thou, if thou know not this, what are all rituals, liturgies, mythologies, mass-chantings, turnings of the rotatory calabash? They are as nothing; in a good many respects they are as *less*. Divorced from this, getting half-divorced from this, they are a thing to fill one with a kind of horror; with a sacred inexpressible pity and fear. The most tragical thing a human eye can look on. It was said to the Prophet, "Behold, I will show thee worse things than these:

women weeping to Thammuz." That was the acme of the Prophet's vision,—then as now.

Rituals, Liturgies, Credos, Sinai Thunder: I know more or less the history of these; the rise, progress, decline and fall of these. Can thunder from all the thirty-two azimuths, repeated daily for centuries of years, make God's Laws more godlike to me? Brother, No. Perhaps I am grown to be a man now; and do not need the thunder and the terror any longer! Perhaps I am above being frightened; perhaps it is not Fear, but Reverence alone, that shall now lead me!—Revelations, Inspirations? Yes: and thy own god-created Soul; dost thou not call that a ' revelation?' Who made THEE? Where didst Thou come from? The Voice of Eternity, if thou be not a blasphemer and poor asphyxied mute, speaks with that tongue of thine! *Thou* art the latest Birth of Nature; it is ' the Inspiration of the Almighty ' that giveth *thee* understanding! My brother, my brother!—

Under baleful Atheisms, Mammonisms, Joe-Manton Dilettantisms, with their appropriate Cants and Idolisms, and whatsoever scandalous rubbish obscures and all but extinguishes the soul of man,—religion now is; its Laws, written if not on stone tables, yet on the Azure of Infinitude, in the inner heart of God's Creation, certain as Life, certain as Death! I say the Laws are there, and thou shalt not disobey them. It were better for thee not. Better a hundred deaths than yes. Terrible ' penalties,' withal, if thou still need ' penalties,' are there for disobeying. Dost thou observe, O redtape Politician, that fiery infernal Phenomenon, which men name FRENCH REVOLUTION, sailing, unlooked-for, unbidden; through thy inane Protocol Dominion:—far-seen, with splendour not of Heaven? Ten centuries will see it. There were Tanneries at Meudon for human skins. And Hell, very truly Hell, had power over God's upper Earth for a season. The cruelest Portent that has risen into created Space these ten centuries: let us hail it, with awestruck repentant hearts, as the voice once more of a God, though of one in wrath. Blessed be the God's-voice; for *it* is true, and Falsehoods have to cease before it! But for that same

preternatural quasi-infernal Portent, one could not know
what to make of this wretched world, in these days, at all.
The deplorablest quack-ridden, and now hunger-ridden,
downtrodden Despicability and *Flebile Ludibrium*, of
redtape Protocols, rotatory Calabashes, Poor-Law Bastilles: who is there that could think of *its* being fated
to continue?—

Penalties enough, my brother! This penalty inclusive
of all: Eternal Death to thy own hapless Self, if thou heed
no other. Eternal Death, I say,—with many meanings
old and new, of which let this single one suffice us here:
The eternal impossibility for thee to be aught but a
Chimera, and swift-vanishing deceptive Phantasm, in God's
Creation;— swift - vanishing, never to reappear: why
should *it* reappear! Thou hadst one chance, thou wilt
never have another. Everlasting ages will roll on, and
no other be given thee. The foolishest articulate-speaking soul now extant, may not he say to himself: "A
whole Eternity I waited to be born; and now I have a
whole Eternity waiting to see what I will do when born!"
This is not Theology, this is Arithmetic. And thou but
half-discernest this; thou but half-believest it? Alas,
on the shores of the Dead Sea, on Sabbath, there goes on
a Tragedy!—

But we will leave this of 'Religion;' of which, to say
truth, it is chiefly profitable in these unspeakable days to
keep silence. Thou needest no 'New Religion;' nor art
thou like to get any. Thou hast already more 'religion'
than thou makest use of. This day thou knowest ten
commanded duties, seest in thy mind ten things which
should be done, for one that thou doest! *Do* one of them;
this of itself will show thee ten others which can and shall
be done. "But my future fate?" Yes, thy future fate,
indeed! Thy future fate, while thou makest *it* the chief
question, seems to me — extremely questionable! I do
not think it can be good. Norse Odin, immemorial
centuries ago, did not he, though a poor Heathen, in the
dawn of Time, teach us that for the Dastard there was,
and could be, no good fate; no harbour anywhere, save
down with Hela, in the pool of Night! Dastards, Knaves,

are they that lust for Pleasure, that tremble at Pain. For this world and for the next Dastards are a class of creatures made to be ' arrested; ' they are good for nothing else, can look for nothing else. A greater than Odin has been here. A greater than Odin has taught us — not a greater Dastardism, I hope! My brother, thou must pray for a *soul;* struggle, as with life-and-death energy, to get back thy soul! Know that ' religion ' is no Morrison's Pill from without, but a reawakening of thy own Self from within:—and, above all, leave me alone of thy ' religions ' and ' new religions ' here and elsewhere! I am weary of this sick croaking for a Morrison's-Pill religion; for any and for every such. I want none such; and discern all such to be impossible. The resuscitation of old liturgies fallen dead; much more, the manufacture of new liturgies that will never be alive: how hopeless! Stylitisms, eremite fanaticisms and fakeerisms; spasmodic agonistic posture-makings, and narrow, cramped, morbid, if forever noble wrestlings: all this is not a thing desirable to me. It is a thing the world *has* done once,—when its beard was not grown as now!

And yet there is, at worst, one Liturgy which does remain forever unexceptionable: that of *Praying* (as the old Monks did withal) *by Working.* And indeed the Prayer which accomplished itself in special chapels at stated hours, and went not with a man, rising up from all his Work and Action, at all moments sanctifying the same,—what was it ever good for? ' Work is Worship: ' yes, in a highly considerable sense,—which, in the present state of all ' worship,' who is there that can unfold! He that understands it well, understands the Prophecy of the whole Future; the last Evangel, which has included all others. *Its* cathedral the Dome of Immensity,—hast thou seen it? coped with the star-galaxies; paved with the green mosaic of land and ocean; and for altar, verily, the Star-throne of the Eternal! Its litany and psalmody the noble acts, the heroic work and suffering, and true heart-utterance of all the Valiant of the Sons of Men. Its choir-music the ancient Winds and Oceans, and deep-toned, inarticulate, but most speaking voices of Destiny and History,—supernal ever as of old. Between two great Silences:

> ' Stars silent rest o'er us,
> Graves under us silent! '

Between which two great Silences, do not, as we said, all human Noises, in the naturalest times, most *preter*-naturally march and roll?—

I will insert this also, in a lower strain, from Sauerteig's *Æsthetische Springwurzeln*. ' Worship? ' says he: ' Before that inane tumult of Hearsay filled men's heads, while the world lay yet silent, and the heart true and open, many things were Worship! To the primeval man what-soever good came, descended on him (as, in mere fact, it ever does) direct from God; whatsoever duty lay visible for him, this a Supreme God had prescribed. To the present hour I ask thee, Who else? For the primeval man, in whom dwelt Thought, this Universe was all a Temple; Life everywhere a Worship.

' What Worship, for example, is there not in mere Washing! Perhaps one of the most moral things a man, in common cases, has it in his power to do. Strip thy-self, go into the bath, or were it into the limpid pool and running brook, and there wash and be clean; thou wilt step out again a purer and a better man. This con-sciousness of perfect outer pureness, that to thy skin there now adheres no foreign speck of imperfection, how it radiates in on thee, with cunning symbolic influences, to thy very soul! Thou hast an increase of tendency towards all good things whatsoever. The oldest Eastern Sages, with joy and holy gratitude, had felt it so,—and that it was the Maker's gift and will. Whose else *is* it? It remains a religious duty, from oldest times, in the East. —Nor could Herr Professor Strauss, when I put the question, deny that for us at present it is still such here in the West! To that dingy fuliginous Operative, emerg-ing from his soot-mill, what is the first duty I will prescribe, and offer help towards? That he clean the skin of him. *Can* he pray, by any ascertained method? One knows not entirely:—but with soap and a sufficiency of water, he can wash. Even the dull English feel something of this; they have a saying, "Cleanliness is near akin to Godliness:"—yet never, in any country, saw I operative men worse washed, and, in a climate drenched with the softest cloud-water, such a scarcity of baths!'—Alas, Sauerteig, our 'operative men' are at present short even of potatoes: what 'duty' can you prescribe to them?

Or let us give a glance at China. Our new friend, the Emperor there, is Pontiff of three hundred million men; who do all live and work, these many centuries now; authentically patronised by Heaven so far; and therefore must have some 'religion' of a kind. This Emperor-Pontiff has, in fact, a religious belief of certain Laws of Heaven; observes, with a religious rigour, his 'three thousand punctualities,' given out by men of insight, some sixty generations since, as a legible transcript of the same,—the Heavens do seem to say, not totally an incorrect one. He has not much of a ritual, this Pontiff-Emperor; believes, it is likest, with the old Monks, that 'Labour is Worship.' His most public Act of Worship, it appears, is the drawing solemnly at a certain day, on the green bosom of our Mother Earth, when the Heavens, after dead black winter, have again with their vernal radiances awakened her, a distinct red Furrow with the Plough,—signal that all the Ploughs of China are to begin ploughing and worshipping! It is notable enough. He, in sight of the Seen and Unseen Powers, draws his distinct red Furrow there; saying, and praying, in mute symbolism, so many eloquent things!

If you ask this Pontiff, "Who made him? What is to become of him and us?" he maintains a dignified reserve; waves his hand and pontiff-eyes over the unfathomable deep of Heaven, the 'Tsien,' the azure kingdoms of Infinitude; as if asking, "Is it doubtful that we are right *well* made? Can aught that is *wrong* become of us?"—He and his three hundred millions (it is their chief 'punctuality') visit yearly the Tombs of their Fathers; each man the Tomb of his Father and his Mother: alone there, in silence, with what of 'worship' or of other thought there may be, pauses solemnly each

man; the divine Skies all silent over him; the divine
Graves, and this divinest Grave, all silent under him; the
pulsings of his own soul, if he have any soul, alone audible.
Truly it may be a kind of worship! Truly, if a man
cannot get some glimpse into the Eternities, looking
through this portal,—through what other need he try it?

Our friend the Pontiff-Emperor permits cheerfully,
though with contempt, all manner of Buddists, Bonzes,
Talapoins and suchlike, to build brick Temples, on the
voluntary principle; to worship with what of chantings,
paper-lanterns and tumultuous brayings, pleases them;
and make night hideous, since they find some comfort in
so doing. Cheerfully, though with contempt. He is a
wiser Pontiff than many persons think! He is as yet the
one Chief Potentate or Priest in this Earth who has made
a distinct systematic attempt at what we call the ultimate
result of all religion, ' *Practical* Hero-worship: ' he does
incessantly, with true anxiety, in such way as he can,
search and sift (it would appear) his whole enormous
population for the Wisest born among them; by which
Wisest, as by born Kings, these three hundred million
men are governed. The Heavens, to a certain extent, do
appear to countenance him. These three hundred millions
actually make porcelain, souchong tea, with innumerable
other things; and fight, under Heaven's flag, against
Necessity;—and have fewer Seven-Years Wars, Thirty-
Years Wars, French-Revolution Wars, and infernal fight-
ings with each other, than certain millions elsewhere have!

Nay in our poor distracted Europe itself, in these
newest times, have there not religious voices risen,—with
a religion new and yet the oldest; entirely indisputable
to all hearts of men? Some I do know, who did not call
or think themselves ' Prophets,' far enough from that;
but who were, in very truth, melodious Voices from the
eternal Heart of Nature once again; souls forever venerable to all that have a soul. A French Revolution is one
phenomenon; as complement and spiritual exponent
thereof, a poet Goethe and German Literature is to me
another. The old Secular or Practical World, so to speak,

having gone up in fire, is not here the prophecy and dawn of a new Spiritual World, parent of far nobler, wider, new Practical Worlds? A Life of Antique devoutness, Antique veracity and heroism, has again become possible, is again *seen* actual there, for the most modern man. A phenomenon, as quiet as it is, comparable for greatness to no other! 'The great event for the world is, now as always, the arrival in it of a new Wise Man.' Touches there are, be the Heavens ever thanked, of new Sphere-melody; audible once more, in the infinite jargoning discords and poor scrannel-pipings of the thing called Literature;— priceless there, as the voice of new Heavenly Psalms! Literature, like the old Prayer-Collections of the first centuries, were it 'well selected from and burnt,' contains precious things. For Literature, with all its printing-presses, puffing-engines and shoreless deafening triviality, *is* yet 'the Thought of Thinking Souls.' A sacred 'religion,' if you like the name, does live in the heart of that strange froth-ocean, not wholly froth, which we call Literature; and will more and more disclose itself therefrom;—not now as scorching Fire: the red smoky scorching Fire has purified itself into white sunny Light. Is not Light grander than Fire? It is the same element in a state of purity.

My ingenuous readers, we will march out of this Third Book with a rhythmic word of Goethe's on our lips; a word which perhaps has already sung itself, in dark hours and in bright, through many a heart. To me, finding it devout yet wholly credible and veritable, full of piety yet free of cant; to me, joyfully finding much in it, and joyfully missing so much in it, this little snatch of music, by the greatest German Man, sounds like a stanza in the grand *Road-Song* and *Marching-Song* of our great Teutonic Kindred, wending, wending, valiant and victorious, through the undiscovered Deeps of Time! He calls it *Mason-Lodge*,—not Psalm or Hymn:

> The Mason's ways are
> A type of Existence,
> And his persistence
> Is as the days are
> Of men in this world.

The Future hides in it
Gladness and sorrow;
We press still thorow.
Nought that abides in it
Daunting us,—onward.

And solemn before us,
Veiled, the dark Portal,
Goal of all mortal:—
Stars silent rest o'er us,
Graves under us silent!

While earnest thou gazest,
Comes boding of terror,
Comes phantasm and error,
Perplexes the bravest
With doubt and misgiving.

But heard are the Voices,—
Heard are the Sages,
The Worlds and the Ages:
" Choose well; your choice is
Brief and yet endless:

Here eyes do regard you,
In Eternity's stillness;
Here is all fulness,
Ye brave, to reward you;
Work, and despair not."

BOOK IV.—HOROSCOPE

CHAPTER I

ARISTOCRACIES

To predict the Future, to manage the Present, would not be so impossible, had not the Past been so sacrilegiously mishandled; effaced, and what is worse, defaced! The Past cannot be seen; the Past, looked at through the medium of ' Philosophical History ' in these times, cannot even be *not* seen: it is misseen; affirmed to have existed, —and to have been a godless impossibility. Your Norman Conquerors, true royal souls, crowned kings as such, were vulturous irrational tyrants: your Becket was a noisy egoist and hypocrite; getting his brains spilt on the floor of Canterbury Cathedral, to secure the main chance,— somewhat uncertain how! ' Policy, Fanaticism; ' or say ' Enthusiasm,' even ' honest Enthusiasm,'—ah yes, of course:

> ' The Dog, to gain his private ends,
> *Went* mad, and bit the Man! '—

For in truth, the eye sees in all things ' what it brought with it the means of seeing.' A godless century, looking back on centuries that were godly, produces portraitures more miraculous than any other. All was inane discord in the Past; brute Force bore rule everywhere; Stupidity, savage Unreason, fitter for Bedlam than for a human World! Whereby indeed it becomes sufficiently natural that the like qualities, in new sleeker habiliments, should continue in our time to rule. Millions enchanted in Bastille Workhouses; Irish Widows proving their relationship by typhus-fever: what would you have? It was ever so, or worse. Man's History, was it not always even this: The cookery and eating-up of imbecile Dupedom by successful Quackhood; the battle, with various weapons,

of vulturous Quack and Tyrant against vulturous Tyrant
and Quack? No God was in the Past Time; nothing but
Mechanisms and Chaotic Brute-Gods:—how shall the
poor ' Philosophic Historian,' to whom his own century
is all godless, see any God in other centuries?

Men believe in Bibles, and disbelieve in them: but of
all Bibles the frightfulest to disbelieve in is this ' Bible of
Universal History.' This is the Eternal Bible and God's-
Book, ' which every born man,' till once the soul and
eyesight are extinguished in him, ' can and must, with
his own eyes, see the God's-Finger writing!' To dis-
credit this, is an *infidelity* like no other. Such infidelity
you would punish, if not by fire and faggot, which are
difficult to manage in our times, yet by the most peremptory order, To hold its peace till it got something
wiser to say. Why should the blessed Silence be broken
into noises, to communicate only the like of this? If
the Past have no God's-Reason in it, nothing but Devil's-
Unreason, let the Past be eternally forgotten: mention
it no more;—we whose ancestors were all hanged, why
should we talk of ropes!

It is, in brief, not true that men ever lived by Delirium,
Hypocrisy, Injustice, or any form of Unreason, since they
came to inhabit this Planet. It is not true that they
ever did, or ever will, live except by the reverse of these.
Men will again be taught this. Their acted History will
then again be a Heroism; their written History, what it
once was, an Epic. Nay, forever it is either such, or
else it virtually is—Nothing. Were it written in a
thousand volumes, the Unheroic of such volumes hastens
incessantly to be forgotten: the net content of an Alex-
andrian Library of Unheroics is, and will ultimately show
itself to be, *zero*. What man is interested to remember
it ; have not all men, at all times, the liveliest interest to
forget it?—' Revelations,' if not celestial, then infernal,
will teach us that God is; we shall then, if needful,
discern without difficulty that He has always been! The
Dryasdust Philosophisms and enlightened Scepticisms of
the Eighteenth Century, historical and other, will have
to survive for a while with the Physiologists, as a

memorable *Nightmare-Dream*. All this haggard epoch,
with its ghastly Doctrines, and death's-head Philosophies
'teaching by example' or otherwise, will one day have
become, what to our Moslem friends their godless ages
are, 'the Period of Ignorance.'

If the convulsive struggles of the last Half-Century
have taught poor struggling convulsed Europe any truth,
it may perhaps be this as the essence of innumerable
others: That Europe requires a real Aristocracy, a real
Priesthood, or it cannot continue to exist. Huge French
Revolutions, Napoleonisms, then Bourbonisms with their
corollary of Three Days, finishing in very unfinal Louis-
Philippisms: all this ought to be didactic! All this
may have taught us, That False Aristocracies are insupportable; that No-Aristocracies, Liberty-and-Equali-
ties are impossible; that true Aristocracies are at once
indispensable and not easily attained.

Aristocracy and Priesthood, a Governing Class and a
Teaching Class: these two, sometimes separate, and endeavouring to harmonise themselves, sometimes conjoined
as one, and the King a Pontiff-King:—there did no Society
exist without these two vital elements, there will none
exist. It lies in the very nature of man: you will visit
no remotest village in the most republican country of
the world, where virtually or actually you do not find
these two powers at work. Man, little as he may suppose
it, is necessitated to obey superiors. He is a social being
in virtue of this necessity; nay he could not be gregarious
otherwise. He obeys those whom he esteems better than
himself, wiser, braver; and will forever obey such; and
even be ready and delighted to do it.

The Wiser, Braver: these, a Virtual Aristocracy everywhere and everywhen, do in all Societies that reach any
articulate shape, develop themselves into a ruling class,
an Actual Aristocracy, with settled modes of operating,
what are called laws and even *private-laws* or privileges,
and so forth; very notable to look upon in this world.—
Aristocracy and Priesthood, we say, are sometimes united.
For indeed the Wiser and the Braver are properly but

one class; no wise man but needed first of all to be a brave man, or he never had been wise. The noble Priest was always a noble *Aristos* to begin with, and something more to end with. Your Luther, your Knox, your Anselm, Becket, Abbot Samson, Samuel Johnson, if they had not been brave enough, by what possibility could they ever have been wise?—If, from accident or forethought, this your Actual Aristocracy have got discriminated into Two Classes, there can be no doubt but the Priest Class is the more dignified; supreme over the other, as governing head is over active hand. And yet in practice again, it is likeliest the reverse will be found arranged;—a sign that the arrangement is already vitiated; that a split is introduced into it, which will widen and widen till the whole be rent asunder.

In England, in Europe generally, we may say that these two Virtualities have unfolded themselves into Actualities, in by far the noblest and richest manner any region of the world ever saw. A spiritual Guideship, a practical Governorship, fruit of the grand conscious endeavours, say rather of the immeasurable unconscious instincts and necessities of men, have established themselves; very strange to behold. Everywhere, while so much has been forgotten, you find the King's Palace, and the Viceking's Castle, Mansion, Manorhouse; till there is not an inch of ground from sea to sea but has both its King and Viceking, long due series of Vicekings, its Squire, Earl, Duke or whatever the title of him,—to whom you have given the land, that he may govern you in it.

More touching still, there is not a hamlet where poor peasants congregate, but, by one means and another, a Church-Apparatus has been got together,—roofed edifice, with revenues and belfries; pulpit, reading-desk, with Books and Methods: possibility, in short, and strict prescription, That a man stand there and speak of spiritual things to men. It is beautiful;—even in its great obscuration and decadence, it is among the beautifulest, most touching objects one sees on the Earth. This Speaking Man has indeed, in these times, wandered terribly from the point; has, alas, as it were, totally lost sight of the point: yet, at bottom, whom have we to compare with him? Of all public functionaries boarded and lodged on the Industry of Modern Europe, is there one worthier of the board he has? A man even professing, and never so languidly making still some endeavour, to save the souls of men: contrast him with a man professing to do little but shoot the partridges of men! I wish he could find the point again, this Speaking One; and stick to it with tenacity, with deadly energy; for there is need of him yet! The Speaking Function, this of Truth coming to us with a living voice, nay in a living shape, and as a concrete practical exemplar: this, with all our Writing and Printing Functions, has a perennial place. Could he but find the point again,—take the old spectacles off his nose, and looking up discover, almost in contact with him, what the *real* Satanas, and soul-devouring, world-devouring *Devil*, now is! Original Sin and suchlike are bad enough, I doubt not: but distilled Gin, dark Ignorance, Stupidity, dark Corn-Law, Bastille and Company, what are they! *Will* he discover our new real Satan, whom he has to fight; or go on droning through his old nose-spectacles about old extinct Satans; and never see the real one, till he *feel* him at his own throat and ours? That is a question, for the world! Let us not intermeddle with it here.

Sorrowful, phantasmal as this same Double Aristocracy of Teachers and Governors now looks, it is worth all men's while to know that the purport of it is and remains noble and most real. Dryasdust, looking merely at the surface, is greatly in error as to those ancient Kings. William Conqueror, William Rufus or Redbeard, Stephen Curthose himself, much more Henry Beauclerc and our brave Plantagenet Henry: the life of these men was not a vulturous Fighting; it was a valorous Governing,—to which occasionally Fighting did, and alas must yet, though far seldomer now, superadd itself as an accident, a distressing impedimental adjunct. The fighting too was indispensable, for ascertaining who had the might over whom, the right over whom. By much hard fighting, as we once said, ' the unrealities, beaten into dust, flew gradually off; ' and left the plain reality and fact, " Thou

stronger than I; thou wiser than I; thou king, and subject I," in a somewhat clearer condition.

Truly we cannot enough admire, in those Abbot-
Samson and William-Conqueror times, the arrangement
they had made of their Governing Classes. Highly
interesting to observe how the sincere insight, on their
part, into what did, of primary necessity, behove to be
accomplished, had led them to the way of accomplishing
it, and in the course of time to get it accomplished! No
imaginary Aristocracy would serve their turn; and accordingly they attained a real one. The Bravest men, who,
it is ever to be repeated and remembered, are also on the
whole the Wisest, Strongest, everyway Best, had here,
with a respectable degree of accuracy, been got selected;
seated each on his piece of territory, which was lent him,
then gradually given him, that he might govern it. These
Vicekings, each on his portion of the common soil of
England, with a Head King over all, were a ' Virtuality
perfected into an Actuality ' really to an astonishing extent.

For those were rugged stalwart ages; full of earnestness,
of a rude God's-truth:—nay, at any rate, their *quilting*
was so unspeakably *thinner* than ours; Fact came swiftly
on them, if at any time they had yielded to Phantasm!
' The Knaves and Dastards ' had to be ' arrested ' in some
measure; or the world, almost within year and day, found
that it could not live. The Knaves and Dastards accordingly were got arrested. Dastards upon the very throne
had to be got arrested, and taken off the throne,—by such
methods as there were; by the roughest method, if there
chanced to be no smoother one! Doubtless there was
much harshness of operation, much severity; as indeed
government and surgery are often somewhat severe.
Gurth, born thrall of Cedric, it is like, got cuffs as often
as pork-parings, if he misdemeaned himself; but Gurth
did belong to Cedric: no human creature then went about
connected with nobody; left to go his way into Bastilles
or worse, under *Laissez-faire ;* reduced to prove his relationship by dying of typhus-fever!—Days come when
there is no King in Israel, but every man is his own king,
doing that which is right in his own eyes;—and tarbarrels

are burnt to 'Liberty,' 'Tenpound Franchise' and the like, with considerable effect in various ways!—

That Feudal Aristocracy, I say, was no imaginary one. To a respectable degree, its *Jarls*, what we now call Earls, were *Strong-Ones* in fact as well as etymology; its Dukes *Leaders*; its Lords *Law-wards*. They did all the Soldiering and Police of the country, all the Judging, Law-making, even the Church-Extension; whatsoever in the way of Governing, of Guiding and Protecting could be done. It was a Land Aristocracy; it managed the Governing of this English People, and had the reaping of the Soil of England in return. It is, in many senses, the Law of Nature, this same Law of Feudalism;—no right Aristocracy but a Land one! The curious are invited to meditate upon it in these days. Soldiering, Police and Judging, Church-Extension, nay real Government and Guidance, all this was actually *done* by the Holders of the Land in return for their Land. How much of it is now done by them; done by anybody? Good Heavens, "Laissez-faire, Do ye nothing, eat your wages and sleep," is everywhere the passionate half-wise cry of this time; and they will not so much as do nothing, but must do mere Corn-Laws! We raise Fifty-two millions, from the general mass of us, to get our Governing done—or, alas, to get ourselves persuaded that it is done: and the 'peculiar burden of the Land' is to pay, not all this, but to pay, as I learn, one twenty-fourth part of all this. Our first Chartist Parliament, or Oliver *Redivivus*, you would say, will know where to lay the new taxes of England! —Or, alas, taxes? If we made the Holders of the Land pay every shilling still of the expense of Governing the Land, what were all that? The Land, by mere hired Governors, cannot be got governed. You cannot hire men to govern the Land; it is by a mission not contracted for in the Stock-Exchange, but felt in their own hearts as coming out of Heaven, that men can govern a Land. The mission of a Land Aristocracy is a *sacred* one, in both the senses of that old word. The footing it stands on, at present, might give rise to thoughts other than of Corn-Laws!—

But truly a 'Splendour of God,' as in William Conqueror's rough oath, did dwell in those old rude veracious ages; did inform, more and more, with a heavenly nobleness, all departments of their work and life. Phantasms could not yet walk abroad in mere Cloth Tailorage; they were at least Phantasms 'on the rim of the horizon,' pencilled there by an eternal Lightbeam from within. A most 'practical' Hero-worship went on, unconsciously or half-consciously, everywhere. A Monk Samson, with a maximum of two shillings in his pocket, could, without ballot-box, be made a Viceking of, being seen to be worthy. The difference between a good man and a bad man was as yet felt to be, what it forever is, an immeasurable one. Who *durst* have elected a Pandarus Dogdraught, in those days, to any office, Carlton Club, Senatorship, or place whatsoever? It was felt that the arch Satanas and no other had a clear right of property in Pandarus; that it were better for you to have no hand in Pandarus, to keep out of Pandarus his neighbourhood! Which is, to this hour, the mere fact; though for the present, alas, the forgotten fact. I think they were comparatively blessed times those, in their way! 'Violence,' 'war,' 'disorder:' well, what is war, and death itself, to such a perpetual life-in-death, and 'peace, peace, where there is no peace'! Unless some Hero-worship, in its new appropriate form, can return, this world does not promise to be very habitable long.

Old Anselm, exiled Archbishop of Canterbury, one of the purest-minded 'men of genius,' was travelling to make his appeal to Rome against King Rufus,—a man of rough ways, in whom the 'inner Lightbeam' shone very fitfully. It is beautiful to read, in Monk Eadmer, how the Continental populations welcomed and venerated this Anselm, as no French population now venerates Jean-Jacques or giant-killing Voltaire; as not even an American population now venerates a Schnüspel the distinguished Novelist! They had, by phantasy and true insight, the intensest conviction that a God's-Blessing dwelt in this Anselm,—as is my conviction too. They crowded round, with bent knees and enkindled hearts, to receive his blessing, to hear his voice, to see the light of his face. My blessings on them and on him!—But the notablest was a certain necessitous or covetous Duke of Burgundy, in straitened circumstances we shall hope,—who reflected that in all likelihood this English Archbishop, going towards Rome to appeal, must have taken store of cash with him to bribe the Cardinals. Wherefore he of Burgundy, for his part, decided to lie in wait and rob him. ' In an open space of a wood,' some ' wood ' then green and growing, eight centuries ago, in Burgundian Land,—this fierce Duke, with fierce steel followers, shaggy, savage, as the Russian bear, dashes out on the weak old Anselm; who is riding along there, on his small quiet-going pony; escorted only by Eadmer and another poor Monk on ponies; and, except small modicum of roadmoney, not a gold coin in his possession. The steelclad Russian bear emerges, glaring: the old white-bearded man starts not,—paces on unmoved, looking into him with those clear old earnest eyes, with that venerable sorrowful time-worn face; of whom no man or thing need be afraid, and who also is afraid of no created man or thing. The fire-eyes of his Burgundian Grace meet these clear eye-glances, convey them swift to his heart: he bethinks him that probably this feeble, fearless, hoary Figure has in it something of the Most High God; that probably he shall be damned if he meddle with it,—that, on the whole, he had better not. He plunges, the rough savage, from his war-horse, down to his knees; embraces the feet of old Anselm: he too begs his blessing; orders men to escort him, guard him from being robbed, and under dread penalties see him safe on his way. *Per os Dei,* as his Majesty was wont to ejaculate!

Neither is this quarrel of Rufus and Anselm, of Henry and Becket uninstructive to us. It was, at bottom, a great quarrel. For, admitting that Anselm was full of divine blessing, he by no means included in him all forms of divine blessing:—there were far other forms withal, which he little dreamed of; and William Redbeard was unconsciously the representative and spokesman of these. In truth, could your divine Anselm, your divine Pope

Gregory have had their way, the results had been very notable. Our Western World had all become a European Thibet, with one Grand Lama sitting at Rome; our one honourable business that of singing mass, all day and all night. Which would not in the least have suited us. The Supreme Powers willed it not so.

It was as if King Redbeard unconsciously, addressing Anselm, Becket and the others, had said: "Right Reverend, your Theory of the Universe is indisputable by man or devil. To the core of our heart we feel that this divine thing, which you call Mother Church, does fill the whole world hitherto known, and is and shall be all our salvation and all our desire. And yet—and yet— Behold, though it is an unspoken secret, the world is *wider* than any of us think, Right Reverend! Behold, there are yet other immeasurable Sacrednesses in this that you call Heathenism, Secularity! On the whole, I, in an obscure but most rooted manner, feel that I cannot comply with you. Western Thibet and perpetual mass-chanting,—No. I am, so to speak, in the family-way; with child, of I know not what,—certainly of something far different from this! I have — *Per os Dei*, I have Manchester Cotton-trades, Bromwicham Iron-trades, American Commonwealths, Indian Empires, Steam Mechanisms, and Shakspeare Dramas, in my belly; and cannot do it, Right Reverend!"—So accordingly it was decided: and Saxon Becket spilt his life in Canterbury Cathedral, as Scottish Wallace did on Tower-hill, and as generally a noble man and martyr has to do,—not for nothing; no, but for a divine something other than *he* had altogether calculated. We will now quit this of the hard, organic, but limited Feudal Ages; and glance timidly into the immense Industrial Ages, as yet all inorganic, and in a quite pulpy condition, requiring desperately to harden themselves into some organism!

Our Epic having now become *Tools and the Man*, it is more than usually impossible to prophesy the Future. The boundless Future does lie there, predestined, nay already extant though unseen; hiding, in its Continents of Darkness, 'gladness and sorrow:' but the supremest intelligence of man cannot prefigure much of it:—the united intelligence and effort of All Men in all coming generations, this alone will gradually prefigure it, and figure and form it into a seen fact! Straining our eyes hitherto, the utmost effort of intelligence sheds but some most glimmering dawn, a little way into its dark enormous Deeps: only huge outlines loom uncertain on the sight; and the ray of prophecy, at a short distance, expires. But may we not say, here as always, Sufficient for the day is the evil thereof! To shape the whole Future is not our problem; but only to shape faithfully a small part of it, according to rules already known. It is perhaps possible for each of us, who will with due earnestness inquire, to ascertain clearly what he, for his own part, ought to do: this let him, with true heart, do, and continue doing. The general issue will, as it has always done, rest well with a Higher Intelligence than ours.

One grand ' outline,' or even two, many earnest readers may perhaps, at this stage of the business, be able to prefigure for themselves,—and draw some guidance from. One prediction, or even two, are already possible. For the Life-Tree Igdrasil, in all its new developments, is the selfsame world-old Life-tree: having found an element or elements there, running from the very roots of it in Hela's Realms, in the Well of Mimer and of the Three Nornas or TIMES, up to this present hour of it in our own hearts, we conclude that such will have to continue. A man has, in his own soul, an Eternal; can read something of the Eternal there, if he will look! He already knows what will continue; what cannot, by any means or appliance whatsoever, be made to continue!

One wide and widest ' outline ' ought really, in all ways, to be becoming clear to us; this namely: That a ' Splendour of God,' in one form or other, will have to unfold itself from the heart of these our Industrial Ages too; or they will never get themselves ' organised;' but continue chaotic, distressed, distracted evermore, and have to perish in frantic suicidal dissolution. A second ' outline ' or prophecy, narrower, but also wide enough, seems not less certain: That there will again be a King in Israel; a system of Order and Government; and every man shall, in some measure, see himself constrained to do that which is right in the King's eyes. This too we may call a sure element of the Future; for this too is of the Eternal;—this too is of the Present, though hidden from most; and without it no fibre of the Past ever was. An actual new Sovereignty, Industrial Aristocracy, real not imaginary Aristocracy, is indispensable and indubitable for us.

But what an Aristocracy; on what new, far more complex and cunningly devised conditions than that old Feudal fighting one! For we are to bethink us that the Epic verily is not *Arms and the Man,* but *Tools and the Man,*—an infinitely wider kind of Epic. And again we are to bethink us that men cannot now be bound to men by *brass-collars,*—not at all: that this brass-collar method, in all figures of it, has vanished out of Europe forevermore! Huge Democracy, walking the streets everywhere in its Sack Coat, has asserted so much; irrevocably, brooking no reply! True enough, man *is* forever the ' born thrall ' of certain men, born master of certain other men, born equal of certain others, let him acknowledge the fact or not. It is unblessed for him when he cannot acknowledge this fact; he is in the chaotic state, ready to perish, till he do get the fact acknowledged. But no man is, or can henceforth be, the brass-collar thrall of any man; you will have to bind him by other, far nobler and cunninger methods. Once for all, he is to be loose of the brass collar, to have a scope *as* wide as his faculties now are:—will he not be all the usefuler to you in that new state? Let him go abroad as a trusted one, as a free one; and return home to you with rich earnings at night! Gurth could only tend pigs; this one will build cities, conquer waste worlds.— How, in conjunction with inevitable Democracy, indispensable Sovereignty is to exist: certainly it is the hugest question ever heretofore propounded to Mankind! The solution of which is work for long years and centuries. Years and centuries, of one knows not what complexion;—blessed or unblessed, according as they shall, with earnest valiant effort, make progress therein, or, in slothful unveracity and dilettantism, only talk of making progress.

For either progress therein, or swift and ever swifter progress towards dissolution, is henceforth a necessity.

It is of importance that this grand reformation were begun; that Corn-Law Debatings and other jargon, little less than delirious in such a time, had fled far away, and left us room to begin! For the evil has grown practical, extremely conspicuous; if it be not seen and provided for, the blindest fool will have to feel it ere long. There is much that can wait; but there is something also that cannot wait. With millions of eager Working Men imprisoned in ‘ Impossibility ’ and Poor-Law Bastilles, it is time that some means of dealing with them were trying to become ‘ possible ’! Of the Government of England, of all articulate-speaking functionaries, real and imaginary Aristocracies, of me and of thee, it is imperatively demanded, “ How do you mean to manage these men? Where are they to find a supportable existence? What is to become of them,—and of you! ”

CHAPTER II

BRIBERY COMMITTEE

IN the case of the late Bribery Committee, it seemed to be the conclusion of the soundest practical minds that Bribery could not be put down; that Pure Election was a thing we had seen the last of, and must now go on without, as we best could. A conclusion not a little startling; to which it requires a practical mind of some seasoning to reconcile yourself at once! It seems, then, we are henceforth to get ourselves constituted Legislators not according to what merit we may have, or even what merit we may seem to have, but according to the length of our purse, and our frankness, impudence and dexterity in laying out the contents of the same. Our theory, written down in all books and law-books, spouted forth from all barrel-heads, is perfect purity of Tenpound Franchise, absolute sincerity of question put and answer given;—and our practice is irremediable bribery; irremediable, unpunishable, which you will do more harm than good by attempting to punish! Once more, a very startling conclusion indeed; which, whatever the soundest practical minds in Parliament may think of it, invites all British men to meditations of various kinds.

A Parliament, one would say, which proclaims itself elected and eligible by bribery, tells the Nation that is governed by it a piece of singular news. Bribery: have we reflected what bribery is? Bribery means not only length of purse, which is neither qualification nor the contrary for legislating well; but it means dishonesty, and even impudent dishonesty;—brazen insensibility to lying and to making others lie; total oblivion, and flinging overboard, for the nonce, of any real thing you can call veracity, morality; with dextrous putting-on the cast-clothes of that real thing, and strutting about in them! What Legislating can you get out of a man in that fatal situation? None that will profit much, one would think! A Legislator who has left his veracity lying on the door-threshold, he, why verily *he*—ought to be sent out to seek it again!

Heavens, what an improvement, were there once fairly in Downing-street an Election-Office opened, with a tariff of Boroughs! Such and such a population, amount of property-tax, ground-rental, extent of trade; returns two Members, returns one Member, for so much money down: Ipswich so many thousands, Nottingham so many,—as they happened, one by one, to fall into this new Downing-street Schedule A! An incalculable improvement, in comparison: for now at least you have it fairly by length of purse, and leave the dishonesty, the impudence, the unveracity all handsomely aside. Length of purse and desire to be a Legislator ought to get a man into Parliament, not *with*, but if possible *without* the unveracity, the impudence and the dishonesty! Length of purse and desire, these are, as intrinsic qualifications, correctly equal to zero; but they are not yet *less* than zero,—as the smallest addition of that latter sort will make them!

And is it come to this? And does our venerable
Parliament announce itself elected and eligible in this
manner? Surely such a Parliament promulgates strange
horoscopes of itself. What is to become of a Parliament
elected or eligible in this manner? Unless Belial and
Beelzebub have got possession of the throne of this
Universe, such Parliament is preparing itself for new
Reform-bills. We shall have to try it by Chartism, or any
conceivable *ism*, rather than put-up with this! There is
already in England 'religion' enough to get six hundred
and fifty-eight Consulting Men brought together who do
not begin work with a lie in their mouth. Our poor old
Parliament, thousands of years old, is still good for something, for several things;—though many are beginning to
ask, with ominous anxiety, in these days: For what
thing? But for whatever thing and things Parliament be
good, indisputably it must start with other than a lie in its
mouth! On the whole, a Parliament working with a lie
in its mouth, will have to take itself away. To no Parliament or thing, that one has heard of, did this Universe
ever long yield harbour on that footing. At all hours
of the day and night, some Chartism is advancing,
some armed Cromwell is advancing, to apprise such
Parliament: "Ye are no Parliament. In the name of
God,—go!"

In sad truth, once more, how is our whole existence, in
these present days, built on Cant, Speciosity, Falsehood,
Dilettantism; with this one serious Veracity in it: Mammonism! Dig down where you will, through the Parlia-
ment-floor or elsewhere, how infallibly do you, at spade's
depth below the surface, come upon this universal *Liars*-
rock substratum! Much else is ornamental; true on barrel-
heads, in pulpits, hustings, Parliamentary benches; but
this is forever true and truest: "Money does bring
money's worth; Put money in your purse." Here, if
nowhere else, is the human soul still in thorough earnest;
sincere with a prophet's sincerity: and 'the Hell of the
English,' as Sauerteig said, 'is the infinite terror of Not
getting on, especially of Not making money.' With
results!

To many persons the horoscope of Parliament is more interesting than to me: but surely all men with souls must admit that sending members to Parliament by bribery is an infamous solecism; an act entirely immoral, which no man can have to do with more or less, but he will soil his fingers more or less. No Carlton Clubs, Reform Clubs, nor any sort of clubs or creatures, or of accredited opinions or practices, can make a Lie Truth, can make Bribery a Propriety. The Parliament should really either punish and put away Bribery, or legalise it by some Office in Downing-street. As I read the Apocalypses, a Parliament that can do neither of these things is not in a good way.— And yet, alas, what of Parliaments and their Elections? Parliamentary Elections are but the topmost ultimate outcome of an electioneering which goes on at all hours, in all places, in every meeting of two or more men. It is *we* that vote wrong, and teach the poor ragged Freemen of Boroughs to vote wrong. We pay respect to those worthy of no respect.

Is not Pandarus Dogdraught a member of select clubs, and admitted into the drawing-rooms of men? Visibly to all persons he is of the offal of Creation; but he carries money in his purse, due lacquer on his dog-visage, and it is believed will not steal spoons. The human species does not with one voice, like the Hebrew Psalmist, ' shun to sit ' with Dogdraught, refuse totally to dine with Dogdraught; men called of honour are willing enough to dine with him, his talk being lively, and his champagne excellent. We say to ourselves, "The man is in good society," — others have already voted for him; why should not I? We *forget* the indefeasible right of property that Satan has in Dogdraught,—we are not afraid to be near Dogdraught! It is we that vote wrong; blindly, nay with falsity prepense! It is we that no longer know the difference between Human Worth and Human Unworth; or feel that the one is admirable and alone admirable, the other detestable, damnable! How shall *we* find out a Hero and Viceking Samson with a maximum of two shillings in his pocket? We have no chance to do such a thing. We have got out of the Ages of Heroism,

deep into the Ages of Flunkyism,—and must return or
die. What a noble set of mortals are we, who, because
there is no Saint Edmund threatening us at the rim of
the horizon, are not afraid to be whatever, for the day
and hour, is smoothest for us!

And now, in good sooth, why should an indigent discerning Freeman give his vote without bribes? Let us
rather honour the poor man that he does discern clearly
wherein lies, for him, the true kernel of the matter.
What is it to the ragged grimy Freeman of a Tenpound-
Franchise Borough, whether Aristides Rigmarole Esq.
of the Destructive, or the Hon. Alcides Dolittle of the
Conservative Party be sent to Parliament;—much more,
whether the two-thousandth part of them be sent, for
that is the amount of his faculty in it? Destructive or
Conservative, what will either of them destroy or conserve of vital moment to this Freeman? Has he found
either of them care, at bottom, a sixpence for him or his
interests, of those of his class or of his cause, or of any
class or cause that is of much value to God or to man?
Rigmarole and Dolittle have alike cared for themselves
hitherto; and for their own clique, and self-conceited
crotchets,—their greasy dishonest interests of pudding,
or windy dishonest interests of praise; and not very
perceptibly for any other interest whatever. Neither
Rigmarole nor Dolittle will accomplish any good or any
evil for this grimy Freeman, like giving him a five-pound
note, or refusing to give it him. It will be smoothest to
vote according to value received. That is the veritable
fact; and he indigent, like others that are not indigent,
acts conformably thereto.

Why, reader, truly, if they asked thee or me, Which
way we meant to vote?—were it not our likeliest answer:
Neither way! I, as a Tenpound Franchiser, will receive
no bribe; but also I will not vote for either of these men.
Neither Rigmarole nor Dolittle shall, by furtherance of
mine, go and make laws for this country. I will have no
hand in such a mission. How dare I! If other men
cannot be got in England, a totally other sort of men,
different as light is from dark, as star-fire is from street-

mud, what is the use of votings, or of Parliaments in England? England ought to resign herself; there is no hope or possibility for England. If England cannot get her Knaves and Dastards ' arrested,' in some degree, but only get them ' elected,' what is to become of England?

I conclude, with all confidence, that England will verily have to put an end to briberies on her Election Hustings and elsewhere, at what cost soever;—and likewise that we, Electors and Eligibles, one and all of us, for our own behoof and hers, cannot too soon begin, at what cost soever, to put an end to *bribeabilities* in ourselves. The death-leprosy, attacked in this manner, by purifying lotions from without and by rallying of the vital energies and purities from within, will probably abate somewhat! It has otherwise no chance to abate.

CHAPTER III

THE ONE INSTITUTION

WHAT our Government can do in this grand Problem of the Working Classes of England? Yes, supposing the insane Corn-Laws totally abolished, all speech of them ended, and ' from ten to twenty years of new possibility to live and find wages ' conceded us in consequence: What the English Government might be expected to accomplish or attempt towards rendering the existence of our Labouring Millions somewhat less anomalous, somewhat less impossible, in the years that are to follow those ' ten or twenty,' if either ' ten ' or ' twenty ' there be?

It is the most momentous question. For all his of the Corn-Law Abrogation, and what can follow therefrom, is but as the shadow on King Hezekiah's Dial: the shadow has gone back twenty years; but will again, in spite of Free-Trades and Abrogations, travel forward its old fated way. With our present system of individual

Mammonism, and Government by Laissez-faire, this Nation cannot live. And if, in the priceless interim, some new life and healing be not found, there is no second respite to be counted on. The shadow on the Dial advances thenceforth without pausing. What Government can do? This that they call 'Organising of Labour' is, if well understood, the Problem of the whole Future, for all who will in future pretend to govern men. But our first preliminary stage of it, How to deal with the Actual Labouring Millions of England? this is the imperatively pressing Problem of the Present, pressing with a truly fearful intensity and imminence in these very years and days. No Government can longer neglect it: once more, what can our Government do in it?

Governments are of very various degrees of activity: some altogether Lazy Governments, in 'free countries' as they are called, seem in these times almost to profess to do, if not nothing, one knows not at first what. To debate in Parliament, and gain majorities; and ascertain who shall be, with a toil hardly second to Ixion's, the Prime Speaker and Spoke-holder, and keep the Ixion's-Wheel going, if not forward, yet round? Not altogether so:—much, to the experienced eye, is not what it seems! Chancery and certain other Law-Courts seem nothing; yet in fact they are, the worst of them, something: chimneys for the devilry and contention of men to escape by;—a very considerable something! Parliament too has its tasks, if thou wilt look; fit to wear-out the lives of toughest men. The celebrated Kilkenny Cats, through their tumultuous congress, cleaving the ear of Night, could they be said to do nothing? Hadst thou been of them, thou hadst seen! The feline heart laboured, as with steam up—to the bursting point; and death-doing energy nerved every muscle: they had a work there; and did it! On the morrow, two tails were found left, and peaceable annihilation; a neighbourhood *delivered* from despair.

Again, are not Spinning-Dervishes an eloquent emblem, significant of much? Hast thou noticed him, that solemnvisaged Turk, the eyes shut; dingy wool mantle circularly hiding his figure;—bell-shaped; like a dingy bell set spinning on the *tongue* of it? By centrifugal force the dingy wool mantle heaves itself; spreads more and more, like upturned cup widening into upturned saucer: thus spins he, to the praise of Allah and advantage of mankind, fast and faster, till collapse ensue, and sometimes death!—

A Government such as ours, consisting of from seven to eight hundred Parliamentary Talkers, with their escort of Able Editors and Public Opinion; and for head, certain Lords and Servants of the Treasury, and Chief Secretaries and others, who find themselves, at once Chiefs and No-Chiefs, and often commanded rather than commanding, —is doubtless a most complicate entity, and none of the alertest for getting on with business! Clearly enough, if the Chiefs be not self-motive and what we call men, but mere patient lay-figures without self-motive principle, the Government will not move anywhither; it will tumble disastrously, and jumble, round its own axis, as for many years past we have seen it do.—And yet a self-motive man who is not a lay-figure, place him in the heart of what entity you may, will make it move more or less! The absurdest in Nature he will make a little *less* absurd, he. The unwieldiest he will make to move;—that is the use of his existing there. He will at least have the manfulness to depart out of it, if not; to say: " I cannot move in thee, and be a man; like a wretched drift-log dressed in man's clothes and minister s clothes, doomed to a lot baser than belongs to man, I will not continue with thee, tumbling aimless on the Mother of Dead Dogs here:— Adieu! "

For, on the whole, it is the lot of Chiefs everywhere, this same. No Chief in the most despotic country but was a Servant withal; at once an absolute commanding General, and a poor Orderly-Sergeant, ordered by the very men in the ranks,—obliged to collect the vote of the ranks too, in some articulate or inarticulate shape, and weigh well the same. The proper name of all Kings is Minister, Servant. In no conceivable Government can a lay-figure

get forward! *This* Worker, surely he above all others has
to 'spread out his Gideon's Fleece,' and collect the monitions
of Immensity; the poor Localities, as we said, and Parishes
of Palace-yard or elsewhere, having no due monition in
them. A Prime Minister, even here in England, who
shall dare believe the heavenly omens, and address himself
like a man and hero to the great dumb-struggling heart of
England; and speak out for it, and act out for it, the God's-
Justice it is writhing to get uttered and perishing for want
of,—yes, he too will see awaken round him, in passionate
burning all-defiant loyalty, the heart of England, and such
a ' support ' as no Division-List or Parliamentary Majority
was ever yet known to yield a man! Here as there, now
as then, he who can and dare trust the heavenly Immensities, all earthly Localities are subject to him. We
will pray for such a Man and First-Lord;—yes, and far
better, we will strive and incessantly make ready, each
of us, to be worthy to serve and second such a First-Lord!
We shall then be as good as sure of his arriving; sure of
many things, let him arrive or not.

Who can despair of Governments that passes a Soldier's
Guard-house, or meets a redcoated man on the streets!
That a body of men could be got together to kill other
men when you bade them: this, *a priori*, does it not seem
one of the impossiblest things? Yet look, behold it; in
the stolidest of Donothing Governments, that impossibility is a thing done. See it there, with buff belts, red
coats on its back; walking sentry at guard-houses, brush-
ing white breeches in barracks; an indisputable palpable
fact. Out of gray Antiquity, amid all finance-difficulties,
scaccarium-tallies, ship-moneys, coat-and-conduct moneys,
and vicissitudes of Chance and Time, there, down to the
present blessed hour, it is.

Often, in these painfully decadent and painfully nascent
Times, with their distresses, inarticulate gaspings and
' impossibilities; ' meeting a tall Lifeguardsman in his
snow-white trousers, or seeing those two statuesque Life-
guardsmen in their frowning bearskins, pipe-clayed buck-
skins, on their coal-black sleek-fiery quadrupeds, riding

sentry at the Horse-Guards,—it strikes one with a kind of mournful interest, how, in such universal down-rushing and wrecked impotence of almost all old institutions, this oldest Fighting Institution is still so young! Fresh-complexioned, firm-limbed, six feet by the standard, this fighting man has verily been got up, and can fight. While so much has not yet got into being; while so much has gone gradually out of it, and become an empty Semblance or Clothes-suit; and highest king's-cloaks, mere chimeras parading under them so long, are getting unsightly to the earnest eye, unsightly, almost offensive, like a costlier kind of scarecrow's-blanket,—here still is a reality!

The man in horsehair wig advances, promising that he will get me 'justice:' he takes me into Chancery Law-Courts, into decades, half-centuries of hubbub, of distracted jargon; and does *get* me—disappointment, almost desperation; and one refuge: that of dismissing him and his 'justice' altogether out of my head. For I have work to do; I cannot spend my decades in mere arguing with other men about the exact wages of my work: I will work cheerfully with no wages, sooner than with a ten-years gangrene or Chancery Lawsuit in my heart! He of the horsehair wig is a sort of failure; no substance, but a fond imagination of the mind. He of the shovel-hat, again, who comes forward professing that he will save my soul—O ye Eternities, of him in this place be absolute silence! —But he of the red coat, I say, is a success and no failure! He will veritably, if he get orders, draw out a long sword and kill me. No mistake there. He is a fact and not a shadow. Alive in this Year Forty-three, able and willing to do *his* work. In dim old centuries, with William Rufus, William of Ipres, or far earlier, he began; and has come down safe so far. Catapult has given place to cannon, pike has given place to musket, iron mail-shirt to coat of red cloth, saltpetre ropematch to percussion-cap; equipments, circumstances have all changed, and again changed: but the human battle-engine in the inside of any or each of these, ready still to do battle, stands there, six feet in standard size. There are Pay-Offices, Woolwich Arsenals, there is a Horse-Guards, War-Office,

Captain-General; persuasive Sergeants, with tap of drum, recruit in market-towns and villages;—and, on the whole, I say, here is your actual drilled fighting-man; here are your actual Ninety-thousand of such, ready to go into any quarter of the world and fight!

Strange, interesting, and yet most mournful to reflect on. Was this, then, of all the things mankind had some talent for, the one thing important to learn well, and bring to perfection; this of successfully killing one another? Truly you have learned it well, and carried the business to a high perfection. It is incalculable what, by arranging, commanding and regimenting, you can make of men. These thousand straight-standing firmset individuals, who shoulder arms, who march, wheel, advance, retreat; and are, for your behoof, a magazine charged with fiery death, in the most perfect condition of potential activity: few months ago, till the persuasive sergeant came, what were they? Multiform ragged losels, runaway apprentices, starved weavers, thievish valets; an entirely broken population, fast tending towards the treadmill. But the persuasive sergeant came; by tap of drum enlisted, or formed lists of them, took heartily to drilling them;—and he and you have made them this! Most potent, effectual for all work whatsoever, is wise planning, firm combining and commanding among men. Let no man despair of Governments who looks on these two sentries at the Horse-Guards and our United-Service Clubs! I could conceive an Emigration Service, a Teaching Service, considerable varieties of United and Separate Services, of the due thousands strong, all effective as this Fighting Service is; all doing *their* work, like it;—which work, much more than fighting, is henceforth the necessity of these New Ages we are got into! Much lies among us, convulsively, nigh desperately *struggling to be born.*

But mean Governments, as mean-limited individuals do, have stood by the physically indispensable; have realised that and nothing more. The Soldier is perhaps one of the most difficult things to realise; but Governments, had they not realised him, could not have existed: accordingly he is here. O Heavens, if we saw an army ninety-thousand strong, maintained and fully equipt, in continual real action and battle against Human Starvation, against Chaos, Necessity, Stupidity, and our real ' natural enemies,' what a business were it! Fighting and molesting not ' the French,' who, poor men, have a hard enough battle of their own in the like kind, and need no additional molesting from us; but fighting and incessantly spearing down and destroying Falsehood, Nescience, Delusion, Disorder, and the Devil and his Angels! Thou thyself, cultivated reader, hast done something in that alone true warfare; but, alas, under what circumstances was it? Thee no beneficent drill-sergeant, with any effectiveness, would rank in line beside thy fellows; train, like a true didactic artist, by the wit of all past experience, to do thy soldiering; encourage thee when right, punish thee when wrong, and everywhere with wise word-of-command say, Forward on this hand, Forward on that! Ah, no: thou hadst to learn thy small-sword and platoon exercise where and how thou couldst; to all mortals but thyself it was indifferent whether thou shouldst ever learn it. And the rations, and shilling a day, were they provided thee,—reduced as I have known brave Jean-Pauls, learning their exercise, to live on ' water *without* the bread ' ? The rations; or any furtherance of promotion to corporalship, lance-corporalship, or due cat-o'-nine-tails, with the slightest reference to thy deserts, were not provided. Forethought, even as of a pipe-clayed drill-sergeant, did not preside over thee. To corporalship, lance-corporalship, thou didst attain; alas, also to the halberts and cat: but thy rewarder and punisher seemed blind as the Deluge: neither lance-corporalship, nor even drummer's cat, because both appeared delirious, brought thee due profit.

It was well, all this, we know;—and yet it was not well! Forty soldiers, I am told, will disperse the largest Spitalfields mob: forty to ten-thousand, that is the proportion between drilled and undrilled. Much there is which cannot yet be organised in this world; but somewhat also which can, somewhat also which must. When one thinks, for example, what Books are become and becoming for us, what Operative Lancashires are become;

what a Fourth Estate, and innumerable Virtualities not
yet got to be Actualities are become and becoming,—
one sees Organisms enough in the dim huge Future; and
'United Services' quite other than the redcoat one;
and much, even in these years, struggling to be born!

Of Time-Bill, Factory-Bill and other such Bills the
present Editor has no authority to speak. He knows
not, it is for others than he to know, in what specific
ways it may be feasible to interfere, with Legislation,
between the Workers and the Master-Workers;—knows
only and sees, what all men are beginning to see, that
Legislative interference, and interferences not a few are
indispensable; that as a lawless anarchy of supply-and-
demand, on market-wages alone, this province of things
cannot longer be left. Nay interference has begun: there
are already Factory Inspectors,—who seem to have no
lack of work. Perhaps there might be Mine-Inspectors
too:—might there not be Furrowfield Inspectors withal,
and ascertain for us how on seven and sixpence a week
a human family does live! Interference has begun; it
must continue, must extensively enlarge itself, deepen
and sharpen itself. Such things cannot longer be idly
lapped in darkness, and suffered to go on unseen: the
Heavens do see them; the curse, not the blessing of the
Heavens is on an Earth that refuses to see them.

Again, are not Sanitary Regulations possible for a
Legislature? The old Romans had their Ædiles; who
would, I think, in direct contravention to supply-and-
demand, have rigorously seen rammed up into total
abolition many a foul cellar in our Southwarks, Saint-
Gileses, and dark poison-lanes; saying sternly, "Shall a
Roman man dwell there?" The Legislature, at whatever cost of consequences, would have had to answer,
"God forbid!"—The Legislature, even as it now is,
could order all dingy Manufacturing Towns to cease from
their soot and darkness; to let-in the blessed sunlight,
the blue of Heaven, and become clear and clean; to
burn their coal-smoke, namely, and make flame of it.
Baths, free air, a wholesome temperature, ceilings twenty
feet high, might be ordained, by Act of Parliament, in all

establishments licensed as Mills. There are such Mills already extant;—honour to the builders of them! The Legislature can say to others: Go ye and do likewise; better if you can.

Every toiling Manchester, its smoke and soot all burnt, ought it not, among so many world-wide conquests, to have a hundred acres or so of free greenfield, with trees on it, conquered, for its little children to disport in; for its all conquering workers to take a breath of twilight air in? You would say so! A willing Legislature could say so with effect. A willing Legislature could say very many things! And to whatsoever 'vested interest,' or suchlike, stood up, gainsaying merely, "I shall lose profits,"—the willing Legislature would answer, "Yes, but my sons and daughters will gain health, and life, and a soul."—"What is to become of our Cotton trade?" cried certain Spinners, when the Factory Bill was proposed; "What is to become of our invaluable Cotton-trade?" The Humanity of England answered steadfastly: "Deliver me these rickety perishing souls of infants, and let your Cotton-trade take its chance. God Himself commands the one thing; not God especially the other thing. We cannot have prosperous Cotton-trades at the expense of keeping the Devil a partner in them!"—

Bills enough, were the Corn-Law Abrogation Bill once passed, and a Legislature willing! Nay this one Bill, which lies yet unenacted, a right Education Bill, is not this of itself the sure parent of innumerable wise Bills, —wise regulations, practical methods and proposals, gradually ripening towards the state of Bills? To irradiate with intelligence, that is to say, with order, arrangement and all blessedness, the Chaotic, Unintelligent: how, except by educating, *can* you accomplish this? That thought, reflection, articulate utterance and understanding be awakened in these individual million heads, which are the atoms of your Chaos: there is no other way of illuminating any Chaos! The sum-total of intelligence that is found in it, determines the extent of order that is possible for your Chaos,—the feasibility and rationality of what your Chaos will dimly demand from you, and

education for illumination of the chaos.

will gladly obey when proposed by you! It is an exact equation; the one accurately measures the other.—If the whole English People, during these 'twenty years of respite,' be not educated, with at least schoolmaster's educating, a tremendous responsibility, before God and men, will rest somewhere! How dare any man, especially a man calling himself minister of God, stand up in any Parliament or place, under any pretext or delusion, and for a day or an hour forbid God's Light to come into the world, and bid the Devil's Darkness continue in it one hour more! For all light and science, under all shapes, in all degrees of perfection, is of God; all darkness, nescience, is of the Enemy of God. 'The schoolmaster's creed is somewhat awry?' Yes, I have found few creeds entirely correct; few light-beams shining *white*, pure of admixture: but of all creeds and religions now or ever before known, was not that of thoughtless thriftless Animalism, of Distilled Gin, and Stupor and Despair, unspeakably the least orthodox? We will exchange *it* even with Paganism, with Fetishism; and, on the whole, must exchange it with something.

An effective 'Teaching Service' I do consider that there must be; some Education Secretary, Captain-General of Teachers, who will actually contrive to get us *taught*. Then again, why should there not be an 'Emigration Service,' and Secretary, with adjuncts, with funds, forces, idle Navy-ships, and ever-increasing apparatus; in fine an *effective system* of Emigration; so that, at length, before our twenty years of respite ended, every honest willing Workman who found England too strait, and the 'Organisation of Labour' not yet sufficiently advanced, might find likewise a bridge built to carry him into new Western Lands, there to 'organise' with more elbow-room some labour for himself? There to be a real blessing, raising new corn for us, purchasing new webs and hatchets from us; leaving us at least in peace;—instead of staying here to be a Physical-Force Chartist, unblessed and no blessing! Is it not scandalous to consider that a Prime Minister could raise within a year, as I have seen it done, a Hundred and Twenty Millions Sterling

to shoot the French; and we are stopt short for want of
the hundredth part of that to keep the English living?
The bodies of the English living, and the souls of the
English living: — these two 'Services,' an Education
Service and an Emigration Service, these with others will
actually have to be organised!

A free bridge for Emigrants: why, we should then be
on a par with America itself, the most favoured of all
lands that have no government; and we should have,
besides, so many traditions and mementos of priceless
things which America has cast away. We could proceed
deliberately to 'organise Labour,' not doomed to perish
unless we effected it within year and day;—every willing
Worker that proved superfluous, finding a bridge ready
for him. This verily will have to be done; the Time is
big with this. Our little Isle is grown too narrow for
us; but the world is wide enough yet for another Six
Thousand Years. England's sure markets w ll be among
new Colonies of Englishmen in all quarters of the Globe.
All men trade with all men, when mutually convenient;
and are even bound to do it by the Maker of men. Our
friends of China, who guiltily refused to trade, in these
circumstances,—had we not to argue with them, in
cannon-shot at last, and convince them that they ought
to trade! 'Hostile Tariffs' will arise, to shut us out;
and then again will fall, to let us in: but the Sons of
England, speakers of the English language were it nothing
more, will in all times have the ineradicable predisposition
to trade with England. Mycale was the *Pan-Ionion*,
rendezvous of all the Tribes of Ion, for old Greece: why
should not London long continue the *All-Saxon-home*,
rendezvous of all the 'Children of the Harz-Rock,'
arriving, in select samples, from the Antipodes and elsewhere, by steam and otherwise, to the 'season' here!—
What a Future; wide as the world, if we have the heart and
heroism for it,—which, by Heaven's blessing, we shall:

> ' Keep not standing fixed and rooted,
> Briskly venture, briskly roam;
> Head and hand, where'er thou foot it,
> And stout heart are still at home.

In what land the sun does visit
Brisk are we, whate'er betide:
To give space for wandering is it
That the world was made so wide.' [1]

Fourteen hundred years ago, it was by a considerable
' Emigration Service,' never doubt it, by much enlistment,
discussion and apparatus, that we ourselves arrived in
this remarkable Island, — and got into our present
difficulties among others!

It is true the English Legislature, like the English
People, is of slow temper; essentially conservative. In
our wildest periods of reform, in the Long Parliament
itself, you notice always the invincible instinct to hold fast
by the Old; to admit the *minimum* of New; to expand,
if it be possible, some old habit or method, already found
fruitful, into new growth for the new need. It is an
instinct worthy of all honour; akin to all strength and all
wisdom. The Future hereby is not dissevered from the
Past, but based continuously on it; grows with all the
vitalities of the Past, and is rooted down deep into the
beginnings of us. The English Legislature is entirely
repugnant to believe in ' new epochs.' The English Legislature does not occupy itself with epochs; has, indeed,
other business to do than looking at the Time-Horologe
and hearing it tick! Nevertheless new epochs do actually
come; and with them new imperious peremptory necessities; so that even an English Legislature has to look up,
and admit, though with reluctance, that the hour has
struck. The hour having struck, let us not say ' impossible: '—it will have to be possible! ' Contrary to the
habits of Parliament, the habits of Government?' Yes:
but did any Parliament or Government ever sit in a Year
Forty-three before? One of the most original, unexampled
years and epochs; in several important respects totally
unlike any other! For Time, all-edacious and all-feracious,
does run on: and the Seven Sleepers, awakening hungry
after a hundred years, find that it is not their old nurses
who can now give them suck!

[1] Goethe, *Wilhelm Meister*.

For the rest, let not any Parliament, Aristocracy, Millocracy, or Member of the Governing Class, condemn with much triumph this small specimen of 'remedial measures;' or ask again, with the least anger, of this Editor, What is to be done, How that alarming problem of the Working Classes is to be managed? Editors are not here, foremost of all, to say How. A certain Editor thanks the gods that nobody pays him three hundred thousand pounds a year, two hundred thousand, twenty thousand, or any similar sum of cash for saying How;— that his wages are very different, his work somewhat fitter for him. An Editor's stipulated work is to apprise *thee* that it must be done. The 'way to do it,'—is to try it, knowing that thou shalt die if it be not done. There is the bare back, there is the web of cloth; thou shalt cut me a coat to cover the bare back, thou whose trade it is. 'Impossible?' Hapless Fraction, dost thou discern Fate there, half unveiling herself in the gloom of the future, with her gibbet-cords, her steel-whips, and very authentic Tailor's Hell; waiting to see whether it is 'possible'? Out with thy scissors, and cut that cloth or thy own windpipe!

CHAPTER IV

CAPTAINS OF INDUSTRY

IF I believed that Mammonism with its adjuncts was to continue henceforth the one serious principle of our existence, I should reckon it idle to solicit remedial measures from any Government, the disease being insusceptible of remedy. Government can do much, but it can in no wise do all. Government, as the most conspicuous object in Society, is called upon to give signal of what shall be done; and, in many ways, to preside over, further, and command the doing of it. But the Government cannot do, by all its signaling and commanding, what the Society is radically indisposed to do. In the long-run every Government is the exact symbol of its People, with their wisdom and unwisdom; we have to say, Like People like Government. — The main substance of this immense Problem of Organising Labour, and first of all of Managing the Working Classes, will, it is very clear, have to be solved by those who stand practically in the middle of it; by those who themselves work and preside over work. Of all that can be enacted by any Parliament in regard to it, the germs must already lie potentially extant in those two classes, who are to obey such enactment. A Human Chaos *in* which there is no light, you vainly attempt to irradiate by light shed *on* it: order never can arise there.

But it is my firm conviction that the 'Hell of England' will *cease* to be that of 'not making money;' that we shall get a nobler Hell and a nobler Heaven! I anticipate light *in* the Human Chaos, glimmering, shining more and more; under manifold true signals from without That light shall shine. Our deity no longer being Mammon, — O Heavens, each man will then say to himself: "Why such deadly haste to make money? I shall not go to Hell, even if I do not make money! There is another Hell, I am told!" Competition, at railway-speed, in all branches of commerce and work will then abate:—good felt-hats for the head, in every sense, instead of seven-feet lath-and-plaster hats on wheels, will then be discoverable! Bubble-periods, with their panics and commercial crises, will again become infrequent; steady modest industry will take the place of gambling speculation. To be a noble Master, among noble Workers, will again be the first ambition with some few; to be a rich Master only the second. How the Inventive Genius of England, with the whirr of its bobbins and billy-rollers shoved somewhat into the backgrounds of the brain, will contrive and devise, not cheaper produce exclusively, but fairer distribution of the produce at its present cheapness! By degrees, we shall again have a Society with something of Heroism in it, something of Heaven's Blessing on it; we shall again have, as my German friend asserts, 'instead of Mammon-Feudalism with unsold cotton-shirts and Preservation of the Game, noble just Industrialism and Government by the Wisest!'

It is with the hope of awakening here and there a

British man to know himself for a man and divine soul, that a few words of parting admonition, to all persons to whom the Heavenly Powers have lent power of any kind in this land, may now be addressed. And first to those same Master-Workers, Leaders of Industry; who stand nearest and in fact powerfulest, though not most prominent, being as yet in too many senses a Virtuality rather than an Actuality.

The Leaders of Industry, if Industry is ever to be led, are virtually the Captains of the World; if there be no nobleness in them, there will never be an Aristocracy more. But let the Captains of Industry consider: once again, are they born of other clay than the old Captains of Slaughter; doomed forever to be no Chivalry, but a mere gold-plated *Doggery*,—what the French well name *Canaille*, ' Doggery ' with more or less gold carrion at its disposal? Captains of Industry are the true Fighters, henceforth recognisable as the only true ones: Fighters against Chaos, Necessity and the Devils and Jötuns; and lead on Mankind in that great, and alone true, and universal warfare; the stars in their courses fighting for them, and all Heaven and all Earth saying audibly, Well done! Let the Captains of Industry retire into their own hearts, and ask solemnly, If there is nothing but vulturous hunger, for fine wines, valet reputation and gilt carriages, discoverable there? Of hearts made by the Almighty God I will not believe such a thing. Deep-hidden under wretchedest god-forgetting Cants, Epicurisms, Dead-Sea Apisms; forgotten as under foulest fat Lethe mud and weeds, there is yet, in all hearts born into this God's - World, a spark of the Godlike slumbering. Awake, O nightmare sleepers; awake, arise, or be forever fallen! This is not playhouse poetry; it is sober fact. Our England, our world cannot live as it is. It will connect itself with a God again, or go down with nameless throes and fire-consummation to the Devils. Thou who feelest aught of such a Godlike stirring in thee, any faintest intimation of it as through heavy-laden dreams, follow *it*, I conjure thee. Arise, save thyself, be one of those that save thy country.

Bucaniers, Chactaw Indians, whose supreme aim in fighting is that they may get the scalps, the money, that they may amass scalps and money: out of such came no Chivalry, and never will! Out of such came only gore and wreck, infernal rage and misery; desperation quenched in annihilation. Behold it, I bid thee, behold there, and consider! What is it that thou have a hundred thousand-pound bills laid-up in thy strong-room, a hundred scalps hung-up in thy wigwam? I value not them or thee. Thy scalps and thy thousand-pound bills are as yet nothing, if no nobleness from within irradiate them; if no Chivalry, in action, or in embryo ever struggling towards birth and action, be there.

Love of men cannot be bought by cash-payment; and without love men cannot endure to be together. You cannot lead a Fighting World without having it regimented, chivalried: the thing, in a day, becomes impossible; all men in it, the highest at first, the very lowest at last, discern consciously, or by a noble instinct, this necessity. And can you any more continue to lead a Working World unregimented, anarchic? I answer, and the Heavens and Earth are now answering, No! The thing becomes not 'in a day' impossible; but in some two generations it does. Yes, when fathers and mothers, in Stockport hunger-cellars, begin to eat their children, and Irish widows have to prove their relationship by dying of typhus-fever; and amid Governing 'Corporations of the Best and Bravest,' busy to preserve their game by 'bushing,' dark millions of God's human creatures start up in mad Chartisms, impracticable Sacred-Months, and Manchester Insurrections;—and there is a virtual Industrial Aristocracy as yet only half-alive, spell-bound amid money-bags and ledgers; and an actual Idle Aristocracy seemingly near dead in somnolent delusions, in trespasses and double-barrels; 'sliding,' as on inclined-planes, which every new year they *soap* with new Hansard's-jargon under God's sky, and so are 'sliding,' ever faster, towards a 'scale' and balance-scale whereon is written *Thou art found Wanting* :—in such days, after a generation or two, I say, it does become, even to the low and simple, very palpably impossible! No Working World, any more than a Fighting World, can be led on without a noble Chivalry of Work, and laws and fixed rules which follow out of that, — far nobler than any Chivalry of Fighting was. As an anarchic multitude on mere Supply-and-demand, it is becoming inevitable that we dwindle in horrid suicidal convulsion and self-abrasion, frightful to the imagination, into *Chactaw* Workers. With wigwams and scalps,—with palaces and thousand-pound bills; with savagery, depopulation, chaotic desolation! Good Heavens, will not one French Revolution and Reign of Terror suffice us, but must there be two? There will be two if needed; there will be twenty if needed; there will be precisely as many as are needed. The Laws of Nature will have themselves fulfilled. That is a thing certain to me.

Your gallant battle-hosts and work-hosts, as the others did, will need to be made loyally yours; they must and will be regulated, methodically secured in their just share of conquest under you; — joined with you in veritable brotherhood, sonhood, by quite other and deeper ties than those of temporary day's wages! How would mere red-coated regiments, to say nothing of chivalries, fight for you, if you could discharge them on the evening of the battle, on payment of the stipulated shillings,—and they discharge you on the morning of it! Chelsea Hospitals, pensions, promotions, rigorous lasting covenant on the one side and on the other, are indispensable even for a hired fighter. The Feudal Baron, much more, — how could he subsist with mere temporary mercenaries round him, at sixpence a day; ready to go over to the other side, if sevenpence were offered? He could not have subsisted;—and his noble instinct saved him from the necessity of even trying! The Feudal Baron had a Man's Soul in him; to which anarchy, mutiny, and the other fruits of temporary mercenaries, were intolerable: he had never been a Baron otherwise, but had continued a Chactaw and Bucanier. He felt it precious, and at last it became habitual, and his fruitful enlarged existence included it as a necessity, to have men round him who in heart loved him; whose life he watched over with rigour yet with love; who were prepared to give their life for him, if need came. It was beautiful; it was human! Man lives not otherwise, nor can live contented, anywhere or anywhen. Isolation is the sum-total of wretchedness to man. To be cut off, to be left solitary: to have a world alien, not your world; all a hostile camp for you; not a home at all, of hearts and faces who are yours, whose you are! It is the frightfulest enchantment; too truly a work of the Evil One. To have neither superior, nor inferior, nor equal, united manlike to you. Without father, without child, without brother. Man knows no sadder destiny. 'How is each of us,' exclaims Jean Paul, 'so lonely in the wide bosom of the All!' Encased each as in his transparent 'ice-palace;' our brother visible in his, making signals and gesticulations to us; — visible, but forever unattainable: on his bosom we shall never rest, nor he on ours. It was not a God that did this; no!

Awake, ye noble Workers, warriors in the one true war: all this must be remedied. It is you who are already half-alive, whom I will welcome into life; whom I will conjure, in God's name, to shake off your enchanted sleep, and live wholly! Cease to count scalps, gold-purses; not in these lies your or our salvation. Even these, if you count only these, will not long be left. Let bucaniering be put far from you; alter, speedily abrogate all laws of the bucaniers, if you would gain any victory that shall endure. Let God's justice, let pity, nobleness and manly valour, with more gold-purses or with fewer, testify themselves in this your brief Life-transit to all the Eternities, the Gods and Silences. It is to you I call; for ye are not dead, ye are already half-alive: there is in you a sleepless dauntless energy, the prime-matter of all nobleness in man. Honour to you in your kind. It is to you I call: ye know at least this, That the mandate of God to His creature man is: Work! The future Epic of the World rests not with those that are near dead, but with those that are alive, and those that are coming into life.

Look around you. Your world-hosts are all in mutiny, in confusion, destitution; on the eve of fiery wreck and madness! They will not march farther for you, on the sixpence a day and supply-and-demand principle: they will not; nor ought they, nor can they. Ye shall reduce them to order, begin reducing them. To order, to just subordination; noble loyalty in return for noble guidance. Their souls are driven nigh mad; let yours be sane and ever saner. Not as a bewildered bewildering mob; but as a firm regimented mass, with real captains over them, will these men march any more. All human interests, combined human endeavours, and social growths in this world, have, at a certain stage of their development, required organising: and Work, the grandest of human interests, does now require it.

God knows, the task will be hard: but no noble task was ever easy. This task will wear away your lives, and the lives of your sons and grandsons: but for what purpose, if not for tasks like this, were lives given to men? Ye shall cease to count your thousand-pound scalps, the noble of you shall cease! Nay the very scalps, as I say, will not long be left if you count only these. Ye shall cease wholly to be barbarous vulturous Chactaws, and become noble European Nineteenth-Century Men. Ye shall know that Mammon, in never such gigs and flunky 'respectabilities,' is not the alone God; that of himself he is but a Devil, and even a Brute-god.

Difficult? Yes, it will be difficult. The short-fibre cotton; that too was difficult. The waste cotton-shrub, long useless, disobedient, as the thistle by the wayside,— have ye not conquered it; made it into beautiful bandana webs; white woven shirts for men; bright tinted air-garments wherein flit goddesses? Ye have shivered mountains asunder, made the hard iron pliant to you as soft putty: the Forest-giants, Marsh-jötuns bear sheaves of golden-grain; Ægir the Sea-demon himself stretches his back for a sleek highway to you, and on Fire-horses and Windhorses ye career. Ye are most strong. Thor red-bearded, with his blue sun-eyes, with his cheery heart and strong thunder-hammer, he and you have prevailed. Ye are most strong, ye Sons of the icy North, of the far East,—far marching from your rugged Eastern Wilder-

nesses, hitherward from the gray Dawn of Time! Ye
are Sons of the *Jötun*-land; the land of Difficulties Conquered. Difficult? You must try this thing. Once
try it with the understanding that it will and shall have
to be done. Try it as ye try the paltrier thing, making
of money! I will bet on you once more, against all
Jötuns, Tailor-gods, Double-barrelled Law-wards, and
Denizens of Chaos whatsoever!

CHAPTER V

PERMANENCE

STANDING on the threshold, nay as yet outside the
threshold, of a ' Chivalry of Labour,' and an immeasurable
Future which it is to fill with fruitfulness and verdant
shade; where so much has not yet come even to the rudi-
mental state, and all speech of positive enactments were
hazardous in those who know this business only by the
eye,—let us here hint at simply one widest universal
principle, as the basis from which all organisation hitherto
has grown up among men, and all henceforth will have to
grow: The principle of Permanent Contract instead of
Temporary.

Permanent not Temporary:—you do not hire the mere
redcoated fighter by the day, but by the score of years!
Permanence, persistence is the first condition of all fruitfulness in the ways of men. The ' tendency to persevere,'
to persist in spite of hindrances, discouragements and
' impossibilities: ' it is this that in all things distinguishes
the strong soul from the weak; the civilised burgher from
the nomadic savage,—the Species Man from the Genus
Ape! The Nomad has his very house set on wheels; the
Nomad, and in a still higher degree the Ape, are all for
' liberty; ' the privilege to flit continually is indispensable
for them. Alas, in how many ways, does our humour, in
this swift-rolling, self-abrading Time, show itself nomadic,

apelike; mournful enough to him that looks on it with
eyes! This humour will have to abate; it is the first
element of all fertility in human things, that such 'liberty'
of apes and nomads do by freewill or constraint abridge
itself, give place to a better. The civilised man lives
not in wheeled houses. He builds stone castles, plants
lands, makes lifelong marriage-contracts;—has long-dated
hundred-fold possessions, not to be valued in the money-
market; has pedigrees, libraries, law-codes; has memories
and hopes, even for this Earth, that reach over thousands
of years. Lifelong marriage-contracts: how much preferable were year-long or month-long—to the nomad or
ape!

Month-long contracts please me little, in any province
where there can by possibility be found virtue enough for
more. Month-long contracts do not answer well even
with your house-servants; the liberty on both sides to
change every month is growing very apelike, nomadic;—
and I hear philosophers predict that it will alter, or that
strange results will follow: that wise men, pestered with
nomads, with unattached ever-shifting spies and enemies
rather than friends and servants, will gradually, weighing
substance against semblance, with indignation, dismiss
such, down almost to the very shoeblack, and say,
"Begone; I will serve myself rather, and have peace!"
Gurth was hired for life to Cedric, and Cedric to Gurth.
O Anti - Slavery Convention, loud - sounding long - eared
Exeter-Hall—But in thee too is a kind of instinct towards
justice, and I will complain of nothing. Only black
Quashee over the seas being once sufficiently attended to,
wilt thou not perhaps open thy dull sodden eyes to the
'sixty-thousand valets in London itself who are yearly
dismissed to the streets, to be what they can, when the
season ends;'—or to the hunger-stricken, pallid, *yellow*-
coloured 'Free Labourers' in Lancashire, Yorkshire,
Buckinghamshire, and all other shires! These Yellow-
coloured, for the present, absorb all my sympathies: if
I had a Twenty Millions, with Model-Farms and Niger
Expeditions, it is to these that I would give it! Quashee
has already victuals, clothing; Quashee is not dying of

such despair as the yellow-coloured pale man's. Quashee, it must be owned, is hitherto a kind of blockhead. The Haiti Duke of Marmalade, educated now for almost half a century, seems to have next to no sense in him. Why, in one of those Lancashire Weavers, dying of hunger, there is more thought and heart, a greater arithmetical amount of misery and desperation, than in whole gangs of Quashees. It must be owned, thy eyes are of the sodden sort; and with thy emancipations, and thy twenty-millionings and long-eared clamourings, thou, like Robes-pierre with his paste-board *Etre Suprême,* threatenest to become a bore to us: *Avec ton Etre Suprême tu commences m'embêter !*—

In a Printed Sheet of the assiduous, much-abused, and truly useful Mr. Chadwick's, containing queries and responses from far and near as to this great question, 'What is the effect of education on working-men, in respect of their value as mere workers?' the present Editor, reading with satisfaction a decisive unanimous verdict as to Education, reads with inexpressible interest this special remark, put in by way of marginal incidental note, from a practical manufacturing Quaker, whom, as he is anonymous, we will call Friend Prudence. Prudence keeps a thousand workmen; has striven in all ways to attach them to him; has provided conversational soirées; play-grounds, bands of music for the young ones; went even 'the length of buying them a drum;' all which has turned out to be an excellent investment. For a certain person, marked here by a black stroke, whom we shall name Blank, living over the way,—he also keeps some-where about a thousand men; but has done none of these things for them, nor any other thing, except due payment of the wages by supply-and-demand. Blank's workers are perpetually getting into mutiny, into broils and coils: every six months, we suppose, Blank has a strike; every one month, every day and every hour, they are fretting and obstructing the shortsighted Blank; pilfering from him, wasting and idling for him, omitting and commit-ting for him. "I would not," says Friend Prudence,

" exchange my workers for his *with seven thousand pounds
to boot.*" [1]

Right, O honourable Prudence; thou art wholly in the
right: Seven thousand pounds even as a matter of profit
for this world, nay for the mere cash-market of this world!
And as a matter of profit not for this world only, but for
the other world and all worlds, it outweighs the Bank of
England!—Can the sagacious reader descry here, as it
were the outmost inconsiderable rock-ledge of a universal
rock-foundation, deep once more as the Centre of the
World, emerging so, in the experience of this good Quaker,
through the Stygian mud-vortexes and general Mother
of Dead Dogs, whereon, for the present, all swags and
insecurely hovers, as if ready to be swallowed?

Some Permanence of Contract is already almost
possible; the principle of Permanence, year by year,
better seen into and elaborated, may enlarge itself,
expand gradually on every side into a system. This once
secured, the basis of all good results were laid. Once
permanent, you do not quarrel with the first difficulty on
your path, and quit it in weak disgust; you reflect that
it cannot be quitted, that it must be conquered, a wise
arrangement fallen on with regard to it. Ye foolish
Wedded Two, who have quarrelled, between whom the
Evil Spirit has stirred-up transient strife and bitterness,
so that 'incompatibility' seems almost nigh, ye are nevertheless the Two who, by long habit, were it by nothing
more, do best of all others suit each other: it is expedient
for your own two foolish selves, to say nothing of the
infants, pedigrees and public in general, that ye agree
again; that ye put away the Evil Spirit, and wisely
on both hands struggle for the guidance of a Good
Spirit!

The very horse that is permanent, how much kindlier
do his rider and he work, than the temporary one, hired
on any hack principle yet known! I am for permanence
in all things, at the earliest possible moment, and to the
latest possible. Blessed is he that continueth where he

---

[1] *Report on the Training of Pauper Children* (1841), p. 18.

is. Here let us rest, and lay-out seedfields; here let us learn to dwell. Here, even here, the orchards that we plant will yield us fruit; the acorns will be wood and pleasant umbrage, if we wait. How much grows everywhere, if we do but wait! Through the swamps we will shape causeways, force purifying drains; we will learn to thread the rocky inaccessibilities; and beaten tracks, worn smooth by mere travelling of human feet, will form themselves. Not a difficulty but can transfigure itself into a triumph; not even a deformity but, if our own soul have imprinted worth on it, will grow dear to us. The sunny plains and deep indigo transparent skies of Italy are all indifferent to the great sick heart of a Sir Walter Scott: on the back of the Apennines, in wild spring weather, the sight of bleak Scotch firs, and snow-spotted heath and desolation, brings tears into his eyes.[1]

O unwise mortals that forever change and shift, and say, Yonder, not Here! Wealth richer than both the Indies lies everywhere for man, if he will endure. Not his oaks only and his fruit-trees, his very heart roots itself wherever he will abide;—roots itself, draws nourishment from the deep fountains of Universal Being! Vagrant Sam-Slicks, who rove over the Earth doing 'strokes of trade,' what wealth have they? Horseloads, shiploads of white or yellow metal: in very sooth, what *are* these? Slick rests nowhere, he is homeless. He can build stone or marble houses; but to continue in them is denied him. The wealth of a man is the number of things which he loves and blesses, which he is loved and blessed by? The herdsman in his poor clay shealing, where his very cow and dog are friends to him, and not a cataract but carries memories for him, and not a mountain-top but nods old recognition: his life, all encircled as in blessed mothers'- arms, is it poorer than Slick's with the ass-loads of yellow metal on his back? Unhappy Slick! Alas, there has so much grown nomadic, apelike, with us: so much will have, with whatever pain, repugnance and ' impossibility,' to alter itself, to fix itself again—in some wise way, in any not delirious way!

[1] Lockhart's *Life of Scott*.

A question arises here: Whether, in some ulterior, perhaps some not far-distant stage of this 'Chivalry of Labour,' your Master-Worker may not find it possible, and needful, to grant his Workers permanent *interest* in his enterprise and theirs? So that it become, in practical result, what in essential fact and justice it ever is, a joint enterprise; all men, from the Chief Master down to the lowest Overseer and Operative, economically as well as loyally concerned for it? — Which question I do not answer. The answer, near or else far, is perhaps, Yes;— and yet one knows the difficulties. Despotism is essential in most enterprises; I am told, they do not tolerate 'freedom of debate' on board a Seventy-four! Republican senate and *plebiscita* would not answer well in Cotton-Mills. And yet observe there too: Freedom, not nomad's or ape's Freedom, but man's Freedom; this is indispensable. We must have it, and will have it! To reconcile Despotism with Freedom:—well, is that such a mystery? Do you not already know the way? It is to make your Despotism *just*. Rigorous as Destiny; but just too, as Destiny and its Laws. The Laws of God: all men obey these, and have no 'Freedom' at all but in obeying them. The way is already known, part of the way;—and courage and some qualities are needed for walking on it!

CHAPTER VI

THE LANDED

A MAN with fifty, with five hundred, with a thousand pounds a day, given him freely, without condition at all, —on condition, as it now runs, that he will sit with his hands in his pockets and do no mischief, pass no Corn-Laws or the like,—he too, you would say, is or might be a rather strong Worker! He is a Worker with such tools as no man in this world ever before had. But in practice, very astonishing, very ominous to look at, he proves not a strong Worker;—you are too happy if he will prove but a No-worker, do nothing, and not be a Wrong-worker.

You ask him, at the year's end: " Where is your three-hundred thousand pound; what have you realised to us with that? " He answers, in indignant surprise: " Done with it? Who are you that ask? I have eaten it; I and my flunkies, and parasites, and slaves two-footed and four-footed, in an ornamental manner; and I am here alive by it; *I* am realised by it to you!"—It is, as we have often said, such an answer as was never before given under this Sun. An answer that fills me with boding apprehension, with foreshadows of despair. O stolid Use-and-wont of an atheistic Half-century, O Ignavia, Tailor-godhood, soul-killing Cant, to what passes art thou bringing us!—Out of the loud-piping whirlwind, audibly to him that has ears, the Highest God is again announcing in these days: " Idleness shall not be." God has said it, man cannot gainsay.

Ah, how happy were it, if he this Aristocrat Worker would, in like manner, see *his* work and do it! It is frightful seeking another to do it for him. Guillotines, Meudon Tanneries, and half-a-million men shot dead, have already been expended in that business; and it is yet far from done. This man too is something; nay he is a great thing. Look on him there: a man of manful aspect; something of the 'cheerfulness of pride' still lingering in him. A free air of graceful stoicism, of easy silent dignity sits well on him; in his heart, could we reach it, lie elements of generosity, self-sacrificing justice, true human valour. Why should he, with such appliances, stand an incumbrance in the Present; perish disastrously out of the Future! From no section of the Future would we lose these noble courtesies, impalpable yet all-controlling; these dignified reticences, these kingly simplicities;—lose aught of what the fruitful Past still gives us token of, memento of, in this man. Can we not save him;—can he not help us to save him! A brave man, he too; had not undivine Ignavia, Hearsay, Speech without meaning,—had not Cant, thousandfold Cant within him and around him, enveloping him like choke-damp, like thick Egyptian darkness, thrown his soul into asphyxia, as it were extinguished his soul; so that he sees not, hears not, and Moses and all the Prophets address him in vain.

Will he awaken, be alive again, and have a soul; or is this death-fit very death? It is a question of questions, for himself and for us all! Alas, is there no noble work for this man too? Has not he thickheaded ignorant boors; lazy, enslaved farmers, weedy lands? Lands! Has not he weary heavy-laden ploughers of land; immortal souls of men, ploughing, ditching, day-drudging; bare of back, empty of stomach, nigh desperate of heart; and none peaceably to help them but he, under Heaven? Does he find, with his three-hundred thousand pounds, no noble thing trodden down in the thoroughfares, which it were godlike to help up? Can he do nothing for his Burns but make a Gauger of him; lionise him, bedinner him, for a foolish while; then whistle him down the wind, to desperation and bitter death?—His work too is difficult, in these modern, far-dislocated ages. But it may be done; it may be tried;—it must be done.

A modern Duke of Weimar, not a god he either, but a human duke, levied, as I reckon, in rents and taxes and all incomings whatsoever, less than several of our English Dukes do in rent alone. The Duke of Weimar, with these incomings, had to govern, judge, defend, everyway administer *his* Dukedom. He does all this as few others did: and he improves lands besides all this, makes river-embankments, maintains not soldiers only but Universities and Institutions;—and in his Court were these four men: Wieland, Herder, Schiller, Goethe. Not as parasites, which was impossible; not as table-wits and poetic Katerfeltoes; but as noble Spiritual Men working under a noble Practical Man. Shielded by him from many miseries; perhaps from many shortcomings, destructive aberrations. Heaven had sent, once more, heavenly Light into the world; and this man's honour was that he gave it welcome. A new noble kind of Clergy, under an old but still noble kind of King! I reckon that this one Duke of Weimar did more for the Culture of his Nation than all the English Dukes and *Duces* now extant, or that were extant since Henry the Eighth gave them the Church Lands to eat, have done for theirs!—I am ashamed, I am alarmed for my English Dukes: what word have I to say? *If* our Actual Aristocracy, appointed ' Best-and-Bravest,' will be wise, how inexpressibly happy for us! If not,—the voice of God from the whirlwind is very audible to me. Nay, I will thank the Great God, that He has said, in whatever fearful ways, and just wrath against us, " Idleness shall be no more! " Idleness? The awakened soul of man, all but the asphyxied soul of man, turns from it as from worse than death. It is the life-in-death of Poet Coleridge. That fable of the Dead-Sea Apes ceases to be a fable. The poor Worker starved to death is not the saddest of sights. He lies there, dead on his shield; fallen down into the bosom of his old Mother; with haggard pale face, sorrow-worn, but stilled now into divine peace, silently appeals to the Eternal God and all the Universe,—the most silent, the most eloquent of men.

Exceptions,—ah yes, thank Heaven, we know there are exceptions. Our case were too hard, were there not exceptions, and partial exceptions not a few, whom we know, and whom we do not know. Honour to the name of Ashley,—honour to this and the other valiant Abdiel, found faithful still; who would fain, by work and by word, admonish their Order not to rush upon destruction! These are they who will, if not save their Order, postpone the wreck of it;—by whom, under blessing of the Upper Powers, ' a quiet euthanasia spread over generations, instead of a swift torture-death concentred into years,' may be brought about for many things. All honour and success to these. The noble man can still strive nobly to save and serve his Order;—at lowest, he can remember the precept of the Prophet: " Come out of her, my people; come out of her! "

To sit idle aloft, like living statues, like absurd Epicurus'-gods, in pampered isolation, in exclusion from the glorious fateful battlefield of this God's-World: it is a poor life for a man, when all Upholsterers and

French-Cooks have done their utmost for it!—Nay what
a shallow delusion is this we have all got into, That
any man should or can keep himself apart from men,
have 'no business' with them, except a cash-account
'business'! It is the silliest tale a distressed generation
of men ever took to telling one another. Men cannot
live isolated: we *are* all bound together, for mutual good
or else for mutual misery, as living nerves in the same
body. No highest man can disunite himself from any
lowest. Consider it. Your poor 'Werter blowing out
his distracted existence because Charlotte will not have
the keeping thereof:' this is no peculiar phasis; it is
simply the highest expression of a phasis traceable
wherever one human creature meets another! Let the
meanest crookbacked Thersites teach the supremest
Agamemnon that he actually does not reverence him, the
supremest Agamemnon's eyes flash fire responsive; a
real pain and partial insanity has seized Agamemnon.
Strange enough: a many-counselled Ulysses is set in
motion by a scoundrel-blockhead; plays tunes, like a
barrel-organ, at the scoundrel-blockhead's touch,—has
to snatch, namely, his sceptre-cudgel, and weal the
crooked back with bumps and thumps! Let a chief of
men reflect well on it. Not in having 'no business' with
men, but in having no unjust business with them, and
in *having* all manner of true and just business, can either
his or their blessedness be found possible, and this waste
world become, for both parties, a home and peopled
garden.

Men do reverence men. Men do worship in that 'one
temple of the world,' as Novalis calls it, the Presence of
a Man! Hero-worship, true and blessed, or else mistaken,
false and accursed, goes on everywhere and everywhen.
In this world there is one godlike thing, the essence of
all that was or ever will be of godlike in this world: the
veneration done to Human Worth by the hearts of men.
Hero-worship, in the souls of the heroic, of the clear and
wise,—it is the perpetual presence of Heaven in our poor
Earth: when it is not there, Heaven is veiled from us;
and all is under Heaven's ban and interdict, and there

is no worship, or worth-ship, or worth or blessedness in
the Earth any more!—

Independence, 'lord of the lion-heart and eagle-eye,'
—alas, yes, he is one we have got acquainted with in
these late times: a very indispensable one, for spurning-
off with due energy innumerable sham-superiors, Tailor-
made: honour to him, entire success to him! Entire
success is sure to him. But he must not stop there, at
that small success, with his eagle-eye. He has now a
second far greater success to gain: to seek out his real
superiors, whom not the Tailor but the Almighty God has
made superior to him, and see a little what he will do
with these! Rebel against these also? Pass by with
minatory eagle-glance, with calm-sniffing mockery, or
even without any mockery or sniff, when these present
themselves? The lion-hearted will never dream of such
a thing. Forever far be it from him! His minatory
eagle-glance will veil itself in softness of the dove: his
lion-heart will become a lamb's; all its just indignation
changed into just reverence, dissolved in blessed floods of
noble humble love, how much heavenlier than any pride,
nay, if you will, how much prouder! I know him, this
lion-hearted, eagle-eyed one; have met him, rushing on,
'with bosom bare,' in a very distracted dishevelled
manner, the times being hard;—and can say, and
guarantee on my life, That in him is no rebellion; that
in him is the reverse of rebellion, the needful preparation
for obedience. For if you do mean to obey God-made
superiors, your first step is to sweep out the Tailor-made
ones; order them, under penalties, to vanish, to make
ready for vanishing!

Nay, what is best of all, he cannot rebel, if he would.
Superiors whom God has made for us we cannot order
to withdraw! Not in the least. No Grand-Turk himself, thickest-quilted tailor-made Brother of the Sun and
Moon can do it: but an Arab Man, in cloak of his own
clouting; with black beaming eyes, with flaming sovereign-
heart direct from the centre of the Universe; and also, I
am told, with terrible ' horseshoe vein ' of swelling wrath
in his brow, and lightning (if you will not have it as

light) tingling through every vein of him,—he rises; says authoritatively: "Thickest-quilted Grand-Turk, tailor-made Brother of the Sun and Moon, No:—*I* withdraw not; thou shalt obey me or withdraw!" And so accordingly it is: thickest-quilted Grand-Turks and all their progeny, to this hour, obey that man in the remarkablest manner; preferring *not* to withdraw.

O brother, it is an endless consolation to me, in this disorganic, as yet so quack-ridden, what you may well call hag-ridden and hell-ridden world, to find that disobedience to the Heavens, when they send any messenger whatever, is and remains impossible. It cannot be done; no Turk grand or small can do it. 'Show the dullest clodpole,' says my invaluable German friend, 'show the haughtiest feather-head, that a soul higher than himself is here; were his knees stiffened into brass, he must down and worship.'

CHAPTER VII

THE GIFTED

YES, in what tumultuous huge anarchy soever a Noble human Principle may dwell and strive, such tumult is in the way of being calmed into a fruitful sovereignty. It is inevitable. No Chaos can continue chaotic with a soul in it. Besouled with earnest human Nobleness, did not slaughter, violence and fire-eyed fury, grow into a Chivalry; into a blessed Loyalty of Governor and Governed? And in Work, which is of itself noble, and the only true fighting, there shall be no such possibility? Believe it not; it is incredible; the whole Universe contradicts it. Here too the Chactaw Principle will be subordinated; the Man Principle will, by degrees, become superior, become supreme.

I know Mammon too; Banks-of-England, Credit-Systems, world-wide possibilities of work and traffic; and applaud and admire them. Mammon is like Fire; the usefulest of all servants, if the frightfulest of all masters!

The Cliffords, Fitzadelms and Chivalry Fighters 'wished to gain victory,' never doubt it: but victory, unless gained in a certain spirit, was no victory; defeat, sustained in a certain spirit, was itself victory. I say again and again, had they counted the scalps alone, they had continued Chactaws, and no Chivalry or lasting victory had been. And in Industrial Fighters and Captains is there no nobleness discoverable? To them, alone of men, there shall forever be no blessedness but in swollen coffers? To see beauty, order, gratitude, loyal human hearts around them, shall be of no moment; to see fuliginous deformity, mutiny, hatred and despair, with the addition of half-a-million guineas, shall be better? Heaven's blessedness not there; Hell's cursedness, and your half-million bits of metal, a substitute for that! Is there no profit in diffusing Heaven's blessedness, but only in gaining gold?—If so, I apprise the Mill-owner and Millionaire, that he too must prepare for vanishing; that neither is *he* born to be of the sovereigns of this world; that he will have to be trampled and chained down in whatever terrible ways, and brass-collared safe, among the born thralls of this world! We cannot have *Canailles* and Doggeries that will not make some Chivalry of themselves: our noble Planet is impatient of such; in the end, totally intolerant of such!

For the Heavens, unwearying in their bounty, do send other souls into this world, to whom yet, as to their fore runners in Old Roman, in Old Hebrew and all noble times, the omnipotent guinea is, on the whole, an impotent guinea. Has your half-dead avaricious Corn-Law Lord, your half-alive avaricious Cotton-Law Lord, never seen one such? Such are, not one, but several: are, and will be, unless the gods have doomed this world to swift dire ruin. These are they, the elect of the world; the born champions, strong men, and liberatory Samsons of this poor world: whom the poor Delilah-wo ld will not always shear of their strength and eyesight, and set to grind in darkness at *its* poor gin-wheel! Such souls are, in the se days, getting somewhat out of humour with the world. Your very Byron, in these days, is at least driven mad;

flatly refuses fealty to the world. The world with its
injustices, its golden brutalities, and dull yellow guineas,
is a disgust to such souls: the ray of Heaven that is in
them does at least predoom them to be very miserable
here. Yes:—and yet all misery is faculty misdirected,
strength that has not yet found its way. The black whirlwind is mother of the lightning. No *smoke*, in any sense,
but can become flame and radiance! Such soul, once
graduated in Heaven's stern University, steps out
superior to your guinea.

Dost thou know, O sumptuous Corn-Lord, Cotton-Lord,
O mutinous Trades-Unionist, gin-vanquished, undeliverable; O much-enslaved World,—this man is not a slave
with thee! None of thy promotions is necessary for him.
His place is with the stars of Heaven: to thee it may
be momentous, to thee it may be life or death, to him
it is indifferent, whether thou place him in the lowest
hut, or forty feet higher at the top of thy stupendous
high tower, while here on Earth. The joys of Earth that
are precious, they depend not on thee and thy promotions.
Food and raiment, and, round a social hearth, souls who
love him, whom he loves: these are already his. He
wants none of thy rewards; behold also, he fears none of
thy penalties. Thou canst not answer even by killing
him: the case of Anaxarchus thou canst kill; but the
self of Anaxarchus, the word or act of Anaxarchus, in no
wise whatever. To this man death is not a bugbear; to
this man life is already as earnest and awful, and beautiful
and terrible, as death.

Not a May-game is this man's life; but a battle and a
march, a warfare with principalities and powers. No
idle promenade through fragrant orange-groves and green
flowery spaces, waited on by the choral Muses and the
rosy Hours: it is a stern pilgrimage through burning
sandy solitudes, through regions of thick-ribbed ice. He
walks among men; loves men, with inexpressible soft
pity,—as they *cannot* love him: but his soul dwells in
solitude, in the uttermost parts of Creation. In green
oases by the palm-tree wells, he rests a space; but anon
he has to journey forward, escorted by the Terrors and

the Splendours, the Archdemons and Archangels. All
Heaven, all Pandemonium are his escort. The stars
keen-glancing, from the Immensities, send tidings to
him; the graves, silent with their dead, from the
Eternities. Deep calls for him unto Deep.

Thou, O World, how wilt thou secure thyself against
this man? Thou canst not hire him by thy guineas;
nor by thy gibbets and law-penalties restrain him. He
eludes thee like a Spirit. Thou canst not forward him,
thou canst not hinder him. Thy penalties, thy poverties,
neglects, contumelies: behold, all these are good for him.
Come to him as an enemy; turn from him as an un-
friend; only do not this one thing,—infect him not with
thy own delusion: the benign Genius, were it by very
death, shall guard him against this!—What wilt thou do
with him? He is above thee, like a god. Thou, in thy
stupendous three-inch pattens, art under him. He is
thy born king, thy conqueror and supreme lawgiver: not
all the guineas and cannons, and leather and prunella,
under the sky can save thee from him. Hardest thick-
skinned Mammon-world, ruggedest Caliban shall obey
him, or become not Caliban but a cramp. Oh, if in this
man, whose eyes can flash Heaven's lightning, and make
all Calibans into a cramp, there dwelt not, as the essence
of his very being, a God's justice, human Nobleness,
Veracity and Mercy,—I should tremble for the world.
But his strength, let us rejoice to understand, is even this:
The quantity of Justice, of Valour and Pity that is in
him. To hypocrites and tailored quacks in high places
his eyes are lightning; but they melt in dewy pity softer
than a mother's to the downpressed, maltreated; in his
heart, in his great thought, is a sanctuary for all the
wretched. This world's improvement is forever sure.

'Man of Genius?' Thou hast small notion, meseems,
O Mæcenas Twiddledee, of what a Man of Genius is.
Read in thy New Testament and elsewhere,—if, with
floods of mealy-mouthed inanity; with miserable froth-
vortices of Cant now several centuries old, thy New
Testament is not all bedimmed for thee. *Canst* thou
read in thy New Testament at all? The Highest Man of

Genius, knowest thou him; Godlike and a God to this hour? His crown a Crown of Thorns? Thou fool, with *thy* empty Godhoods, Apotheoses *edge-gilt ;* the Crown of Thorns made into a poor jewel-room crown, fit for the head of blockheads; the bearing of the Cross changed to a riding in the Long-Acre Gig! Pause in thy mass-chantings, in thy litanyings, and Calmuck prayings by machinery; and pray, if noisily, at least in a more human manner. How with thy rubrics and dalmatics, and cloth-webs and cobwebs, and with thy stupidities and grovelling baseheartedness, hast thou hidden the Holiest into all but invisibility!—

'Man of Genius:' O Mæcenas Twiddledee, hast thou any notion what a Man of Genius is? Genius is 'the inspired gift of God.' It is the clearer presence of God Most High in a man. Dim, potential in all men; in this man it has become clear, actual. So says John Milton, who ought to be a judge; so answer him the Voices of all Ages and all Worlds. Wouldst thou commune with such a one? *Be* his real peer, then: does that lie in thee? Know thyself and thy real and thy apparent place, and know him and his real and his apparent place, and act in some noble conformity with all that. What! The star-fire of the Empyrean shall eclipse itself, and illuminate magic-lanterns to amuse grown children? He, the god-inspired, is to twang harps for thee, and blow through scrannel-pipes, to soothe thy sated soul with visions of new, still wider Eldorados, Houri Paradises, richer Lands of Cockaigne? Brother, this is not he; this is a counterfeit, this twangling, jangling, vain, acrid, scrannel-piping man. Thou dost well to say with sick Saul, " It is nought, such harping! "—and in sudden rage, to grasp thy spear, and try if thou canst pin such a one to the wall. King Saul was mistaken in his man, but thou art right in thine. It is the due of such a one: nail him to the wall, and leave him there. So ought copper shillings to be nailed on counters; copper geniuses on walls, and left there for a sign!—

I conclude that the Men of Letters too may become a 'Chivalry,' an actual instead of a virtual Priesthood, with result immeasurable,—so soon as there is nobleness in themselves for that. And, to a certainty, not sooner! Of intrinsic Valetisms you cannot, with whole Parliaments to help you, make a Heroism. Doggeries never so gold-plated, Doggeries never so escutcheoned, Doggeries never so diplomaed, bepuffed, gas-lighted, continue Doggeries, and must take the fate of such.

CHAPTER VIII

THE DIDACTIC

CERTAINLY it were a fond imagination to expect that any preaching of mine could abate Mammonism; that Bobus of Houndsditch will love his guineas less, or his poor soul more, for any preaching of mine! But there is one Preacher who does preach with effect, and gradually persuade all persons: his name is Destiny, is Divine Providence, and his Sermon the inflexible Course of Things. Experience does take dreadfully high school-wages; but he teaches like no other!

I revert to Friend Prudence the good Quaker's refusal of ' seven thousand pounds to boot.' Friend Prudence's practical conclusion will, by degrees, become that of all rational practical men whatsoever. On the present scheme and principle, Work cannot continue. Trades' Strikes, Trades' Unions, Chartisms; mutiny, squalor, rage and desperate revolt, growing ever more desperate, will go on their way. As dark misery settles down on us, and our refuges of lies fall in pieces one after one, the hearts of men, now at last serious, will turn to refuges of truth. The eternal stars shine out again, so soon as it is dark *enough*.

Begirt with desperate Trades' Unionism and Anarchic Mutiny, many an Industrial *Law-ward*, by and by, who has neglected to make laws and keep them, will be heard saying to himself: " Why have I realised five hundred thousand pounds? I rose early and sat late, I toiled and moiled,

and in the sweat of my brow and of my soul I strove to
gain this money, that I might become conspicuous, and
have some honour among my fellow-creatures. I wanted
them to honour me, to love me. The money is here,
earned with my best lifeblood: but the honour? I am
encircled with squalor, with hunger, rage, and sooty
desperation. Not honoured, hardly even envied; only
fools and the flunky-species so much as envy me. I am
conspicuous,—as a mark for curses and brickbats. What
good is it? My five hundred scalps hang here in my
wigwam: would to Heaven I had sought something else
than the scalps; would to Heaven I had been a Christian
Fighter, not a Chactaw one! To have been ruled and fought
not in a Mammonish but in a Godlike spirit; to have had
the hearts of the people bless me, as a true ruler and
captain of my people; to have felt my own heart bless me,
and that God above instead of Mammon below was blessing me,—this had been something. Out of my sight, ye
beggarly five hundred scalps of banker's-thousands: I
will try for something other, or account my life a tragical
futility! "

Friend Prudence's ' rock-ledge,' as we called it, will
gradually disclose itself to many a man; to all men.
Gradually, assaulted from beneath and from above, the
Stygian mud-deluge of Laissez-faire, Supply-and-demand,
Cash-payment the one Duty, will abate on all hands;
and the everlasting mountain-tops, and secure rock-founda-
tions that reach to the centre of the world, and rest on
Nature's self, will again emerge, to found on, and to build
on. When Mammon-worshippers here and there begin
to be God-worshippers, and bipeds-of-prey become men,
and there is a Soul felt once more in the huge-pulsing
elephantine mechanic Animalism of this Earth, it will be
again a blessed Earth.

" Men cease to regard money? " cries Bobus of Houndsditch: " What else do all men strive for? The very
Bishop informs me that Christianity cannot get on without a minimum of Four thousand five hundred in its
pocket. Cease to regard money? That will be at
Doomsday in the afternoon! "—O Bobus, my opinion is

somewhat different. My opinion is, that the Upper Powers have not yet determined on destroying this Lower World. A respectable, ever-increasing minority, who do strive for something higher than money, I with confidence anticipate; ever-increasing, till there be a sprinkling of them found in all quarters, as salt of the Earth once more. The Christianity that cannot get on without a minimum of Four thousand five hundred, will give place to something better that can. Thou wilt not join our small minority, thou? Not till Doomsday in the afternoon? Well; *then*, at least, thou wilt join it, thou and the majority in mass!

But truly it is beautiful to see the brutish empire of Mammon cracking everywhere; giving sure promise of dying, or of being changed. A strange, chill, almost ghastly dayspring strikes up in Yankeeland itself: my Transcendental friends announce there, in a distinct, though somewhat lankhaired, ungainly manner, that the Demiurgus Dollar is dethroned; that new unheard-of Demuirgusships, Priesthoods, Aristocracies, Growths and Destructions, are already visible in the gray of coming Time. Chronos is dethroned by Jove; Odin by St. Olaf: the Dollar cannot rule in Heaven forever. No; I reckon, not. Socinian Preachers quit their pulpits in Yankeeland, saying, " Friends, this is all gone to coloured cobweb, we regret to say! "—and retire into the fields to cultivate onion-beds, and live frugally on vegetables. It is very notable. Old godlike Calvinism declares that its old body is now fallen to tatters, and done; and its mournful ghost, disembodied, seeking new embodiment, pipes again in the winds;—a ghost and spirit as yet, but heralding new Spirit-worlds, and better Dynasties than the Dollar one.

Yes, here as there, light is coming into the world; men love not darkness, they do love light. A deep feeling of the eternal nature of Justice looks out among us every-where,—even through the dull eyes of Exeter Hall; an unspeakable religiousness struggles, in the most helpless manner, to speak itself, in Puseyisms and the like. Of our Cant, all condemnable, how much is not condemnable without pity; we had almost said, without respect! The *in*articulate worth and truth that is in England goes down yet to the Foundations.

Some ' Chivalry of Labour,' some noble Humanity and practical Divineness of Labour, will yet be realised on this Earth. Or why *will ;* why do we pray to Heaven, without setting our own shoulder to the wheel? The Present, if it will have the Future accomplish, shall itself commence. Thou who prophesiest, who believest, begin thou to fulfil. Here or nowhere, now equally as at any time! That outcast help-needing thing or person, trampled down under vulgar feet or hoofs, no help ' possible ' for it, no prize offered for the saving of it,—canst not thou save it, then, without prize? Put forth thy hand, in God's name; know that ' impossible,' where Truth and Mercy and the everlasting Voice of Nature order, has no place in the brave man's dictionary. That when all men have said " Impossible," and tumbled noisily elsewhither, and thou alone art left, then first thy time and possibility have come. It is for thee now; do thou that, and ask no man's counsel, but thy own only, and God's. Brother, thou hast possibility in thee for much: the possibility of writing on the eternal skies the record of a heroic life. That noble down-fallen or yet unborn ' Impossibility,' thou canst lift it up, thou canst, by thy soul's travail, bring it into clear being. That loud inane Actuality, with millions in its pocket, too ' possible ' that, which rolls along there, with quilted trumpeters blaring round it, and all the world escorting it as mute or vocal flunky,—escort it not thou; say to it, either nothing, or else deeply in thy heart: " Loud-blaring Nonentity, no force of trumpets, cash, Long-acre art, or universal flunkyhood of men, makes thee an Entity; thou art a *Non*entity, and deceptive Simulacrum, more accursed than thou seemest. Pass on in the Devil's name, unworshipped by at least one man, and leave the thorough-fare clear! "

Not on Ilion's or Latium's plains; on far other plains and places henceforth can noble deeds be now done. Not on Ilion's plains; how much less in Mayfair's drawing-rooms! Not in victory over poor brother French or Phryg'ans; but in v:ctory over Frost-jötuns, Marshgiants, over demons of Discord, Idleness, Injustice, Unreason, and Chaos come again. None of the old Epics is longer possible. The Epic of French and Phrygians was comparatively a small Epic: but that of Flirts and Fribbles, what is that? A thing that vanishes at cock-crowing,— that already begins to scent the morning air! Game-preserving Aristocracies, let them ' bush ' never so effectually, cannot escape the Subtle Fowler. Game seasons will be excellent, and again will be indifferent, and by and by they will not be at all. The Last Partridge of England, of an England where millions of men can get no corn to eat, will be shot and ended. Aristocracies with beards on their chins will find other work to do than amuse themselves with trundling-hoops.

But it is to you, ye Workers, who do already work, and are as grown men, noble and honourable in a sort, that the whole world calls for new work and nobleness. Subdue mutiny, discord, wide-spread despair, by manfulness, justice, mercy and wisdom. Chaos is dark, deep as Hell; let light be, and there is instead a green flowery World. Oh, it is great, and there is no other greatness. To make some nook of God's Creation a little fruitfuller, better, more worthy of God; to make some human hearts a little wiser, manfuler, happier,—more blessed, less accursed! It is work for a God. Sooty Hell of mutiny and savagery and despair can, by man's energy, be made a kind of Heaven; cleared of its soot, of its mutiny, of its need to mutiny; the everlasting arch of Heaven's azure overspanning *it* too, and its cunning mechanisms and tall chimney-steeples, as a birth of Heaven; God and all men looking on it well pleased.

Unstained by wasteful deformities, by wasted tears or heart's-blood of men, or any defacement of the Pit, noble fruitful Labour, growing ever nobler, will come forth,—the grand sole miracle of Man; whereby Man has risen from the low places of this Earth, very literally, into divine Heavens. Ploughers, Spinners, Builders; Prophets, Poets, Kings; Brindleys and Goethes, Odins and Arkwrights; all martyrs, and noble men, and gods are of one grand

Host; immeasurable; marching ever forward since the
beginnings of the World. The enormous, all-conquering,
flame-crowned Host, noble every soldier in it; sacred,
and alone noble. Let him who is not of it hide himself;
let him tremble for himself. Stars at every button cannot
make him noble; sheaves of Bath-garters, nor bushels of
Georges; nor any other contrivance but manfully enlisting
in it, valiantly taking place and step in it. O Heavens,
will he not bethink himself; he too is so needed in the
Host! It were so blessed, thrice-blessed, for himself and
for us all! In hope of the Last Partridge, and some Duke
of Weimar among our English Dukes, we will be patient
yet a while.

> 'The Future hides in it
> Gladness and sorrow;
> We press still thorow,
> Nought that abides in it
> Daunting us,—onward.'

SUMMARY

BOOK I.—PROEM

Chap. I. *Midas*

THE condition of England one of the most ominous ever seen in this world: Full of wealth in every kind, yet dying of inanition. Workhouses, in which no work can be done. Destitution in Scotland. Stockport Assizes. (p. 1.)—England's unprofitable success: Human faces glooming discordantly on one another. Midas longed for gold, and the gods gave it him. (5.)

Chap. II. *The Sphinx*

The grand unnamable Sphinx-riddle, which each man is called upon to solve. Notions of the foolish concerning justice and judgment. Courts of Westminster, and the general High Court of the Universe. The one strong thing, the just thing, the true thing. (p. 7.)—A noble Conservatism, as well as an ignoble. In all battles of men each fighter, in the end, prospers according to his right: Wallace of Scotland. (11.)—Fact and Semblance. What is Justice? As many men as there are in a Nation who can *see* Heaven's Justice, so many are there who stand between it and perdition. (13.)

Chap. III. *Manchester Insurrection*

Peterloo not an unsuccessful Insurrection. Governors who wait for Insurrection to instruct them, getting into the fatalest courses. Unspeakable County Yeomanry. Poor Manchester operatives, and their huge inarticulate question: Unhappy Workers, unhappier idlers, of this actual England! (p. 14.)—Fair day's-wages for fair day's-work: Milton's 'wages;' Cromwell's. Pay to each man what he has earned and done and deserved; what more have we to ask?—Some not *in*supportable approximation indispensable and inevitable. (18.)

Chap. IV. *Morrison's Pill*

A state of mind worth reflecting on. No Morrison's Pill for curing the maladies of Society: Universal alteration of regimen and way of life: Vain jargon giving place to some genuine Speech again. (p. 22.)—If we walk according to the Law of this Universe, the Law-Maker will befriend us; if not, not. Quacks, sham heroes, the one bane of the world. Quack and Dupe, upper side and under of the selfsame substance. (24.)

Chap. V. *Aristocracy of Talent*

All misery the fruit of unwisdom: Neither with individuals nor with Nations is it fundamentally otherwise. Nature in late centuries universally supposed to be dead; but now everywhere asserting herself to be alive and miraculous. The guidance of this country not sufficiently wise. (p. 26.)—Aristocracy of talent, or government by the Wisest, a dreadfully difficult affair to get started. The true *eye* for talent; and the flunky eye for respectabilities, warm garnitures and larders dropping fatness: Bobus and Bobissimus. (30.)

Chap. VI. *Hero-worship*

Enlightened Egoism, never so luminous, not the rule by which man's life can be led: A *soul*, different from a stomach in any sense of the word. Hero-worship done differently in every different epoch of the world. Reform, like Charity, must begin at home. 'Arrestment of the knaves and dastards,' beginning by arresting our own poor selves out of that fraternity. (p. 32.)—The present Editor's purpose to himself full of hope. A Loadstar in the eternal sky: A glimmering of light, for here and there a human soul. (35.)

BOOK II.—THE ANCIENT MONK

Chap. I. *Jocelin of Brakelond*

How the Centuries stand lineally related to each other. The one Book not permissible, the kind that has nothing in it. Jocelin's 'Chronicle,' a private Boswellean Note-book, now seven centuries old. How Jocelin, from under his monk's cowl, looked out on that narrow section of the world in a really *human* manner: A wise simplicity in him; a *veracity* that goes deeper than words. Jocelin's Monk-Latin; and Mr. Rokewood's editorial helpfulness and fidelity. (p. 38.)— A veritable Monk of old Bury St. Edmunds worth attending to. This England of ours, of the year 1200: Cœur-de-Lion: King Lackland, and his thirteenpenny mass. The poorest historical Fact, and the grandest imaginative Fiction. (42.)

Chap. II. *St. Edmundsbury*

St. Edmund's Bury, a prosperous brisk Town: Extensive ruins of the Abbey still visible. Assiduous Pedantry, and its rubbish-heaps called 'History.' Another world it was, when those black ruins first saw the sun as walls. At lowest, O dilettante friend, let us know always that it *was* a world. No easy matter to get across the chasm of Seven Centuries: Of all helps, a Boswell, even a small Boswell, the welcomest. (p. 45.)

CHAP. III. *Landlord Edmund*

' Battle of Fornham,' a fact, though a forgotten one. Edmund, Landlord of the Eastern Counties: A very singular kind of ' landlord.' How he came to be ' sainted.' Seen and felt to have done verily a man's part in this life-pilgrimage of his. How they took up the slain body of their Edmund, and reverently embalmed it. (p. 49.)—Pious munificence, ever growing by new pious gifts. Certain Times do crystallise themselves in a magnificent manner; others in a rather shabby one. (54.)

CHAP. IV. *Abbot Hugo*

All things have two faces, a light one and a dark: The Ideal has to grow in the Real, and to seek its bed and board there, often in a very sorry manner. Abbot Hugo, grown old and feeble. Jew debts and Jew creditors. How approximate justice strives to accomplish itself. (p. 55.)—In the old monastic Books almost no mention whatever of ' personal religion.' A poor Lord Abbot, all stuck-over with horse-leeches: A ' royal commission of inquiry,' to no purpose. A monk's first duty, obedience. Magister Samson, Teacher of the Novices. The Abbot's providential death. (58.)

CHAP. V. *Twelfth Century*

Inspectors or Custodiars; the King not in any breathless haste to appoint a new Abbot. Dim and very strange looks that monk-life to us. Our venerable ancient spinning grand-mothers, shrieking, and rushing out with their distaffs. Laken-heath eels too slippery to be caught. (p. 60.)—How much is alive in England, in that Twelfth Century; how much not yet come into life. Feudal Aristocracy; Willelmus Con-quæstor: Not a steeple-chimney yet got on end from sea to sea. (63).

CHAP. VI. *Monk Samson*

Monk-Life and Monk-Religion: A great heaven-high Unquestionability, encompassing, interpenetrating all human Duties. Our modern Arkwright Joe - Manton ages: All human dues and reciprocities changed into one great due of ' cash-payment.' The old monks but a limited class of creatures, with a somewhat dull life of it. (p. 64.)—One Monk of a taciturn nature distinguishes himself among those bab-bling ones. A Son of poor Norfolk parents. Little Samson's awful dream: His poor Mother dedicates him to St. Edmund. He grows to be a learned man, of devout grave nature. Sent to Rome on business; and returns *too* successful: Method of travelling thither in those days. His tribulations at home: Strange conditions under which Wisdom has sometimes to struggle with folly. (67.)

Chap. VII. *The Canvassing*

A new Abbot to be elected. Even gossip, seven centuries off, has significance. The Prior with Twelve Monks, to wait on his Majesty at Waltham. An ' election ' the one important social act: Given the Man a People choose, the worth and worthlessness of the People itself is given. (p. 71.)

Chap. VIII. *The Election*

Electoral methods and manipulations. Brother Samson ready oftenest with some question, some suggestion that has wisdom in it. The Thirteen off to Waltham, to choose their Abbot: In the solitude of the Convent, Destiny thus big and in her birthtime, what gossiping, babbling, dreaming of dreams! (p. 74.)—King Henry II. in his high Presence-chamber. Samson chosen Abbot: the King's royal acceptation. (77.)—St. Edmundsbury Monks, without express ballot-box or other winnowing machine. In every nation and Community there is at all times *a fittest*, wisest, bravest, best. Human Worth and human Worthlessness. (80.)

Chap. IX. *Abbot Samson*

The Lord Abbot's arrival at St. Edmundsbury: The self-same Samson yesterday a poor mendicant, this day finds himself a *Dominus Abbas* and mitred Peer of Parliament. (p. 81.)—Depth and opulence of true social vitality in those old barbarous ages. True Governors go about under all manner of disguises now as then. Genius, Poet; what these words mean. George the Third, head charioteer of England; and Robert Burns, gauger of ale in Dumfries. (82.)—How Abbot Samson found a Convent all in dilapidation. His life-long harsh apprenticeship to governing, namely obeying. First get your Man; all is got. Danger of blockheads. (84.)

Chap. X. *Government*

Beautiful, how the chrysalis governing-soul, shaking off its dusty slough and prison, starts forth winged, a true royal soul! One first labour, to institute a strenuous review and radical reform of his economics. Wheresoever Disorder may stand or lie, let it have a care; here is a man that has declared war with it. (p. 87.)—In less than four years the Convent debts are all liquidated, and the harpy Jews banished from St. Edmundsbury. New life springs beneficent everywhere: Spiritual rubbish as little tolerated as material. (89.)

Chap. XI. *The Abbot's Ways*

Reproaches, open and secret, of ingratitude, unsociability: Except for ' fit men ' in all kinds, hard to say for whom Abbot Samson had much favour. Remembrance of benefits. (p. 91). —An eloquent man, but intent more on substance than on ornament. A just clear heart the basis of all true talent.

One of the justest of judges: His invaluable ' talent of silence.'
Kind of people he liked worst. Hospitality and stoicism.
(92.)—The country in those days still dark with noble wood
and umbrage: How the old trees gradually died out, no man
heeding it. Monachism itself, so rich and fruitful once, now
all rotted into *peat*. Devastations of four-footed cattle and
Henry-the-Eighths. (95.)

CHAP. XII. *The Abbot's Troubles*

The troubles of Abbot Samson more than tongue can tell.
Not the spoil of victory, only the glorious toil of battle, can
be theirs who really govern. An insurrection of the Monks:
Behave better, ye remiss Monks, and thank Heaven for such
an Abbot. (p. 96.)—Worn down with incessant toil and
tribulation: Gleams of hilarity too; little snatches of encouragement granted even to a Governor. How my Lord of Clare,
coming to claim his *un*due ' debt,' gets a Roland for his Oliver.
A Life of Literature, noble and ignoble. (98.)

CHAP. XIII. *In Parliament*

Confused days of Lackland's usurpation, while Cœur-de-
Lion was away: Our brave Abbot took helmet himself,
excommunicating all who should favour Lackland. King
Richard a captive in Germany. (p. 101.)—St. Edmund's
Shrine not meddled with: A heavenly Awe overshadowed
and encompassed, as it still ought and must, all earthly
Business whatsoever. (102.)

CHAP. XIV. *Henry of Essex*

How St. Edmund punished terribly, yet with mercy;
A Narrative significant of the Time. Henry Earl of Essex,
standard-bearer of England: No right reverence for the
Heavenly in Man. A traitor or a coward. Solemn Duel,
by the King's appointment. An evil Conscience doth make
cowards of us all. (p. 103.)

CHAP. XV. *Practical-Devotional*

A Tournament proclaimed and held in the Abbot's domain,
in spite of him. Roystering young dogs brought to reason.
The Abbot a man that generally remains master at last:
The importunate Bishop of Ely outwitted. A man that dare
abide King Richard's anger, with justice on his side. Thou
brave Richard, thou brave Samson! (p. 107.)—The basis of
Abbot Samson's life truly religion. His zealous interest in
the Crusades. The great antique heart, like a child's in its
simplicity, like a man's in its earnest solemnity and depth.
His comparative silence as to his religion precisely the
healthiest sign of him and it. Methodism, Dilettantism,
Puseyism. (111.)

Chap. XVI. *St. Edmund*

Abbot Samson built many useful, many pious edifices: All ruinous, incomplete things an eye-sorrow to him. Rebuilding the great Altar: A glimpse of the glorious Martyr's very Body. What a scene; how far vanished from us, in these unworshipping ages of ours! The manner of men's Hero-worship, verily the innermost fact of their existence, determining all the rest. (p. 114.)—On the whole, who knows how to reverence the Body of Man? Abbot Samson, at the culminating point of his existence: Our real-phantasmagory of St. Edmundsbury plunges into the bosom of the Twelfth Century again, and all is over. (119.)

Chap. XVII. *The Beginnings*

Formulas the very skin and muscular tissue of a Man's Life: Living Formulas and dead. Habit the deepest law of human nature. A pathway through the pathless. Nationalities. Pulpy infancy, kneaded, baked into any form you choose: The Man of Business; the hard-handed Labourer; the genus Dandy. No Mortal out of the depths of Bedlam but lives by Formulas. (p. 122.)—The hosts and generations of brave men Oblivion has swallowed: Their crumbled dust, the soil our life-fruit grows on. Invention of Speech; Forms of Worship; Methods of Justice. This English Land, here and now, the summary of what was wise and noble, and accordant with God's Truth, in all the generations of English Men. The thing called 'Fame.' (125.)

BOOK III.—THE MODERN WORKER

Chap. I. *Phenomena*

How men have 'forgotten God;' taken the Fact of this Universe as it is *not ;* God's Laws become a Greatest-Happiness Principle, a Parliamentary Expediency. Man has lost the *soul* out of him, and begins to find the want of it. (p. 131.) —The old Pope of Rome, with his stuffed dummy to do the kneeling for him. Few men that worship by the rotatory Calabash, do it in half so great, frank or effectual a way. (132.)—Our Aristocracy no longer able to *do* its work, and not in the least conscious that it has any work to do. The Champion of England 'lifted into his saddle.' The Hatter in the Strand, mounting a huge lath-and-plaster Hat. Our noble ancestors have fashioned for us, in how many thousand senses, a 'life-road;' and we their sons are madly, literally enough, 'consuming the way.' (134.)

Chap. II. *Gospel of Mammonism*

Heaven and Hell, often as the words are on our tongue, got to be fabulous or semi-fabulous for most of us. The real

' Hell ' of the English.   Cash-payment, *not* the sole or even chief relation of human beings.   Practical Atheism, and its despicable fruits. (p. 139.)—One of Dr. Alison's melancholy facts: A poor Irish Widow, in the Lanes of Edinburgh, *proving* her sisterhood.   Until we get a human *soul* within us, all things are *im*possible: Infatuated geese, with feathers and without. (143.)

Chap. III. *Gospel of Dilettantism*

Mammonism at least works; but ' Go gracefully idle in Mayfair,' what does or can that mean?—Impotent, insolent Donothingism in Practice and Saynothingism in Speech.   No man now speaks a plain word: Insincere Speech the prime material of insincere Action. (p. 144.)—Moslem parable of Moses and the Dwellers by the Dead Sea: The Universe *become* a Humbug to the Apes that thought it one. (146.)

Chap. IV. *Happy*

All work noble; and every noble crown a crown of thorns. Man's pitiful pretension to be what he calls ' happy: ' His Greatest-Happiness Principle fast becoming a rather un-happy one.   Byron's large audience.   A philosophical Doctor: A disconsolate Meat-jack, gnarring and creaking with rust and work. (p. 147.)—The only ' happiness ' a brave man ever troubled himself much about, the happiness to get his work done. (150.)

Chap. V. *The English*

With all thy theoretic platitudes, what a depth of practical sense in thee, great England!   A dumb people, who can do great acts, but not describe them.   The noble Warhorse, and the Dog of Knowledge: The freest utterances not by any means the best. (p. 151.)—The done Work, much more than the spoken Word, an epitome of the man.   The Man of Practice, and the Man of Theory: Ineloquent Brindley.   The English, of all Nations the stupidest in speech, the wisest in action: Sadness and seriousness: Unconsciously this great Universe is great to them.   The silent Romans.   John Bull's admirable insensibility to Logic. (152.)—All great Peoples conservative.   Kind of Ready-Reckoner a Solecism in East-cheap.   Berserkir rage.   Truth and Justice alone *capable* of being ' conserved.'   Bitter indignation engendered by the Corn-Laws in every just English heart. (156.)

Chap. VI. *Two Centuries*

The ' Settlement ' of the year 1660 one of the mournfulest that ever took place in this land of ours.   The true end of Government, to guide men in the way they should go: The true good of this life, the portal of infinite good in the life to come. Oliver Cromwell's body hung on the Tyburn gallows, the type of Puritanism found futile, inexecutable, execrable. The Spiritualism of England, for two godless centuries, utterly forgettable: Her practical material Work alone memorable. (p. 160.) — Bewildering obscurations and impediments: Valiant Sons of Toil enchanted, by the million, in their Poor-Law Bastille. Giant Labour yet to be King of this Earth. (163.)

CHAP. VII. *Over-Production*

An idle Governing Class addressing its Workers with an indictment of ' Over-production.' Duty of justly apportioning the Wages of Work done. A game-preserving Aristocracy, guiltless of producing or apportioning anything. Owning the soil of England. (p. 164.)—The Working Aristocracy steeped in ignoble Mammonism: The Idle Aristocracy, with its yellow parchments and pretentious futilities. (166.)

CHAP. VIII. *Unworking Aristocracy*

Our Land the *Mother* of us all: No true Aristocracy but must possess the Land. Men talk of ' selling ' Land! Whom it belongs to. Our much-consuming Aristocracy: By the law of their position bound to furnish guidance and governance. Mad and miserable Corn-Laws. (p. 168.)—The Working Aristocracy, and its terrible New-Work: The Idle Aristocracy, and its horoscope of despair. (170.)—A High Class without duties to do, like a tree planted on precipices. In a valiant suffering for others, not in a slothful making others suffer for us, did nobleness ever lie. The Pagan Hercules; the Czar of Russia. (172.)—Parchments, venerable and not venerable. Benedict the Jew, and his usuries. No Chapter on the Corn-Laws: The Corn-Laws too mad to have a Chapter. (174.)

CHAP. IX. *Working Aristocracy*

Many things for the Working Aristocracy, in their extreme need, to consider. A National Existence supposed to depend on ' selling cheaper ' than any other People. Let inventive men try to invent a little how cotton at its present cheapness could be somewhat justlier divided. Many ' impossibles ' will have to become possible. (p. 176.)—Supply-and-demand: For what noble work was there ever yet any audible ' demand ' in that poor sense? (179.)

CHAP. X. *Plugson of Undershot*

Man's Philosophies usually the ' supplement of his practice: ' Symptoms of social death. Cash-Payment: The Plugson Ledger, and the Tablets of Heaven's Chancery, discrepant exceedingly. (p. 181.)—All human things do require to have an Ideal in them. How murderous fighting became a ' glorious

Chivalry.' Noble devout - hearted Chevaliers. Ignoble
Bucaniers and Chactaw Indians: Howel Davies. Napoleon
flung out, at last, to St. Helena; the latter end of him sternly
compensating for the beginning. (183.)—The indomitable
Plugson, as yet a Bucanier and Chactaw. William Conqueror
and his Norman followers. Organisation of Labour: Courage, there are yet many brave men in England! (185.)

CHAP. XI. *Labour*

A perennial nobleness and even sacredness in Work.
Significance of the Potter's Wheel. Blessed is he who has
found his Work; let him ask no other blessedness. (p. 189.)—
A brave Sir Christopher, and his Paul's Cathedral: Every
noble work at first 'impossible.' Columbus royalest Sea-
king of all: A depth of Silence, deeper than the Sea; a
Silence unsoundable; known to God only. (191.)

CHAP. XII. *Reward*

Work is Worship: Labour, wide as the Earth, has its
summit in Heaven. One monster there is in the world, the
idle man. (p. 193.)—' Fair day's-wages for a fair day's-work,'
the most unrefusable demand. The ' wages ' of every noble
Work in Heaven, or else Nowhere: The brave man has to
give his Life away. He that works bodies forth the form of
Things Unseen. Strange mystic affinity of Wisdom and
Insanity: All Work, in its degree, a making of Madness sane.
(196.)—Labour not a devil, even when encased in Mammonism: The unredeemed ugliness, a slothful People. The
vulgarest Plugson of a Master-Worker, not a man to strangle
by Corn-Laws and Shotbelts. (199.)

CHAP. XIII. *Democracy*

Man must actually have his debts and earnings a little
better paid by man. At no time was the lot of the dumb
millions of toilers so entirely unbearable as now. Sisterhood,
brotherhood often forgotten, but never before so expressly
denied. Mungo Park and his poor Black Benefactress.
(p. 201.)—Gurth, born thrall of Cedric the Saxon: Liberty
a divine thing; but ' liberty to die by starvation ' not so
divine. Nature's Aristocracies. William Conqueror, a resident
House-Surgeon provided by Nature for her beloved English
People. (204.)—Democracy, the despair of finding Heroes to
govern us, and contented putting-up with the want of them.
The very Tailor unconsciously symbolising the reign of
Equality. Wherever ranks do actually exist, strict division
of costumes will also be enforced. (207.)—Freedom from
oppression, an indispensable yet most insignificant portion
of Human Liberty. A *best path* does exist for every man;
a thing which, here and now, it were of all things *wisest* for
him to do. Mock Superiors and Real Superiors. (210.)

Chap. XIV. *Sir Jabesh Windbag*

Oliver Cromwell, the remarkablest Governor we have had for the last five centuries or so: No volunteer in Public Life, but plainly a balloted soldier: The Government of England put into his hands. (p. 214.)—Windbag, weak in the faith of a God; strong only in the faith that Paragraphs and Plausibilities bring votes. Five years of popularity or unpopularity; and *after* those five years, an Eternity. Oliver has to appear before the Most High Judge: Windbag, appealing to ' Posterity.' (215.)

Chap. XV. *Morrison again*

New Religions: This new stage of progress, proceeding ' to invent God,' a very strange one indeed. (p. 217.)—Religion, the Inner Light or Moral Conscience of a man's soul. Infinite difference between a Good man and a Bad. The Great Soul of the World, just and not unjust: Faithful, unspoken, but not ineffectual ' prayer.' Penalties: The French Revolution; cruelest Portent that has risen into created Space these ten centuries. Man needs no ' New Religion ; ' nor is like to get it: Spiritual Dastardism, and sick folly. (218.)—One Liturgy which does remain forever unexceptionable, that of *Praying by Working.* Sauerteig on the symbolic influences of Washing. Chinese Pontiff-Emperor and his significant ' punctualities.' (224.) — Goethe and German Literature. The great event for the world, now as always, the arrival in it of a new Wise Man. Goethe's *Mason-Lodge.* (227.)

BOOK IV.—HOROSCOPE

Chap. I. *Aristocracies*

To predict the Future, to manage the Present, would not be so impossible, had not the Past been so sacrilegiously mishandled: a godless century, looking back to centuries that were godly. (p. 230.)—A new real Aristocracy and Priesthood. The noble Priest always a noble *Aristos* to begin with, and something more to end with. Modern Preachers, and the *real* Satanas that now is. Abbot-Samson and William-Conqueror times. The mission of a Land Aristocracy a *sacred* one, in both senses of that old word. Truly a ' Splendour of God ' did dwell in those old rude veracious ages. Old Anselm travelling to Rome, to appeal against King Rufus. Their quarrel at bottom a great quarrel. (232.)—The boundless Future, predestined, nay already extant though unseen. Our Epic, not *Arms and the Man,* but *Tools and the Man ;* an infinitely wider kind of Epic. Important that our grand Reformation were begun. (239.)

CHAP. II. *Bribery Committee*

Our theory, perfect purity of Tenpound Franchise; our practice, irremediable bribery. Bribery, indicative not only of length of purse, but of brazen dishonesty: Proposed improvements. A Parliament, starting with a lie in its mouth, promulgates strange horoscopes of itself. (p. 242.)—Respect paid to those worthy of no respect: Pandarus Dogdraught. The indigent discerning Freeman; and the kind of men he is called upon to vote for. (245.)

CHAP. III. *The one Institution*

The 'Organisation of Labour,' if well understood, the Problem of the whole Future. Governments of various degrees of utility. Kilkenny Cats; Spinning-Dervishes; Parliamentary Eloquence. A Prime-Minister who would dare believe the heavenly omens. (p. 247.)—Who can despair of Governments, that passes a Soldier's Guardhouse?— Incalculable what, by arranging, commanding and regimenting, can be made of men. Organisms enough in the dim huge Future; and 'United Services' quite other than the red-coat one. (250.)—Legislative interference between Workers and Master-Workers increasingly indispensable. Sanitary Reform: People's Parks: A right Education Bill, and effective Teaching Service. Free bridge for Emigrants: England's sure markets among her Colonies. London the *All-Saxon-Home*, rendezvous of all the 'Children of the Harz-Rock.' (254.)—The English essentially conservative: Always the invincible instinct to hold fast by the Old, to admit the *minimum* of New. Yet new epochs do actually come; and with them new peremptory necessities. A certain Editor's stipulated work. (258.)

CHAP. IV. *Captains of Industry*

Government can do much, but it can in nowise do all. Fall of Mammon: To be a noble Master among noble Workers, will again be the first ambition with some few. (p. 259.)—The Leaders of Industry, virtually the Captains of the World: Doggeries and Chivalries. Isolation, the sum-total of wretchedness to man. All social growths in this world have required organising; and Work, the grandest of human interests, does now require it. (261.)

CHAP. V. *Permanence*

The 'tendency to persevere,' to persist in spite of hindrances, discouragements and 'impossibilities,' that which distinguishes the Species Man from the Genus Ape. Month-long contracts, and Exeter-Hall purblindness. A practical manufacturing Quaker's care for his workmen. (p. 266.)— Blessing of Permanent Contract: Permanence in all things,

at the earliest possible moment, and to the latest possible.
Vagrant Sam-Slicks. The wealth of a man the number of
things he loves and blesses, which he is loved and blessed by.
(269.)—The Worker's *interest* in the enterprise with which
he is connected. How to reconcile Despotism with Freedom.
(271.)

Chap. VI. *The Landed*

A man with fifty, with five hundred, with a thousand pounds
a day, given him freely, without condition at all, might be a
rather strong Worker: The sad reality, very ominous to look
at. Will he awaken, be alive again; or is this death-fit very
death?—Goethe's Duke of Weimar. Doom of Idleness.
(p. 271.)—To sit idle aloft, like absurd Epicurus'-gods, a poor
life for a man. Independence, ' lord of the lion-heart and
eagle-eye: ' Rejection of sham Superiors, the needful
preparation for obedience to *real* Superiors. (274.)

Chap. VII. *The Gifted*

Tumultuous anarchy calmed by noble effort into fruitful
sovereignty. Mammon, like Fire, the usefulest of servants,
if the frightfulest of masters. Souls to whom the omnipotent
guinea is, on the whole, an impotent guinea: Not a May-
game is this man's life; but a battle and stern pilgrimage:
God's justice, human Nobleness, Veracity and Mercy, the
essence of his very being. (p. 277.)—What a man of Genius is.
The Highest ' Man of Genius.' Genius, the clearer presence
of God Most High in a man. Of intrinsic Valetism you cannot, with whole Parliaments to help you, make a Heroism.
(280.)

Chap. VIII. *The Didactic*

One preacher who does preach with effect, and gradually
persuade all persons. Repentant Captains of Industry:
A Chactaw Fighter become a Christian Fighter. (p. 282.)—
Doomsday in the afternoon. The ' Christianity ' that cannot
get on without a minimum of Four-thousand-five-hundred,
will give place to something better that can. Beautiful to
see the brutish empire of Mammon cracking everywhere:
A strange, chill, almost ghastly dayspring in Yankeeland
itse'f. Here as there, Light is coming into the world. Whoso
believes, let him begin to fulfil: ' Impossible,' where Truth
and Mercy and the everlasting Voice of Nature order, can
have no place in the brave man's dictionary. (284.)—Not
on Ilion's or Latium's plains; on far other plains and places
henceforth can noble deeds be done. The last Partridge of
England shot and ended: Aristocracies with beards on their
chins. O, it is great, and there is no other greatness: To
make some nook of God's Creation a little fruitfuler; to make
some human hearts a little wiser, manfuler, happier: It is
work for a God! (285.)

INDEX

resiliences
vibrations

Law of Duty
Patience
Justice
Ygdrasil
Essence of universe Unmeasurable
Nature's laws eternal
Veracity
Work – Deeds greater than words worship
Silence
Conservative
order
valour
pity